About the Author

Dr. Gary Botting—lawyer, legal scholar, journalist, playwright, and poet—was born at Frilford Heath near Oxford, England, in 1943. He has written several books of nonfiction, including *The Orwellian World of Jehovah's Witnesses* (University of Toronto Press, 1984) and most recently two books on extradition: *Canadian Extradition Law Practice* (Butterworth's, 2005) and *Extradition Between Canada and the United States* (Transnational, 2005). Many of his thirty plays have been produced nationally, including *Way to Go, Witigo!*, which Botting wrote after he first became inspired by Chief Bob Smallboy's exodus to the Kootenay Plains in 1968.

Before becoming a lawyer in 1991, Botting taught creative writing and English literature at several colleges and universities. He obtained his Ph.D. in English literature from University of Alberta in 1975, and his Ph.D. in law from University of British Columbia in 2004. Now, he divides his time between his Vancouver Island home at Deep Bay and the University of Washington School of Law in Seattle, where he is a visiting scholar and SSHRC post-doctoral fellow.

Chief SMALLBOY

In Pursuit of Freedom

GARY BOTTING

FIFTH
HOUSE

Cover and interior design by Articulate Eye

Cover images by Darwin Wiggett (Kootenay Plains) and Gary Botting (Chief Bobtail Smallboy)

Edited by Kirsten Craven

Copyedited by Geri Rowlatt

Proofread by Lesley Reynolds

Scans by ABL Imaging

The publisher gratefully acknowledges the support of The Canada Council for the Arts and the Department of Canadian Heritage.

 Canada Council   Conseil des Arts
for the Arts   du Canada

We acknowledge the financial support of the Government of Canada through the Book Publishing Industry Development Program (BPIDP) for our publishing activities.

Printed in Canada by Friesens

05 06 07 08 09 / 5 4 3 2 1

First published in the United States in 2006 by

Fitzhenry & Whiteside
121 Harvard Avenue, Suite 2
Allston, MA 02134

Library and Archives Canada Cataloguing in Publication

Botting, Gary, 1943-

Chief Smallboy : in pursuit of freedom / Gary Botting.

Includes bibliographical references and index.

ISBN 1-894856-78-3

1. Smallboy, Bob 2. Cree Indians—Alberta. 3. Cree Indians-
Alberta—Kings and rulers—Biography. 4. Cree Indians—Biography.

5. Oral history. I. Title.

E99.C88S588 2005   971.23004'97323'0092

C2005-904625-2

Fifth House Ltd.
A Fitzhenry & Whiteside Company
1511, 1800-4 St. SW
Calgary, Alberta T2S 2S5
1-800-387-9776
www.fitzhenry.ca

Harold Cardinal

1945–2005

In Memoriam

For Aidan
Mosôm's "*Nosisim*"

In memory of my beloved niece
Lisa Ann Cole Lightning
1963–1986

Contents

Foreword

The life of Bob Smallboy harkens back to an earlier time when his great uncle, Big Bear, said "no" to the government. Big Bear was right, but the forces of westward settlement were so overpowering that there was no way he could win the concessions he sought for his Cree people. In the end, he was broken and jailed. Not so Bob Smallboy. He also said "no" to the authorities but was more successful in stemming the tide of western society that was corrupting and destroying his people. He succeeded where his great uncle failed.

Bob (Bobtail) Smallboy, born about 1898, was descended from two great families of the Cree nation—Big Bear and Bobtail. From them he inherited his natural ability for leadership, which was reinforced by the people who influenced his life. These included the prophet Yellowface, Bobtail's son, Coyote, and his own parents, who gave him much wise advice. He became an industrious mixed farmer in the 1920s, and by the end of the decade he had a well-operating and successful business. From there he went on to become chief of the Ermineskin Reserve in 1959.

Soon after becoming chief, he led a delegation to Ottawa, where he listed the problems of his people. They needed more land; there was too much unemployment; family units were crumbling; alcoholism was rampant; child neglect was common; too many Indians were in jail; suicide was common; children were failing in school; and there was a general loss of pride, dignity, religion, and social order, leaving the people with little meaning in their lives. However, his pleas for change fell on deaf ears.

As oil development and modernization engulfed his reserve, Smallboy was saddened by the increasing use of alcohol and drugs, his people's loss of culture and language due to television, and their movement away from traditional rituals and medicine. As oil revenues increased, people gave up farming while domestic disputes, suicides, and traffic deaths increased dramatically. Smallboy could find only one solution: to take his followers away from this harmful environment and to embrace a more natural way of life based upon the principles of his forefathers.

He concluded that he must abandon the Ermineskin Reserve "for the future of his children and grandchildren and for a good, peaceful life for them in a place far from the influences of the modern world." In the summer of 1968, Smallboy, together with Simon Omeasoo, Lazarus Roan, Alex Shortneck, and some 140 persons, left the reserve and established a camp in the wilderness of the Kootenay Plains near the Rocky Mountains. There they pitched a large council teepee, twenty tents, and had a portable schoolroom. They had no intention of reverting to the role of nomadic plainsmen, but sought isolation, while at the same time providing an acceptable level of education for their children and taking government contracts to clear areas for roads and dams.

Smallboy was adamant in maintaining the integrity of his camp and successfully avoided government efforts to close it down. This camp was an inspiration to Native people everywhere and became a centre for learning about Cree spiritual life. While there were disagreements and breakaways, Smallboy's philosophy remained unchanged: that the people must escape the pitfalls of modern society if they were to survive. The simple way of life in the wilderness provided this sanctuary for many years.

If this book dealt only with Smallboy's life, it would be a significant contribution in itself. But it is greatly enriched by vivid accounts of the many factors that influenced the man's life. The quest of Big Bear, the long struggle of Little Bear to find a haven in Montana, and the detailed and personal look at the life of Yellowface add immeasurably to this volume. The author's own involvement with Smallboy is also recounted, providing a personal touch to this very human story.

Hugh A. Dempsey

Preface

In the summer of 1970, I moved to Alberta from Ontario to pursue graduate studies at the University of Alberta. This was about the same time that Chief Bob Smallboy led his attack on the Trudeau White Paper, which sought to abolish the reserve system. Smallboy's stand, and the reasons he gave for taking his band from the Ermineskin Reserve to the Kootenay Plains, inspired me to write a short story, "The Aliens," and a play, *Way to Go, Witigo!*, both published in 1972.[1]

The following year, as a faculty member and media relations coordinator at Red Deer College, I presented a personally drafted proposal to the Ermineskin Band for the establishment of a multi-faceted adult education program on the reserve at Hobbema, Alberta. Two years later, Maskwachees Cultural College was established by the Four Bands in Hobbema in an old, two-room schoolhouse on the Samson Reserve under the direction of Bob Silverthorne, who arranged for the University of Calgary to offer courses for university transfer credit through its outreach program. When I taught the first of these courses in 1974–75, my students included members of the Smallboy Band, who despite having lived in comparative isolation seemed to be every bit as articulate as their fellows. The students went on to the University of Calgary to complete their Bachelor of Education degrees, and most of them continue to teach in Alberta.

Besides teaching English and creative writing at Red Deer College and Maskwachees Cultural College, I was at the time president of the Alberta Publishers Association and editor-in-chief of Red Deer College Press, in which capacity I had accepted and edited for publication several titles on First Nations themes. In 1982, Chief Gordon Lee of the Ermineskin First Nation, the husband of one of my students and then administrator of the Four Bands Council in Hobbema, requested my assistance in recording and preserving the thoughts, memories, and oral history of Chief Bob Smallboy, especially Smallboy's narrative of how and why he came to take a good portion of the Ermineskin Band with him to the foothills of the Rocky Mountains in 1968, declaring it to be Indian land. In addition to earlier interviews he had recorded with the Chief, starting in July 1982,

Gordon and I conducted a series of interviews with Smallboy in which he explained in detail the life he was trying to lead in the foothills. During this time, my family lived in Hobbema in the house of Smallboy's long-time friend and fellow-traveller Albert Lightning. I usually took my son, Aidan, then seven, on my visits to see Smallboy, and for some reason they hit it off. Smallboy called him *Sipihkopiyesis* (Bluebird)—a name that stuck.

GIFTS FIT FOR A CHIEF

In the late 1970s, I had requested a medicine man from the Smallboy Camp, Wayne Roan, to intercede on my behalf for a medical affliction known as Ménière's syndrome, characterized by dizziness, loss of balance, and tinnitus. The medical doctor who had diagnosed the condition proclaimed it incurable and prescribed medicines such as Gravol to control the symptoms. He explained in lay terms that crystals usually resting on cilia in the inner ear, providing a sense of balance, had likely jarred loose from their moorings; without them, I could expect to feel dizzy for the rest of my days. A friend in Hobbema suggested that Wayne was the best medicine man around and interceded with him on my behalf. I was instructed to fast for four days. I brought Wayne as a gift the traditional three yards of different-coloured cotton cloth and a pouch of Amphora pipe tobacco. Suffice to say, after weeks of fasting, ritual sweats, and ritual drumming, my crystals had an attitude adjustment that included a reconciliation with my cilia. The symptoms of Ménière's syndrome eventually disappeared altogether, leading my physician to declare, tongue-in-cheek, that from then on he would prescribe a visit to a medicine man for patients suffering from the affliction. Ever the rationalist, he speculated that the loss of fatty tissue in my ear, combined with the repeated vibration from the drumming in an enclosed space, must have drummed my crystals back into place.

This was my first encounter with the power and apparent efficacy of Cree medicine, for which I retain a great deal of respect. I learned then that gifts should be given upon any approach to an elder, medicine man, or chief, and these most appropriately were lengths of cloth and tobacco. When I learned that Gordon had set up a meeting with Chief Smallboy, I prepared exactly the same gifts as I had given to Wayne Roan. As a mark of his esteem for the Chief, Gordon brought him a colourful blanket, which to our delight he immediately modelled for us, showing his good sense of humour by retrieving his favourite hat, which had been hanging from a nail on the wall of his cabin. The photograph of Chief Smallboy on the cover is the first of a series of photographs I took of him on the occasion of our first meeting.

Each time we went out to the camp, I drove my Ford F-150 Club Cab with a canoe and camping equipment in the back, ready for any eventuality. On one occasion, Gordon asked me to stop at a grocery store in Rocky Mountain House—he said he had forgotten something. He ran in and came back out again moments later with a plastic bag of groceries, including a loaf of Wonderbread. We headed west on the David Thompson Highway towards Nordegg, then north up the winding Forestry Trunk Road towards the Brazeau River, where Smallboy and his band had set up their permanent camp. As we negotiated the mountain roads, Gordon dug into the plastic grocery bag and pulled out a frozen chicken.

"This is my gift to the Chief," he said teasingly. "What's your gift?"

I had forgotten to bring one—as he had suspected. I racked my brains as to what there was among my camping gear that I could give him. A Coleman stove, perhaps? A propane lamp? A tin of sockeye salmon?

Just then, as we skirted a low mountain, a rabbit shot out onto the road. Reflexively, I swerved, but had very little room to manoeuvre: on one side of the gravel road was sheer cliff going up and on the other side, sheer cliff going down. I clipped the rabbit, which was left kicking in my tracks. Borrowing a hunting knife from Gordon, I ran back to put it out of its misery, then placed it in the back of the truck. I wiped off the knife and gave it back to Gordon.

"Thanks," I said. "Now I have a gift for the Chief!"

We drove on to the camp, each of us lost in thought.

Smallboy was delighted with the chicken, but even more delighted with the rabbit, which he showed Aidan how to skin and clean. As I photographed him, Chief Smallboy cut the rabbit and chicken up in cubes to make a delicious stew.

A HOLY PLACE

Every single meeting with the Chief was memorable for different reasons. Once when we visited him, he told us of a holy place that he wanted to share with us about ten kilometres from his camp, where sweet grass and timothy grew in a mile-long meadow adjacent to the Cardinal River. There were falls there, he said, where the trout fishing was good, dolly varden and brook trout, mostly, and the occasional rainbow. There were bear caves there, and you could often see mule deer and elk and moose—even bighorn sheep came down from the mountains to graze. He had seen cougar and lynx back in there, too—all kinds of animals. The pasture was good for grazing horses in the wintertime when they could paw through to whatever hay was left under the snow. As he was preparing dinner, he asked us to pick some saskatoon berries for dessert.

Off we drove down the dirt road to the west in my Club Cab, my canoe rattling about in the back. Soon Gordon directed me to hang a right into the forest. A trail had been cut through the thick mixed woods, well above the canyon cut by the river. Sure enough, about half a kilometre down the trail there was a turnaround beside a spectacular saskatoon bush laden with berries.

Saskatoon bushes grow much higher than blueberry bushes, and occasionally I had come across copses of saskatoons in the Alberta wilderness. But this saskatoon bush overlooking the Cardinal River was a veritable tree, standing sentinel to a memorable garden of natural delights that the Chief obviously wanted to share with us.

Initially, Gordon told me that the Chief had said to park beside the saskatoons and not to drive any farther down the trail. I took this to mean that we should not befoul the sacred ground with my truck; if we wanted to see the rest of the holy place, we would have to work at it and hike on down.

I did exactly as the Chief instructed, parking in the turnaround beside the laden saskatoon tree. While Aidan and I picked saskatoon berries and admired the view of the Cardinal River rushing through a canyon far below, Gordon hiked down the trail with his o.22 rifle—perhaps intending to bag a rabbit. When he came back, he pronounced the trail to be dry and solid all the way down. "I think the truck'll be okay," he said. "May as well drive down. It's a little sloppy just at the bottom, but as long as we're moving we should be able to get through."

"But didn't the Chief say to park here—not to drive any further?" I said.

"He thought it was wet. He obviously doesn't know that it's dried up."

So against my better judgment we drove on down the trail. When we came to the boggy stretch at the edge of the woods, I stepped on the gas and we sailed through it into a wonderland of mountain, river, woods, meadow, and blue eternal sky with aromatic grasses waving gently in a warm breeze. The meadow itself was transporting with its blended aroma of sweet grass, timothy, and alfalfa.

I skirted the meadow, marvelling at its expanse, accelerating a little, when Gordon yelled a warning. I jammed on the brakes right at the edge of a hidden gully that drained the meadow into the adjacent river. One more metre and my front wheel would have been over the edge.

"That's close enough," said Gordon, in a classic understatement. "We'd better walk from here."

Leaving our truck at what proved to be the first of a series of ravines cleverly disguised by the height of the timothy, the three of us hiked along the southeast bank of the river, skirting the meadow, until we reached a rocky flat, where the river resolved itself in a series of spectacular cataracts. The water was low, but spring runoff through here must be dramatic, I thought, as I sat down on a polished limestone rock. The hundred-metre-square rock slab this side of the waterfalls was as smooth and flat as pavement—a natural platform.

Gordon had wandered over to the falls, but Aidan stood in the middle of the flat slab of rock, intrigued by a butterfly that seemed to be marking out its territory, claiming the entire platform for itself. At the time, Aidan collected butterflies and to see a tortoiseshell butterfly that far up in the mountains was a rare treat. He pointed to the showy insect with his index finger as it soared over the boulder where I was sitting. It landed on another boulder adjacent to mine, opening and closing its wings to the sun in lazy, brilliant arcs. As we watched, the butterfly took off again and spiralled right around the rock towards the water, past Gordon, past some more saskatoon bushes, past me again, gradually spiralling inwards towards the centre of the slab. It flew another complete circle around Aidan—and alighted on his outstretched finger.

He examined it minutely, then glanced across at me.

"It's a tortoiseshell," he said in awe.

"Uh-huh."

"A female." He gulped as he stared at the prize, then added breathlessly, "I don't have one in my collection."

I didn't say a word.

Aidan looked around, drinking in the landscape. He looked back at the motionless butterfly still perched on his finger.

"But she has eggs to lay," he sighed, working it out, "and *Mosôm* says this is a holy place."

He raised his hand high in the air towards the sun, and with the gentlest flick of his finger the butterfly soared off over the rocks, circling again outwards over the rock, over the river, over the saskatoons, and into the sweet grass and timothy meadow beyond, no doubt searching for an appropriate food plant on which to lay her eggs. But Aidan's innocent remark about *Mosôm* (Grandpa) Smallboy and his holy place said more to me about the Chief's method of teaching than volumes of psychological theory. In my own son, I could see Chief Smallboy's subtle yet effective teaching method at work.

As the sun sank behind the mountains, we hiked back along the length of the meadow to the truck, parked askew at the edge of the first ravine. I turned the truck around and we headed back towards the woods—only to sink into the muskeg bog up to the hubs. High-centred, the truck would not budge in either direction. After half an hour of trying to jack the truck out and build up the road with branches and twigs, Gordon suggested that we hike out before it got too dark and come back for the truck tomorrow. We grabbed some necessities and began to hike out, but

I hadn't walked six metres before being hit with a wave of nausea and dizziness that signalled a return of Ménière's syndrome. I lost my balance and had to kneel to regain any semblance of equilibrium. Gasping, I returned to the truck, then walked beyond it into the open meadow, whereupon I almost instantly recovered.

Gordon, cradling his 0.22, looked on with a measure of concern. Aidan offered to carry my pack. Feeling foolish, I apologized and we started out again, but the same thing happened at the same spot. It seemed I just could not walk beyond the barrier of the bog at the edge of the woods. The nausea triggered by the woods was overwhelming. Yet each time I returned to the meadow, my sense of balance returned. On the fourth unsuccessful attempt, I declared that we would pitch the tent in the meadow before it got any darker. Gordon said he would hike out alone and bring help in the morning.

As soon as Gordon disappeared up the trail, still cradling his rifle, Aidan and I set up camp. Later, dizziness overwhelmed me as I lay down in my sleeping bag. Aidan made me some tea from a wild sunflower, which he steeped in boiling water, roots and all.

"Who taught you how to do that?" I asked.

"Chief," he replied.

The concoction helped settle my stomach and seemed to drive the dizziness away. That night, the temperature fell below freezing, and in the morning frost tipped the grasses of the meadow, sparkling in the first light of dawn, lighting up the mountains to the west with an orange glow as if the whole horizon was ablaze. The muskeg in which my truck was stuck had become relatively solid overnight, and so as soon as the sun came up above the eastern treeline, I tried to dislodge it from the mire. Although the truck wouldn't move ahead, it inched its way back into the meadow. We quickly collapsed the tent and were loading it into the back of the truck when a large four-wheel-drive pickup with raised rear suspension appeared on the trail above us. "Chief's truck!" said Aidan. It sailed without any hesitation whatsoever through the boggy patch where my own pickup had been stuck.

At the wheel was Chief Smallboy's grandson. On the passenger's side, his elbow stuck out the open window, was Gordon Lee. In the centre, wearing a huge grin, was Chief Smallboy. For him, it was clearly an "I told you so!" moment. I grinned back sheepishly.

The truck turned in a lazy loop and pulled up alongside. "Follow us!" Chief Smallboy said. For good measure, Gordon hopped out and jumped into my truck. We followed the Chief and his grandson out, passing through the bog, and drove up the trail past the amazing saskatoon tree.

At the end of the lane, near the road, Gordon got out and ran to pick up his rifle, which he had stowed under a tree the night before so he could hitch a ride to camp without drivers thinking they were in danger of being hijacked.

If he had developed a respect for me when I produced the rabbit with a story of how I had picked it off with my truck on a hair-raising mountain road without damaging the meat, I now respected more than ever Chief Smallboy's wisdom, which, I learned, was not to be challenged lightly. He'd had good reason for telling us not to drive beyond the saskatoon bush.

MEMOIRS

To supplement his narratives, Chief Smallboy gave Gordon and me custody of his personal photo albums and scrapbooks. I collected these together, along with other documents (some translated or interpreted by Eugene Steinhauer), to produce a manuscript entitled "The Indian Way: The Memoirs of Chief Bob Smallboy." Mel Hurtig of Hurtig Publishers in Edmonton expressed an interest in publishing this book, as did the University of Toronto Press, which that year had published one of my earlier books, *The Orwellian World of Jehovah's Witnesses*. At the time of Smallboy's death in July 1984, the manuscript was being reviewed by external readers, who ultimately rejected a publication grant, opining that the manuscript was not academic enough to warrant government subsidy.

At Smallboy's funeral, Gordon, then administrator of the Four Bands, took possession of the original manuscript, Smallboy's photo albums, and all of my photographs of Smallboy, including negatives, on the understanding that the manuscript, including illustrations, would be published by the Ermineskin Band. However, it was never published. More than twenty years later, I was informed by Muriel Lee, Gordon's ex, that the manuscript and photographs had been stored in a safe in Gordon's house. The house had burned to the ground, destroying all the contents, including the contents of the safe. Many of the images contained in this book are therefore copies of copies, the negatives having been destroyed along with the manuscript of the memoirs. Fortunately, I had kept a copy of an early draft of the narratives, which I have relied upon as a source for some of the material in this book.

I visited the Chief many times between 1982 and 1984, sometimes driving out to the camp alone or with Aidan, sometimes with colleagues from Red Deer College. Chief Smallboy's son, Joe, who eventually became chief of the Smallboy Band in his own right, sometimes acted as interpreter for his father in Gordon's absence. He and his wife, Dorothy, Wayne Roan's sister, frequently visited me and my ex-wife, Heather Botting, at our home in Bentley, Alberta, a logical stop between the camp and Hobbema.

Dorothy often used to joke that Joe paid us a visit whenever he got into a storytelling mood. She would at times insert her editorial comments or remind him of details that he had overlooked. Occasionally, he would arrive alone, and once he brought his daughter Jessie to meet us and listen to the stories. His familiarity with his father's oral history allowed him to flesh out the narratives of accounts initially outlined by his father.

With Joe's encouragement and input, I set out to write a biography of Chief Smallboy that vastly expanded on the Chief's own early narratives. Heather and I moved to Calgary and eventually to the west coast, where I embarked on a new and demanding career path—the practice of law. We lost contact with Joe and Dorothy (they did not have a phone), and although I attempted to find a publisher for the biography, I forgot all about the memoirs. In 1999, I found both an early copy of the memoirs and the manuscript of the biography, which eventually I reworked into the present text.

In this retelling of the Smallboy saga, I have relied on the biography written with Joe Smallboy's help between 1984 and 1986 and have quoted liberally from the narratives of Bob Smallboy contained in the early draft of the memoirs. I have travelled wherever their storytelling has led me. Where possible, I have corroborated their accounts with references to parallel oral accounts and to the written record in the form of newspaper articles, reservation rolls, censuses, and historical treatments of the circumstances within which the child *Keskayo Apitchitchiw* (Bobtail Smallboy) grew up to become one of the most influential First Nations chiefs in Canadian history.

ORAL HISTORY

Sometimes the oral history expressed by the Smallboys seemed more accurate, coherent, and consistent than the fragmentary written record found within the archives. Conforming to academic tradition, where there appeared to be a conflict between the written record and the Smallboys' version of events, I followed the written record unless the Smallboys' account was corroborated elsewhere, which was usually the case. For example, Chief Smallboy said many times that his mother, Isabelle Coyote, was 112 when she died in 1977, which meant she was born sometime during 1865. This seemed problematic at first, since the initial Rocky Boy Reservation roll compiled in 1917 listed her year of birth as 1862. Other accounts, including that of Smallboy's granddaughter Jessie, listed her year of birth as 1867, the year of Canadian Confederation. However, Marie Smallboy recalled visiting her great-grandmother in hospital in 1976 when Isabelle told her that she had been twelve years old when her grandfather Bobtail signed the adhesion to Treaty Six at Blackfoot Crossing in 1877.

Re-examination of the census data revealed that the dates of birth and ages of the members of the Cree Indians in Montana, where Isabelle lived for forty years, pegged the ages at multiples of five for people born in 1867 or earlier. Smallboy's mother was thought to be fifty-five when the census was taken in 1917, while ten members of the core group of Canadian-born Cree were thought to be fifty, and *none* was thought to be fifty-one. This apparent arbitrariness in assessing age tends to discredit the roll where year of birth is concerned.

That the author of the Rocky Boy census roll, Roger St. Pierre, resorted to creative guesswork is not surprising given evidence of his personal political agenda. Canadian-born Cree, as opposed to American-born Chippewa, faced possible disenfranchisement, leaving more land for the "legitimate" Chippewa. A half-Chippewa man of mixed blood married to a Chippewa member of the reservation, St. Pierre was likely aware that bestowing on Cree members a disproportionately high "Canadian-born" status (i.e., a birth year of 1867 or later) put those putative Canadians in jeopardy of losing their American Indian status, leaving more land to American-born members.[2] Be that as it may, St. Pierre's estimates in the rolls make the corroborated oral tradition of the Smallboys that Isabelle Coyote was born in 1865 seem the more credible by comparison.

At other times, the oral history seems so at odds with historical sources that it must be re-evaluated. This is especially the case in the interface between Indian and white worlds. For example, basing his knowledge on the oral tradition passed down to him by his mother, Chief Smallboy clearly believed that his maternal great-grandfather, Bobtail, was the first Cree chief to sign Treaty Six. In point of fact, Bobtail did not sign the original Treaty Six at Fort Carlton in 1876, but rather an adhesion to it more than a year later. Bobtail was the first Cree chief to sign the adhesion to Treaty Six at Blackfoot Crossing on the Bow River on 25 September 1877, and his name also appears beside his "+" (he and his band consistently did not mark an "x") at the top of the list of names in subsequent treaty adhesions, one at Blackfoot Crossing and another at Tail Creek, which Bobtail's eldest son, Coyote—Smallboy's maternal grandfather— also signed.

However, this apparent anomaly does not impute the integrity of the oral history as much as it would seem. Bobtail himself, obviously, would have been aware that he had not signed the original treaty. But from Coyote's point of view, Bobtail would have been the first to sign the treaty document; indeed, in two of the adhesions, Coyote had been second to sign with his own "+" immediately below that of his father. Furthermore, Isabelle Coyote, Smallboy's mother, had travelled to Blackfoot Crossing with her parents and grandparents in 1877 and had personally witnessed her grandfather and father sign the adhesion document. There is little doubt that her perception that Bobtail was the first to sign was faithfully transmitted directly and personally to her sons Bob and Johnny Smallboy of the fourth generation, to Joe and James Smallboy of the fifth generation, and to Marie Smallboy of the sixth. Marie, in turn, has passed the account on to her sons in the seventh generation and her grandson in the eighth.

In this manner, the oral history has been preserved, as Marie testified to the Standing Committee on Aboriginal Affairs in 2003: "My great-great-great grandfather, Chief Bobtail, was about my age when he entered into treaty with the Imperial Crown. I carry that history, a history I did not learn from the textbooks provided to me by the missionaries, nor did I learn it at the University of Calgary. This is a history I learned through my own research and validated by my traditional upbringing and oral testimony."[3]

The collective memory reflected in the storytelling of Bob and Joe Smallboy and their kin is a much more fluid and living medium than the one normally required by legal or historical purists. As a lawyer, I am all too aware of the barriers a rigid legalism would raise to accepting oral history as fact. However, Mr. Justice Dickson recognized in 1978, in connection with the right of Indians to hunt on Crown land under Treaty Six, that "claims to aboriginal title are woven with history, legend, politics and moral obligations," all of which had to be given due consideration even in a judicial context.[4] As Marie Smallboy implied in her testimony to the Standing Committee, the "truth" of what Smallboy believed trumps and ultimately transcends the importance of "facts" in history books.

Following Bob Smallboy's death, Joe became informal chief of the Smallboy Band. Tragically, he and his wife, Dorothy, the daughter of Lazarus Roan, one of the triumvirate who led the Smallboy Band to the Kootenay Plains, were both killed in 1995 in a car accident on the same treacherous stretch of mountain road near the Smallboy Camp where thirteen years earlier I had hit the rabbit. More recently, their daughter Jessie and Bob Smallboy's grandnieces Marie Small, whom I met in Hobbema in 2005, and Arlene Small, with whom I had a chance meeting at Stone Child College on the Rocky Bay Reservation in 2002, filled in some remaining gaps and helped sort out names, dates, and relationships. Marie in particular helped answer remaining questions about her great-great-grandparents, which she drew from personal memories of conversations she had with Isabelle in the 1970s.[5]

Early on, Dr. John Tobias of Red Deer College recognized the significance of recording Smallboy's memoirs, and in 1982 he encouraged me in this enterprise, as did Mel Hurtig and, later, Dr. Wes Pue of the University of British Columbia Faculty of Law. I am indebted to my former wife, Dr. Heather Botting-O'Brien, now a professor of anthropology at the University of Victoria, for copying, preserving, and organizing most of Smallboy's photographs.

The late Hon. Eugene Steinhauer, former lieutenant-governor of Alberta, translated Smallboy's public speeches, addresses, and broadcasts, which I have quoted liberally, and Gordon Lee, who also served as chief of the Ermineskin Band, translated some fifteen hours of taped interviews with Smallboy, some of the unpublished transcripts of which were included in "The Indian Way: The Memoirs of Chief Bob Smallboy." The Literary Arts Branch of Alberta Culture provided me with a Senior Writer's grant to complete the original "Memoirs," and more recently the Social Sciences and Humanities Research Council has provided me with doctoral and postdoctoral fellowships that have allowed me to continue to research and write this and other research projects. Professor Walter Walsh of the University of Washington School of Law has, since 2000, provided helpful pointers on archival research in the history of law. The University of British Columbia Faculty of Graduate Studies has provided me, over the years, with generous funding, including the prestigious Paetzold Fellowship two years in a row. Finally, the editorial staff of Fifth House Ltd. is owed much gratitude, especially Charlene Dobmeier, Meaghan Craven, and Kirsten Craven.

My concern throughout this project has been to present an account that approximates how Chief Bob Smallboy viewed himself and his family history. It is also an exposition of the course taken and the decisions made by Smallboy in two personal quests: 1) the pursuit of freedom and 2) the recognition that the mountains of Banff and Jasper national parks and their surrounds—including the Kootenay Plains—were never ceded to the Canadian government and, therefore, remain Indian land to this day.

Gary Botting, Ph.D.
University of Washington School of Law
Seattle, Washington
8 July 2005

CHAPTER 1

Voice In the Wilderness

WHEN IN ROME ...

When Canadian Prime Minister Brian Mulroney met with Pope John Paul II in Rome on 26 January 1987, he expected the Pontiff to be supportive of his efforts to bring sanctions against South Africa for its apartheid policies. He certainly did not expect to get an earful on Canada's own "Indian problem" (as Prime Minister Trudeau had called it), which some critics had suggested was parallel to the situation in South Africa.[1] Prime Minister Mulroney discovered that the Pope already knew a great deal about the rights of Canada's First Nations and the reserve system in Canada, even alluding to a federal-provincial meeting on Native rights scheduled for the following March. Furthermore, the Pope reasserted his intention to visit Fort Simpson later in the year to meet a commitment made to Native groups in 1984. How had the Pope become so knowledgeable and interested in the First Nations of Canada?

Chief Bob Smallboy was among the first Canadian Indians to meet with the Pope during what many First Nations groups considered a constitutional crisis at the time of negotiations on the patriation of the Canadian Constitution. With the help of Eugene Steinhauer, Smallboy presented John Paul II with the First Nations view of the situation and asked the Pontiff to use his power and influence to intervene to ensure that Aboriginal voices were heard. Later, the Pope expressed interest in meeting as many First Nations people as possible during his visit to Canada in September 1984. His disappointment at having to cancel the Fort Simpson leg of his trip was immediately obvious. Smallboy had extended an invitation to him to visit his camp, which by then had become a hamlet. At one point, it was announced that the Pope planned a side trip into the foothills of the Rocky Mountains, raising speculation as to whether he intended to visit the Smallboy Camp. As it turned out, by the time the Pope arrived in Canada, Smallboy was dead.

It is perhaps a paradox that Smallboy, who claimed to be a baptized Roman Catholic, should have become a prophet and inspiration to a whole generation of fellow Indians who came to adopt traditional modes of Native worship and lifestyle. While in Italy, Smallboy held a press conference, during which he was asked by a journalist, a trifle cynically, if he had any advice for Europe: "When in Rome," he replied, "do as the Pope would have you do." This twist on "When in Rome, do as the Romans do," widely reported in the press, was no glib answer. Rather, it reflected wisdom born of Smallboy's true respect for leadership, particularly for the qualities of chieftain and elder that he recognized in Pope John Paul II. "Do as the Pope would have you do," he repeated in his admonition to the scrum of journalists. "He is a great leader. It is for me to give advice to my own people. It is for the Pope to give advice to you."[2]

OUTLASTING TRUDEAU

Brian Mulroney was not the first prime minister to be embarrassed, indirectly, by the enigmatic Cree leader. Smallboy had no time for politics or politicians, but had a knack for setting snares for them that often were not triggered until months or even years later.

Lester Pearson was prime minister when Chief Smallboy, Lazarus Roan, and Simon Omeasoo first plotted to leave Hobbema, Alberta, with a good chunk of the population of the Ermineskin Band, of which Smallboy was undisputed chief. A long-standing struggle with the Department of Indian Affairs, as it was constituted under the Pearson administration, led directly to Smallboy and his followers abandoning their reserve at Hobbema and moving to the Kootenay Plains in the foothills of the Rocky Mountains. The treaty process had been a fraud, Chief Smallboy declared. This land had not been ceded to Queen Victoria. The collected chiefs who signed Treaty Six in 1876 and Treaty Seven in 1877 had no idea what they were giving up. There was never, at any point, a meeting of the minds. More importantly, the undeveloped Crown land east of the Rocky Mountains, where he was then residing, had not been included in Treaties Six and Seven. This omission was not without reason: everyone since David Thompson had recognized that the Kootenay Plains were sacred Indian land. Despite inclusion of that strip of land as the anomalous "panhandle" of Treaty Eight, it remained sacred Indian land and henceforth would be occupied by Smallboy's band and any Indians who chose to follow.

This was the essence of Smallboy's position in 1968, as he pitched his tent along with dozens of other tents and teepees on the Kootenay Plains north of Abraham Lake. He insisted on certain rules: those who chose to join him would have to give up modern influences, such as television, drugs, and alcohol; they would have to follow the "Indian Way," adopting traditional rituals and traditional Indian medicine; and they would have to learn to speak Cree as well as English.

The first tents were erected by Simon Omeasoo, Lazarus Roan, Alex Shortneck, and Frank Nadeau on the very day that Pearson's successor, Pierre Elliott Trudeau, came to power—25 June 1968. On 4 July, Smallboy left Hobbema to lead the breakaway band that was to assume his name. When asked by a journalist from the *Edmonton Journal* how long he would remain at the new "Smallboy Camp," he declared simply that he would outlast Pierre Trudeau. The words were prophetic. Pierre Trudeau finally passed the reins of office to John Turner on 30 June 1984. A week later, on 8 July, Smallboy died at his camp between the Brazeau and Cardinal rivers of complications from diabetes and gangrene poisoning.

"THE LAND OF ANSWERS"

Twenty-five families—in all, about 140 men, women, and children—followed Chief Smallboy to the Kootenay Plains. The move was the culmination of fifteen years of planning and dreaming. An advance guard led by Bob Smallboy's brother, Johnny, and Johnny's son, James, had camped out on the Kootenay Plains on and off for close to four years, beginning in 1964, to find the right place for a permanent camp, a place that would resonate with Johnny as a "Land of Answers," prophesied by Yellowface, an important Cree-Crow chief. For two years, James had lived there with his children, including Marie, Chief Smallboy's grandniece.

Despite all these preparations, the 1968 migration from Hobbema to the Smallboy Camp was so secretive that it took the press—and many Hobbema residents—completely by surprise. The news, when it broke, was huge. After all, Smallboy was not only a hereditary chief, but had also been the elected chief of the Ermineskin Band at Hobbema since 1959. At that time, most Indian chiefs in Alberta were relatively conservative if not complacent people, often chosen for their knack of placating the most outspoken voices among them while knuckling under to the wishes and demands of the federal Department of Indian Affairs. Usually this entailed setting an example of restraint. Smallboy, obviously, did not fit this mould.

Chief Smallboy recognized that something had to be done about the effects of alcohol abuse on the reserves, including increased domestic assault and vehicular deaths from driving while under the influence. He saw that the fathers and mothers of Hobbema, envious of the glamour and prosperity of the "outside" world portrayed by Hollywood, increasingly drank their problems into existence. He saw that television in particular offered the youth of Hobbema impossible dreams and fantasies and led children to become less understanding of their traditional parents and even more traditional grandparents, of whom they grew increasingly contemptuous. Rather than recognize that their elders had something important to say, the children more often than not left home early for the glitz of the city.

Edmonton was just a short hop down Highway 2A to personal destruction. It was usually a sad if not tragic return trip. At first, the night lights of Edmonton's Whyte Avenue glittered prettily. But the reality was harsh. Cree girls in their early teens were exploited by pimps virtually upon their arrival in the big city. Exposed to brutal racial stereotyping, young Cree men could find no jobs. Hungry and lonely, both guys and girls would trust the wrong people, hang out with bad company, and often resort to petty crime to stave off starvation. Many ended up in the drunk tank as vagrants. They would return home in frustration to do the only things that gave them temporary reprieve: watch more television, drink more beer, and perhaps toke away their troubles. Thus emboldened, they would return to the city, where the whole destructive process would start over—this time with a pre-existing criminal record. In the 1960s, most inmates at Fort Saskatchewan Jail north of Edmonton were Cree. When the lifestyle of a revolving prison door became unbearable, suicide was a common way out.

This was the situation Smallboy decided to remedy amid the hoopla of Canadian centennial celebrations in 1967, in his ninth year as chief of the Ermineskin Band.

SMALLBOY'S NAMES

As an infant, Bob Smallboy was named *Keskayo* (Bobtail) by his famous grandfather of the same name. As he grew older, he contracted the English translation of his name to "Bob" to fit in with English custom. Once he came to prominence, newspapers, including the *Edmonton Journal*, followed the *Canadian Press Stylebook* convention of expanding "Bob" to "Robert," in this case, quite inaccurately. That name stuck, in official circles, so that his Order of Canada certificate and a medical scholarship established in his honour are both in the name of "Robert Smallboy." But some sources, such as the *Canadian Encyclopedia*, give his name as "Johnny Bob Smallboy." How did this come about?

Before he could marry Louisa Headman in Hobbema's Our Lady of the Seven Sorrows Church in 1918, Smallboy had to prove he was a baptized Roman Catholic. This he could not do, since he had never actually been baptized. The only record of baptism he had access to was that of his younger brother, Johnny, who had been baptized in the Church on 10 July 1900 at six months of age. Bob "borrowed" the baptismal certificate long enough to get married on 3 June 1918 under the name "Johnny Bob Smallboy."

Later, on 30 January 1964, Bob applied for an official copy of his marriage certificate from the Church and, while he was at it, asked if he could obtain a copy of a certificate of baptism. He gave his name and date of birth. However, while the officials could find an entry for his marriage in the name of "Johnny Bob Smallboy," the only record of baptism on 10 July 1900 at Our Lady of Seven Sorrows Church was for Johnny. No date of birth was given—just a notation that Johnny had been about six months old at the time of baptism. Accordingly, a baptismal certificate in the name of "Johnny *Apitchitchiw* (Smallboy)" was issued, with Bob Smallboy's birth date of 7 November 1898. The name "Bob" was later added to this copy of the certificate of baptism, using a different typewriter, in elite typeface rather than pica. At the time of Smallboy's death in 1984, some popular sources, such as *Alberta Report* and the *Canadian Encyclopedia*, presented with these documents, listed Smallboy's name, erroneously, as "Johnny Bob Smallboy."

The etymology of Smallboy's Cree surname, *Apitchitchiw*, is equally intriguing. A triple diminutive, *apitchitchiw* could be literally translated from the Old Cree as "small young boy." Its variants in modern Cree have been variously translated as "small," "small boy," "small young boy," "short young boy," "young boy," "little boy," and (in the United States) "shorty"! Contemporary Cree syllabics allow for a variety of spellings, including *Apisisiw, Apihcihciw*, and *Apiscisciw*.[3] However, none of these variants capture the full range of meaning given to the original Old Cree word. Thus, throughout this book, when referring to Smallboy's father, I have used the original spelling of *Apitchitchiw*, as it appears on Johnny Smallboy's purloined certificate of baptism.

STORYTELLING

In attempting to reconstruct an idyllic life in the foothills, Smallboy drew heavily from two main sources: his memory of what life had been like as a child living a nomadic existence in Alberta and Montana; and the oral history provided by several mentors, including his mother, Isabelle Coyote, and her stepmother, *Waskahte* (Walking-in-a-Circle), whom he regarded as his *nokôm* (grandma). He explained that storytellers rely on younger men and women in the tribe as a repository of memories. Once the story is told to a younger person and the younger man or woman has told the story in public to the satisfaction of the original storyteller, then the original storyteller can "let go" of the memory.

Thus the Chief would refer to others in his family who had been entrusted with a particular sacred memory, a story that perhaps had its origins in previous generations. His mother and grandmother had entrusted him with the telling of certain memories, and he in turn had entrusted his stories to his son, Joe, and also to his daughters, Elizabeth Monture and Clara Rattlesnake,[4] to his grandsons, Don, Bob, Lorne, and Paul, and to his many granddaughters, Lorrene, Andrea, Audrey, Eleanor, Jessie, Paula, Lisa, and Shannon. His grandniece Marie Smallboy explained the process by analogy to modern technology: "They used the brains of younger people like we use computer memory today," she said. "Then all they had to remember was which folder they'd stored it in—and which drive."[5]

Since this book relies heavily on the storytelling skills of Chief Smallboy and his descendants from generation to generation, it is important to understand the ways in which stories and the information they contain are preserved in memory and how they are transmitted. Chief Smallboy himself emphasized the importance of retelling narratives precisely, in the context of listening carefully to the words of the elders so that sentences could be repeated virtually verbatim after a single hearing. In turn, elders would listen carefully to the men and women who had been entrusted with the family stories and tribal history and would correct any errors in the recitation. He told me that there were many checks and balances to make sure that the storyteller did not deviate from the truth. "Elders listen to young storytellers relate from memory the history of the family or band or tribe, and correct them whenever necessary," he said, adding that his grandmother *Waskahte* was just such a "tribal historian."[6] According to Marie Smallboy, her great-grandmother Isabelle Coyote in particular retained her storytelling ability right up to her death, describing to Marie details of the signing of the treaty at Blackfoot Crossing in 1877 and of the great peace pact concluded among the Plains Indian tribes in 1871—information that she had obtained not only from personal observation but also from her father, Coyote, and her grandfather Bobtail.

The Cree had a reputation for preciseness, which explains why they are called to this day the *Nehiyawak*, literally the "Precise Speakers."

Chief Smallboy himself has been presented by linguists and other academics studying the subject as a prime example of how Cree oral history has been preserved. For example, Smallboy repeated the circumstances leading up to his 1968 exodus from the Ermineskin Reserve to the Kootenay Plains many times, under different circumstances, in many different places; yet he remained remarkably consistent in his narrative. Bruce Cox, who describes the migration as "another example of Cree attempts to redefine their relations with the Indian Affairs Branch," points out that Smallboy's narrative "Decision to Leave Hobbema," as translated by Eugene Steinhauer and published in the very first issue of *The Western Canadian Journal of Anthropology*, "reflects, even in translation, the oratorical tradition of the nayhiyuwayin—the 'precise speakers.'"[7]

Joan Oxendale writes in "Reflections of the Structure of Cree," which accompanies Smallboy's narrative,

> To the people who speak it, the Cree language is known as *nayhiyuwayin*, the way of speaking accurately. In some of the old records, the Cree people were referred to as "the nayhiyways," the precise speakers. The precision of the spoken language is an integral part of Cree tradition.... The emphasis on importance of oratorical ability itself indicates the nature of a society where courtesy and liberality are of paramount value. The Cree are a gracious, hospitable people.[8]

Their oratorical ability translates into a narrative tapestry or oral history, which in this book forms a backdrop to the collective Smallboy psyche.

Oxendale's observation is of course a generalization, but it is also a truism: it implies that, more than most people, the Cree in their own traditional setting listen politely to their storytelling elders and learn from them and that they are generous about sharing their stories with others. But the storytelling process isn't simply a matter of manners; it's also a matter of linguistics: "Cree words are often whole thoughts strung together polysynthetically in a manner so vivid to the listener (or narrator) that they are easily remembered," says Oxendale.[9]

The Cree may have been particularly precise storytellers, but storytelling was by no means exclusive to the Cree. Stoney Chief John Snow explains that storytelling was at the very hub of the education of every traditional Plains Indian: "A very important responsibility of the tribal members was to pass on valuable information to the next generation by the spoken word. Parents, grandparents, and elders told and retold stories and legends to the children by the campfires, in the teepees, on the hillsides, in the forest, and at special gatherings during the day and at night."[10]

THE SMALLBOY CAMP

At first, the Smallboy Camp was located on the Kootenay Plains north of the North Saskatchewan River, not far from the proposed David Thompson Highway, which would eventually provide western Alberta with an easy link to the high mountains of Banff and Jasper national parks. The band had ready employment because the Alberta government had committed to building the Bighorn Dam across the North Saskatchewan, in the process creating a huge artificial reservoir, Lake Abraham, named after Silas Abraham, one of the first Assiniboine (Stoney) settlers in the region. All the trees had to be harvested and the land cleared to make way for the eventual flooding of the dam. As the work progressed, Smallboy changed the location of the camp half a dozen times during the first year.

Reporters visiting Chief Smallboy at the camp were surprised to find not a hotheaded radical, but a dignified, good-humoured gentleman, who, by the time of his move, was already well into his seventies. Cree interpreters reported that he had a distinctive Chippewa or "Old Cree" inflexion, pronunciation, and vocabulary. He steadfastly refused to speak English. Still, reporters generally seemed to be inspired by his resourcefulness and determination. They described him as a leader who had "shepherded" his people, a soldier fighting "a determined battle for his dream."[11]

The initial mobile village consisted of one huge teepee, used as a meeting hall and schoolroom, and about twenty tents. The first site was on a meadow, surrounded by low poplar trees and high mountains near the confluence of the North Saskatchewan and Siffleur rivers; it was accessible only by a network of grassy trails meandering through the trees. Later in the fall of 1968, the camp was moved closer to the barely passable gravel road that was to become the David Thompson Highway.

Alberta's Social Credit government deliberately ignored the new settlement, partly because the Smallboy Band served a useful purpose. In fact, while the *Weekend Magazine* news team was at the camp, provincial officials approached Smallboy and the heavily bearded Lazarus Roan to offer the band jobs clearing the land. The deputy minister of Lands and Forests, Dr. V. A. Wood, admitted that his department was co-operating with the Chief. "We know they're there," he said. "In fact, we even suggested where they should set up their camp. They're running a good camp. It's quite true that they have no authority to be there, but we're just not taking any action. Anybody can go camping—although this is more permanent than usual."[12]

EDUCATION

Classes in Native lore were taught in the central teepee by Simon Omeasoo's daughter-in-law, Violet. "We brought the children away to grow this Indian way, to grow up with it," she told journalist Paul Grescoe of *Weekend Magazine*. "We try to get back to the Indian way. The younger boys learn to hunt. The younger girls, they have to make hides. There's always something to do."[13] In August 1968, the *Edmonton Journal*'s Stan Reid noticed evidence of this traditional Indian education: "The women and girls were all busy," he reported. "Young girls under the supervision of an elderly squaw were scraping fresh hide. Another group was stretching another hide, which looked like that of a deer."[14] Grescoe confirmed that "they are teaching the children to hunt and trap and treat hides, to know the forest and the mountains and the animals, to respect their elders and to despise liquor and the licentiousness it can cause."[15]

The quality of education of the children and teenagers in the Smallboy Camp was, from the beginning, the hottest issue, not only with the local media but also with members of the camp itself. In the fall of 1968, the generally unsympathetic *Red Deer Advocate* ran the headline "INDIANS WARNED: CAN'T SKIP SCHOOL," followed by a front-page attack on Smallboy, quoting Alberta government sources. Stan Reid of the *Edmonton Journal* considered the establishment of the Smallboy Camp the 1968 "Story of the Year" and by September had shifted his attention from berating Smallboy's efforts to speculating, naively, on when they would return to the reserve: "A lever expected to get them back to Hobbema was the legal requirement that their children go to school. There are from 125 to 150 Indians in the group, including 40 children of school age."[16]

In fact, Smallboy was as concerned as anyone else with establishing a school at the camp, and Violet Omeasoo suggested sending some of the teenagers to college for training as teachers—a dream that came true a decade later when her own daughter, Janet, completed her Bachelor of Education degree through Maskwachees Cultural College and the University of Calgary. In 1969, a teacher was assigned, and two mobile construction trailers were supplied by the federal government for use as a teacherage and school. However, the teacher, unsuited for the rigours of the bush, soon packed it in, taking one of the trailers with him. The remaining construction trailer was used for storage until the government supplied larger classroom facilities, a mobile unit that became the feature landmark of the permanent Smallboy Camp. The mobile schoolhouse remains in place, although it has been boarded up since 2003, when the government withdrew support for the school in the amount of $250,000 of annual funding.[17]

FROM POVERTY TO RICHES

In 1970, the Smallboy Camp split in two, one-third of the membership following Joseph Mackinaw to the Buck Lake region within the boundaries of Treaty Six. After the death in the mid-1970s, first, of Simon Omeasoo and, then, of Lazarus Roan, a number of their relatives returned to Hobbema. The remaining members of the Smallboy Band retained their status in the Ermineskin Band as well and so were not deprived of their share of the oil royalties that in the 1970s and 1980s gave each member of the Ermineskin Band, man, woman, and child, about five hundred dollars a month.

Although Smallboy had initially taken his band to the foothills to help alleviate poverty, the Ermineskin Reserve soon became the richest in the land. Smallboy, before leaving Hobbema, had had the foresight along with other chiefs of the Four Bands Council based at Hobbema to allow oil exploration on their reserves, even though this activity did not at first yield high dividends. Once the Province of Alberta imposed a heavy royalty on oil produced in the province, oil on federal Indian reserves could be sold at a commensurately lower price—and the Indian reserves could take the royalties for themselves. The royalties in turn were distributed to members of the reserves and invested in the community.

Given this new wealth, the temptation to remain on the Ermineskin Reserve rather than go "home" to the Smallboy Camp sometimes became overwhelming. Many tried to keep a foot in both worlds, travelling between Hobbema, where they had the most modern amenities, such as large-screen television sets and fancy plumbing, and the camp, where they had no such amenities. Those who, with Smallboy, believed that the abundance of riches was more of a curse than a blessing remained at the camp.

By 1978, Smallboy had become an important influence on Native politics, a living oracle with whom Native leaders consulted and whose advice was often followed. On the tenth anniversary of his bold foray into the wilderness, both Native and white admirers of Smallboy began a campaign to honour him, and in 1979 he was nominated for the Order of Canada by Maurice Strong. The following year, Governor General Ed Schreyer presented him with the Order of Canada medal in Ottawa.

Why did Chief Bob Smallboy return to the land, forsaking his farm and his political ambitions in Hobbema? How successful was he in accomplishing his goals and dreams? What kind of man was he? What moved him to do the things he did, even travelling in his pursuit of freedom to Ottawa, to London, to Rome? If actions speak louder than words, then his was a very loud voice—a voice in the wilderness that insists even now on being heard.

CHAPTER 2

Big Bear
and Little Bear

"A ROPE AROUND MY NECK"

If Chief Bob Smallboy came to be regarded by the press as a maverick among Native leaders, he came by this reputation quite correctly: "It's in our DNA," quipped Marie Smallboy. Just as she regarded Smallboy, her great-uncle on her father's side, as her *mosôm* (grandpa), so Smallboy regarded his great-uncle on his father's side, Big Bear, as his *nimosôm* (grandfather, grand-uncle). Big Bear (*Mistahimaskwa*) was one of several impressive chiefs whom Smallboy claimed among his "grandfathers"—the men he honoured in death as much as in life. Another such leader was Big Bear's son Little Bear, in Canada known as *Ayimisis* or *Imasees* (Little Bad Man), who eventually became the first chief of the Rocky Boy Reservation in Montana. Both chiefs became role models for Bob Smallboy.

One of the metaphors used by Smallboy in 1971 had been repeatedly used by Big Bear during the 1876 treaty negotiations at Fort Pitt (located in what is now western Saskatchewan). Given that treaty negotiations had been represented to the Indians as being, at least in part, "peace" talks—preceded by the ritual smoking of peace pipes—Big Bear's remarks seemed particularly out of place. The words had confounded both interpreters and the lieutenant-governor of the North-West Territories, Alexander Morris. The remarks also seemed out of character for Big Bear, who had a reputation for fearlessness. After galloping across the plains for days to reach the treaty talks, just about the first thing this bold chief is alleged to have said, as translated by the interpreter, was that he was terrified of death by hanging!

Big Bear had turned up several days late for the treaty talks at Fort Pitt, which had commenced on 7 September 1876. He had been out on the plains hunting buffalo when he first heard about the convention. When he finally arrived on 12 September, the commissioners were just packing up to leave. Chief Sweet Grass, the primary spokesman for the assembled Cree, urged Big Bear to sign Treaty Six, as he and all the other assembled chiefs had done. But Big Bear balked. "Stop, stop, my friends," he said, sizing up Morris. "I never saw the Governor before." Then he added: "When I heard he was come, I said I will request him to save me from what I most dread. It was not given to us to have the rope about our necks." The interpreter conveyed to Morris that Big Bear was afraid of "hanging," inserting this word parenthetically after the clause "what I most dread." The official transcriber, A. G. Jackes, M.D., recognized this as a parenthetical insertion by the translator. He transcribed Big Bear's words as:

> Stop, stop, my friends, I have never seen the Governor before; I have seen Mr. Christie many times. I heard the Governor was to come and I said I shall see him; when I see him I will make a request that he will save me from what I most dread, that is: the rope to be about my neck (hanging).[1]

Misunderstanding Big Bear, Morris naturally enough replied that hanging as a form of capital punishment would remain in place. He regarded Big Bear's remark either as a sign of a guilty mind (he must have done something for which he thought he might garner the death penalty) or an intention to do something horrific for which he sought in advance some sort of reprieve from facing the death penalty. Why should Big Bear be so concerned about hanging if he intended to keep the law? "Why are you so anxious about bad men?" Morris asked.[2]

When Big Bear persisted in using the metaphor, Morris wrote, "I informed him that his request would not be granted."[3] This seemed to leave Big Bear in some confusion.

> The Bear remained sitting until all had shaken hands, he then took mine and holding it, said, "If he had known he would have met me with all his people. I am not an undutiful child, I do not throw back your hand, but as my people are not here I do not sign. I will tell them what I have heard, and next year I will come." The Indians then left, but shortly afterwards the Bear came to see me again, fearing I had not fully understood him, and assured me that he accepted the treaty as if he had signed it, and would come next year with all his people and accept it.[4]

This approximated Dr. Jackes's transcription:

The Bear remained sitting until all had said good-bye to the Governor, and then he rose and taking his hand, said, "I am glad to meet you, I am alone; but if I had known the time, I would have been here with all my people. I am not an undutiful child, I do not throw back your hand; but as my people are not here, I do not sign. I will tell them what I have heard, and next year I will come." About an hour afterwards the Big Bear came to the Fort Pitt House to see the Governor, and again repeated that he accepted the treaty as if he had signed it, and would come next year, with all his people, to meet the Commissioners and accept it.[5]

Historian Hugh A. Dempsey's analysis of what happened in this interchange is very instructive, because here, as elsewhere, there was no comprehension on either side—no meeting of the minds. In Dempsey's view, what Big Bear really meant by the expression "It was not given to us to have the rope about our necks" was not hanging by the neck until dead, but a much greater existential conundrum: the loss of freedom. The metaphor was that of a horse, which Big Bear had just been riding for days trying to get to the fort on time. The Indians considered the will of the horse broken by its trainer only when it could be led about and given commands with a simple rope around its neck. Dempsey suggests, "Had the words been properly translated, Big Bear might have received an assurance from [Alexander] Morris that could have changed the course of history."[6] No doubt every Indian chief present knew precisely what Big Bear was talking about, but, partly because of the mistranslation, Morris remained ignorant.

There is yet another dimension to Big Bear's metaphor that rationalist historians may be quick to dismiss, but that remains a credible explanation for his words as far as traditional Cree observers are concerned: that of a prophecy. Big Bear was regarded as powerfully connected to the spirit world.[7] The Cree of today are prepared to accept that Big Bear was indeed referring to hanging, in the context of Big Bear's having had a prophetic vision of the future: eight Cree and Stoney Indians hanged by the neck until dead in what remains the largest mass execution in Canadian history.

Be that as it may, Chief Smallboy used the same metaphor in a speech in 1971: "If they come for me and tell me to leave," he said, "I will do as my grandfather (*omosôma*) would have done. They can put a rope around my neck but I will not move from this land!"[8] He later acknowledged that, in that particular speech, he was alluding to the words of Big Bear, his *omosômâw* (great-uncle), whom Smallboy respected as if he were his actual grandfather. The metaphor of the rope around the neck had not only survived in the oral tradition, but also remained rich with double meaning. Big Bear had said, "It is not given to us to have a rope about our necks"—describing the freedom of the First Nations before the reserve system was put in place. Signing Treaty Six was tantamount to allowing the white establishment to put a rope around their necks. But the mere act of putting a rope around a horse's neck doesn't mean the horse is broken. Smallboy was saying that even if the government puts a rope around his neck, he would resist being controlled—he would remain a wild horse to the end. And, ultimately, that is the same metaphor Big Bear used to convey that the First Nations were not easily tamed.

Just as Morris misunderstood the words and actions of Big Bear in 1876, the people outside Smallboy's camp misunderstood the words and actions of Bob Smallboy. Morris believed, erroneously, that Big Bear was driven by a personal obsession to the point of paranoia—fear of hanging as a form of execution. Similarly, in Hobbema, members of the Ermineskin Band believed that Chief Smallboy was driven by a similar personal obsession to the point of paranoia; after all, the death penalty had been abolished in Canada for everything but treason and military offences, such as desertion in the face of the enemy. They could not make sense of their chief's remarks. Some band members dismissed the Chief as out of touch with reality: he had become "an old hippie."[9]

Embarrassed by the Chief's words and actions, some band members circulated a petition asking the band council to unseat Chief Smallboy "because he has deserted us and no longer has any interest." This petition was eventually signed by a quarter of the remaining members of the Ermineskin Band, and it triggered a referendum that was held among the remaining band members, as a result of which new elections were held. Maurice Wolfe was elected new chief of the Ermineskin Band. Nonetheless, Smallboy continued to claim to be chief of the breakaway Smallboy Band by virtue of his hereditary status as chief dating back to his two *omosômâws*—his great-grandfather Chief Bobtail (after whom he was named) and his great-uncle Chief Big Bear.

Chief Little Bear, whom Smallboy called *Kakikaymuskwa*, meaning "Forever Bear," was technically only his cousin. Like Moses, Little Bear led the Canadian Cree in Montana, who had wandered around the state for more than thirty years, before becoming their first chief in the "Promised Land" of the Rocky Boy Reservation in 1917. Smallboy and his family lived with Little Bear for many years, and Big Bear's second son figured so prominently in Smallboy's early life that Smallboy regarded him, too, as his *nimosôm*.

Like Smallboy, both Big Bear and Little Bear had been late bloomers, at least where politics was concerned. All three tried to stand up for the rights of their followers in the face of the juggernaut of western settlement —none of them without controversy.

BIG BEAR

The life of Big Bear has been well documented by Hugh A. Dempsey and well depicted by Rudy Wiebe.[10] Born in 1825 near Fort Carlton, on the North Saskatchewan River just north of present-day Saskatoon, Big Bear "was the son of an Ojibwa chief named Black Powder, or *Mukatai* … His mother, whose name has been forgotten in the mistiness of the past, was either Cree or Ojibwa."[11] Smallboy said that the mother of both Big Bear and his own grandmother, *Miýweýihtakwan* (Pleasant One), was *Ocepihk* (Root). *Sayos*, the first wife of Big Bear, was also Ojibwa (synonymous with Chippewa), according to Dempsey.[12]

Big Bear received his name after seeing a vision of the Great Parent Bear Spirit at the forks of the South Saskatchewan and Red Deer rivers—the true "crossroads" of the prairies. A bear-paw necklace was subsequently a significant part of his power bundle, and Big Bear wore the claw for protection in battle. David Mandelbaum notes that Big Bear's bundle, known as "Chief's Son's Hand," is now in the American Museum of Natural History:[13]

> The charm itself is simply the tanned hide from a bear paw, with the claws attached. It is sewn on a square collar of scarlet flannel, and was worn as a neckpiece. Big-bear [sic] was visited by the Bear spirit power who told him to make the bundle and taught him a song. The words of the song are "My teeth are my knives; my claws are my knives." Before he unwrapped the bundle, Big-bear would dig a hole and scoop out some clay which he would plaster over his face and streak with outspread fingers in imitation of bear scratches.
>
> When any bundle was unwrapped, pipe offerings had to be made. When Big-bear's bundle was opened a filled pipe was passed through sweetgrass smoke, then held with the stem pointing directly upward. Great *Manito* was addressed and asked to notice that the pipe offering was being made as he had directed. Then the pipe was lit; four puffs were taken, and the pipestem rotated in a counter-clockwise direction so that the mouthpiece described a complete circle. Then the stem was held up again, somewhat lower than before, and the Great Parent Bear spirit was addressed and told the reason for unwrapping the bundle. The cloth to be added to the bundle as a payment offering was mentioned. The pipe was rotated once again and the stem pointed to the forks of the South Saskatchewan and Red Deer

rivers, the place where the vision appeared to Chief Big-bear. The Bear spirit which visited Big-bear was addressed and the circumstances of the vision were recited. The pipe was rotated again and pointed to the ground. It was held over four places on the ground as though being pointed to the four legs of a bear or of a bear hide. The Great Parent of Bear was again addressed.[14]

At the battle of Loon Lake Narrows on 3 June 1885, Big Bear is said to have walked unscathed between the battling parties with the bear's claw resting in the hollow of his throat. "As long as he wore that claw there, nothing could hurt him. It was as if he placed an invisible wall between his people and the soldiers."[15]

At forty, Big Bear became headman of a small band near Fort Pitt. At fifty, he was first recognized as a full-fledged chief in the wake of an attempt to persuade other chiefs, including Bobtail, not to sign Treaty Six. He declined to sign the treaty until he had a chance to consult with other Cree and Assiniboine chiefs in his group.[16] Even though he was forced to sign an adhesion to the treaty in 1882 in order to stave off the starvation of his band, as far as the Canadian government was concerned, he remained a primary threat to peace in the Saskatchewan area until 1885, when, at sixty, he tried but failed to convince the younger men in his band to follow the course of moderation. Lumped in with Louis Riel and Gabriel Dumont as one of the fomenters of the second Riel Rebellion, Big Bear was found guilty of felonious treason and, along with Poundmaker, was sentenced to three years, and jailed for two. His spirit broken, he died soon after his release.[17]

SMALLPOX AND THE BATTLE OF BELLY RIVER

For decades, the Blackfoot and Cree had conducted savage raids on each other, absconding with horses, women, and scalps. Invariably there were casualties on both sides; in a raiding party of thirty men, often only twenty could be expected to return home alive to tell tales of their coups. The Peigans and Crow were considered to be the most dangerous rivals of the Cree, if only because they gave chase with exceptional zeal, often following the Cree marauders for four or five days in order to recover stolen horses.[18]

By 1869, the Peigans in particular roamed throughout Montana to southern Alberta, from the confluence of the Milk and Missouri rivers in the southeast to the Kootenay Plains in the northwest. Armed with repeating rifles and relatively fleet horses, they were proud of their seeming invincibility. To feed the insatiable European demand for buffalo robes, even as the population of the North American bison declined, in 1869 the Blackfoot Confederacy raided and pillaged Cree, Assiniboine, and Chippewa camps, almost at will, taking buffalo robes from people who would surely need them to survive the bitterly cold winter. The Blackfoot traded the looted robes for whisky and rifles at Fort Whoop-Up, located at the confluence of the St. Mary and Oldman rivers. In the most savage of these raids in 1869, the Peigans massacred seventy Assiniboines in the Cypress Hills, sustaining only one loss.[19]

A few of the Peigan warriors felt so invincible that, when the opportunity arose, they raided a river steamer that had run aground on the Missouri at the mouth of the Milk River at the eastern edge of their territory, not knowing that two of the passengers had been quarantined with symptoms of smallpox. In reprisal for the raid, the U.S. Cavalry mounted an assault against the Peigans, massacring two hundred South Peigans in their village (mostly women and children) and pushing the warriors westward across Montana to the mountains and then north across the border into Canada.[20] In the meantime, the Bloods in Canada were doing a brisk trade with American whisky traders. That winter, the Bloods in particular drank away all other inclinations, even as a parallel scourge worked its way through the Peigan, Blood, and Siksika camps—for the blankets originally purloined on the river steamer had been infected with smallpox. The horrible disease spread rapidly through the Blackfoot population, leaving hundreds dead.

Early the following year, Cree raiding parties came across hundreds of abandoned Blackfoot teepees containing the corpses of men, women, and children. They took blankets from the dead and looted the camps, then rode northeast to spread the word, in the process spreading the disease to the Crees. "The disease was brought to the Indians by the Long Knives," said Chief Smallboy, reciting oral history of the epidemic told to him by his step-grandmother *Waskahte*. "They did so deliberately to wipe out the Indian people." The population of the Blackfoot was greatly reduced by the disease, he said. "There were many lodges where one could see an entire family lying on the ground, with everyone dead within the lodge."[21]

Most survivors were disfigured for life, among them Little Bear's second wife (his first died of starvation in 1883, along with their daughter).[22] Big Bear had developed immunity to the disease, having contracted smallpox at age twelve. He had been left disfigured by the epidemic of 1837.[23] To him, history seemed to be repeating itself. As far as he was concerned, smallpox was the first "gift" of the white man to the First Nations—and, this time, the Blackfoot Confederacy had been the agents of the white man in spreading it around.[24]

He blamed the Bloods and Siksikas for the new smallpox epidemic.

When the Assiniboines called upon their allies to attack the Blackfoot in a reprisal for a massacre of almost everybody in their camp in the Cypress Hills, Big Bear was quick to agree. In the summer of 1870, Cree and Assiniboine warriors from all over the plains rode westward from the Qu'Appelle Valley to confront the Blackfoot Confederacy, perhaps not appreciating the extent to which the Blackfoot population had itself been decimated by the disease.

The Cree attack on a small Blood camp on the Belly River, five kilometres north of Fort Whoop-Up, on Halloween and All Saints Day, 1870, was ill-conceived, since the Cree scouts had overlooked the fact that a larger Blood camp was situated on the far side of the river a short distance away. The Cree were armed only with bows and arrows and primitive flintlocks, while the Blackfoot Confederacy had acquired comparatively sophisticated repeating rifles from the whisky traders at Fort Whoop-Up—paying for them with the purloined buffalo robes. Furthermore, hundreds of armed South Peigans were camped at the edge of Fort Whoop-Up, blood running high from having been chased by the U.S. Cavalry across Montana in retaliation for the raid on the river boat. Only five kilometres away from the Blood camp, they were quickly called to arms.[25]

Alerted by the sound of gunfire and possibly by retreating Bloods, the Peigans mounted a counterattack that amounted to a complete rout of the Cree-Assiniboine alliance. One of Hugh Dempsey's sources, John Cotton, stated that 42 Bloods, Peigans, and Blackfeet and 173 Cree were killed—substantially fewer casualties than Dempsey's earlier estimates, in which he stated that the body count for the 1870 Battle of Belly River was the largest ever sustained in intertribal First Nations warfare in Canada. In his book *Firewater* (2002), Dempsey calls the Battle of Belly River "the last great Indian battle on the Canadian frontier." He notes that trader Jerry Potts and freighter Howard Harris had witnessed the fighting. "You could fire with your eyes shut," Potts later told the *Lethbridge News*, "and be sure to kill a Cree," implying that he took part in the massacre.[26]

Big Bear's woes were only just beginning. Opposed to giving up his freedom for the confines of a reserve, he refused to sign Treaty Six in 1876 and resisted the reserve system until 1882, by which time the buffalo had been all but eradicated and Big Bear's nomadic band was on the verge of mass starvation. *Waskahte* vividly described all of this to Bob Smallboy. She told him that it wasn't just the buffalo that disappeared, although that was the root cause: because of the demand on the food chain, everything else edible, including rodents, disappeared. She told Bob that the nomadic Cree were reduced to cooking their moccasins and rawhide ropes to release any nutrients they might contain. "Many, many were those who died from starvation, according to my grandmother," said Smallboy. "Many babies died from starvation, for they were too weak to suck milk from the breasts of their mothers, and there was nothing in the breasts to suck. That is what my grandmother said of that difficult time."[27] As Geoffrey York puts it, "Eventually, the Indians were reduced to eating horses, dogs, gophers and mice."[28] Among those who starved to death were the wife and daughter of *Imasees.*[29] As if that weren't enough suffering, "shortly afterwards, an epidemic of measles wiped out one-third of the band members."[30] Smallboy's paternal grandmother, *Miÿweÿihtakwan,* the first wife of his paternal grandfather, Rocky Boy, died in that epidemic, and his mother, Isabelle Coyote, was blinded by the disease.

THE RIEL REBELLION

Big Bear's alliance of Cree, Chippewa, and Assiniboine Indians, about 750 people in all, sympathized with the uprising led by Louis Riel and Gabriel Dumont, known as the Riel Rebellion—what some Cree sources now refer to as the "Riel Resistance."[31] The band received only self-serving reports from Métis messengers, designed to bring as many Indians into the conflict as possible. These reports fired up younger elements among Big Bear's band, including his son *Imasees.* In the Cree tradition, once war was in the offing, the reins of power were handed to the war chief, in this case, a feisty warrior named Wandering Spirit (*Kapapamahchakwew*), who, fuelled by alcohol-laced painkillers and sacramental wine purloined from the mission, led an attack on the small community of whites at Frog Lake in 1885. Nine men, including two priests, were killed in what became known as the Frog Lake Massacre. The first to die was the hard-nosed Indian agent Tom Quinn, who had adopted a rigid food-for-work policy.

The Cree under Big Bear lingered in the vicinity of Fort Pitt, where they took several white prisoners, whom Big Bear undertook to protect. But the pressure quickly mounted as the army and the North-West Mounted Police combined forces against them, using more sophisticated weaponry, including Gatling guns and cannon. Eventually, Big Bear's band split up into smaller parties, and many surrendered. Big Bear continued to take personal responsibility for the welfare of the white prisoners who had surrendered to them at Fort Pitt.

Big Bear did not participate directly in the Battle of Frenchman's Butte on 28 May, remaining with the prisoners and older members of the band five kilometres behind the front lines. He allowed half a dozen white prisoners and as many Métis and Woodland Cree prisoners to escape, and more escaped on 1 June.[32]

Meanwhile, in the combat zone, Wandering Spirit had become "in every sense a true chief, inspiring confidence and courage … bold, decisive and inspiring." He led the band north through thick forest. "Big Bear no longer had a horse and plodded along with the rest, neither offering help nor being helped by others. Someone had even stolen his blanket. Like the others, he and his small family had only the food they could carry on their backs, or on the few horses and oxen that accompanied the retreating band."[33]

Two days later, they reached Loon Lake, but the group had split in two, perhaps by design.[34] One group of predominantly Woodland Cree, accompanied by Wandering Spirit, headed southwest back to Fort Pitt, where they would eventually surrender, Wandering Spirit apparently deciding to accept responsibility for what had happened at Fort Pitt (where one policeman was killed) and at Frog Lake. "His defection meant that Imasees assumed leadership of his father's band."[35] It also acted as a distraction so that other Plains Cree who were considered fomenters of the rebellion (but who were for the most part innocent) would have a better chance of escape.

Major General Frederick Middleton ordered a multi-pronged invasion of the territory surrounding Loon Lake from Prince Albert to the northeast, from Battleford to the southeast, and from Fort Pitt to the southwest. He himself took four hundred cavalry and infantrymen up the North Saskatchewan from Battleford to Fort Pitt, while ordering Colonel W. D. Otter to march northward from Battleford to Turtle Lake.

> Confident that the Cree could be overtaken, the general hurriedly joined the pursuit with a large mounted force and two Gatling guns. He also ordered three other columns north in an effort to snare the wily old chief if he tried to escape south: Commissioner Irvine of the NWMP would march from Prince Albert to Green Lake; Colonel Otter from Battleford to Turtle Lake; and General Strange from Frog Lake to Cold Lake. But the largest manhunt in Canadian history came up empty-handed.[36]

Most histories have discounted any role that Big Bear may have played in events following the final disintegration of his band on 25 June 1885, when his middle two sons, *Imasees* and Kingbird, declared they were going to make for the U.S. border with the bulk of those remaining—about two hundred men, women, and children. There is every indication that Big Bear, his youngest son, Horsechild, and a faithful headman, Two-and-Two, followed their column, covering their tracks. It is likely that Big Bear contributed more to the successful escape of the remnant of his band than has been credited.

Big Bear had originally been identified with the River People, a large group of Plains Cree who wintered along the North Saskatchewan.[37] As

Mandelbaum suggests, the Cree transition from canoe to horse "was not as great a dislocation as it might have been," had they been a more sedentary people.[38] Big Bear personally demonstrated the skill to build and use river craft, including a raft.[39] Given that the military and police forces were acting in concert in a double-pincer movement in order to capture Big Bear and his band, the Cree fugitives likely resorted not only to the use of horses, but also to their more traditional—but not entirely forgotten—woodland skills.

The Indian Agency had issued them valued tools, including axes, saws, and ropes, in order to clear the land. Now, rather than leaving a swath through the woods for their pursuers to follow as they had earlier on in the chase, they likely used their tools to fell trees to make rafts large enough to carry some—if not many—of their number, especially the women and children, downstream on the North Saskatchewan to a rendezvous point in the Thickwood Hills.

After General Middleton moved most of his troops upstream from Battleford to Fort Pitt, he joined the march north from Fort Pitt to Loon Lake. Colonel Otter marched his brigade from Battleford north to Turtle Lake and came closest to capturing the main group; indeed, forty of those who had followed *Imasees*'s initial route gave themselves up to Otter shortly after his arrival at Turtle Lake. This created a distraction that benefitted *Imasees* and his group, including Big Bear, for whom Otter's troops were on the lookout. Big Bear himself "reached Turtle Lake and almost stumbled into Colonel Otter's camp but managed to pass through his lines without being seen."[40]

Big Bear, Horsechild (then twelve), and Two-and-Two likely followed *Imasees*'s retreat, helping the fugitives to "disappear" by erasing any tracks or other evidence of their passage. This may be one reason why neither Colonel Otter nor Assistant Commander A. G. Irvine of the North-West Mounted Police, whose troops and officers were criss-crossing the country, could not find any evidence of a mass retreat.

After their close shave with Colonel Otter's troops, Big Bear, Horsechild, and Two-and-Two made their way to the Thickwood Hills. It is not known what route the trio took, but assuming they followed the tracks of *Imasees*'s horses east via Birch Lake and then southeast to the Thickwood Hills, they were not at any time very far in the rear, especially if, as the prevailing theory has it, the women and children were on foot. What is known is that in the Thickwood Hills, the trio nearly ran into a patrol of scouts sent out by Assistant Commander Irvine.[41]

It is also known that it took the main body of *Imasees*'s retreating group three weeks to travel from Loon Lake to the Forks of the South Saskatchewan and Red Deer rivers. Most of the group would have been thoroughly exhausted from the trek through the muskeg and from a month of combat, including the original northward retreat to Loon Lake. If in addition the fugitives took an overland route from Loon Lake to the Thickwood Hills, they would have been doubly exhausted. The rough terrain they had to negotiate for those on foot to get to the Thickwood Hills would have determined the schedule of the entire group: it would have taken several days to get from Loon Lake to the Thickwood Hills on foot, via Turtle Lake and Birch Lake.

It seems just as feasible that this first leg of the trip was accomplished by the women and children, accompanied by a few men, plying the river on rafts. True, most of the men may have ridden without detection by a route farther north, past Birch Lake, as Dempsey suggested. But as he himself pointed out, by then the group had few horses.[42] Some of the men may have ridden closer to the river to keep tabs on the progress of the rafts on the swift-flowing river.

It is also known that a week after *Imasees* declared that he would head for the border, Big Bear used a raft to float to an island near the Thickwood Hills, where he and Horsechild camped—only to hear "the whistle of a steamboat, the *Alberta*, coming downstream from Battleford. To Big Bear's horror, the boat passed too close to his little island and became stuck on a sandbar. For a while he had visions of men swarming over the place, looking for logs to work the boat loose, but then breathed a sigh of relief when it worked itself free and continued its journey."[43] Big Bear then headed downriver with Horsechild, intending to surrender at Fort Carlton. En route, on 4 July 1885, just nine days after *Imasees* had first declared his intention to make for the border, Big Bear gave himself up to a Hudson's Bay Company trader, who in turn summoned the police.[44]

By the fall of 1885, most of Big Bear's band—at one time the largest of the prairie Cree bands—had been rounded up and dispersed across the prairies in a forced diaspora designed to foil further opposition to Canadian government plans for the Indian. In August, the *Calgary Herald* opined in an editorial that Indians generally "know very well that they can never be anything more than the pariahs of the civilization which has surrounded them, in spite of pow-wows and promises and treaties."[45] Sir Cecil Denny perhaps best capsulated the attitude of the white man towards the Indian in his memoirs, published in 1939:

The white settler coming into the country to raise cattle or farm cared little what became of the poor Indian. If a cow was killed or a horse stolen, the Indians were to blame. Their land was looked upon with covetous eyes and they were regarded as a nuisance and expense. The right of the native red man was not for a moment considered or acknowledged, though more from ignorance than actual hard-heartedness. He was an inferior being to the lordly white man and doomed to pass before advancing civilization.[46]

By the time Big Bear was released from jail after serving two years of his three-year sentence, only the youngest of his five wives was anywhere to be found, and she had taken up residence with another man.[47] An Indian agent wrote with respect to Big Bear's death: "He has had domestic troubles lately, his wife preferring the society of other men. She would leave the Reserve and the old veteran would follow her for days, until he overdid himself."[48] Truth be told, he wasn't that old—just sixty-three at the time of his death.

LITTLE BEAR

Although there is no evidence to show that he was directly involved in the killings at Frog Lake, *Imasees*, who eventually came to be called Little Bear, is widely regarded as being the fomenter of that particular conflict in 1885, for which his father was eventually incarcerated and Wandering Spirit and seven others were hanged.[49] Thanks to an ambiguously stated opinion of his involvement by William Bleasdell Cameron, a white man with an axe to grind, Little Bear was held as responsible for the Frog Lake Massacre as Wandering Spirit, who, there is no doubt, led the attack on the white and half-Sioux inhabitants of the village and trading post. As late as 1926, Cameron, said to have written "the most detailed eye-witness account of the Frog Lake Massacre of April 2, 1885," maintained that had Little Bear "been captured after the rebellion he would doubtless have swung from the same scaffold as Wandering Spirit, for he was the real instigator of the Frog Lake Massacre."[50] However, Cameron, whose father was killed in the massacre, was not considered an impartial witness. At Little Bear's preliminary hearing in Regina in 1896, Cameron was dropped from the witness list when it was demonstrated that he did not personally witness the murders.

Little Bear claimed to have been on his way to Onion Lake at the time of the confrontation that left nine people dead. There is some independent evidence to support his claim of innocence. Old Keyam, one of the informants cited at length by Edward Ahenakew in *Voices of the Plains Cree*, gave a parallel account:

> Immediately after word came of the fight at Duck Lake, the Indians held a council. Wandering Spirit was present, as one of Big Bear's headmen, and I have been told by those who knew him well that he was utterly wild and reckless, "a no-good man" were the words used of him. The Indians listened

with more confidence to those who, like *A-yi-mi-ses*, Big Bear's son, urged a council meeting with the Chiefs of Onion Lake and Long Lake, who were moderate men.[51]

Certainly Chief *Seekaskootch* of Onion Lake had been summoned by *someone*. On the day following the murders, the one-armed chief arrived late at a council meeting led by Wandering Spirit and confronted him directly: "It is a shame to see how you have butchered innocent white people down there, but you cannot scare me," he said.[52]

It must have been clear to Little Bear that he would be blamed for the massacre. Following the subsequent sacking of Fort Pitt, he invited anyone actively involved in the combat to join him and Little Poplar in the long and risky trek to the border. "By 25 June the supplies of the Cree rebels were exhausted, so a council was held of those who remained. *Imasees*, now the leader, made it clear he had no intention of surrendering and planned to travel to the United States," along with Coyote, Kingbird, Lucky Man, Four Sky Thunder, and Miserable Man.[53] Because this move was for keeps and they feared reprisals against their families, the "rebels" took their wives and children—and even mothers and grandmothers—with them. Little Bear undertook to protect and care for his grandmother, Big Bear's mother, *Ocepihk*, by then already eighty. From their point of view, "This was war! Their women and children, their families, were in danger."[54]

Little Bear clearly believed, with Bobtail, that the Cree-Chippewa alliance had become the object of systematic genocide because of their alleged (and much exaggerated) complicity in the Riel Rebellion. Otherwise he would not have been so concerned about taking the women and children with him. Later, there were complaints that Little Bear "commandeered (for his escape) the best horses and many needed supplies and left his tribal kinsmen as a traitor might leave his comrades."[55] However, the fleeing "rebels" needed reliable horses to fetch and carry food and supplies sufficient to provide for about two hundred people, at the outset, including many women and children who were fleeing with them.[56]

THE FLIGHT TO FREEDOM

There has been some suggestion that Little Bear and his band took a direct path south into Montana, "following a route almost parallel to Saskatchewan's present-day number four highway."[57] However, as noted earlier, there is better evidence that they took a zigzag route, initially following a path southeast from Loon Lake past Turtle Lake and from there either rafting down the river or riding southwest to the Thickwood Hills, "which took them safely down to the Elbow of the North Saskatchewan at the edge of the plains."[58] From there, Little Bear and his remaining 140 or so followers headed south and southwest up Eagle Hills Creek and two weeks later reached the Forks, where the Red Deer River meets the South Saskatchewan.[59]

East of the Forks, the band waited as Little Bear sought guidance from the Great Parent Bear Spirit at the very location where years earlier his father had received a revelation from the selfsame spirit.[60] According to Bob Smallboy, Little Bear, having fasted for days since starting the trek, was soon visited by the Spirit of Bear, who gave him guidance, along with his new spiritual name *Kakikaymaskwa* (Forever Bear.) Later, in the United States, he modified his adopted name to *Maskosis* (Little Bear), perhaps in honour of the *other* Little Bear, who went to the gallows protesting his innocence.[61]

One incident in particular must have seemed like a miracle to the starving fugitives and corroboration of Little Bear's ascendancy in the esteem of the spirit world. North of the river, a stray bullock appeared seemingly from nowhere, as if it were offered to them by the Great Spirit. The band promptly dispatched and feasted upon it, thereby staving off starvation.[62] Later, as they prepared to cross the river, Bull Boy shot at and wounded a white man, George McIvor, as he fried fish on an island in the South Saskatchewan: nobody wanted witnesses to the crossing.[63] McIvor managed to push off in his rowboat and two days later made it as far as Saskatchewan Crossing before gasping out his story with his last breath.[64]

By then, however, Little Bear's entire group was well on its way to the Montana frontier. Crossing the Cypress Hills, the band was careful to avoid the North-West Mounted Police post at Fort Walsh, whose attention was thankfully diverted farther north by the predicament of their compeers at Fort Pitt. From the Cypress Hills, it was a comparatively easy trek across the broad expanse of prairie to Montana. Altogether, the journey took about four weeks.[65] Among those making the trek to Montana with Little Bear were Bob Smallboy's parents, *Apitchitchiw* and Isabelle (who probably first met and may well have commenced a relationship around the time of the trek); his paternal grandfather, Rocky Boy; his maternal grandfather, Coyote; his grandmother *Kakokikanis*; and two great-grandmothers: Rocky Boy's Assiniboine mother, Chippewa Speaker (who was born in Saskatchewan in 1837), and Rocky Boy's mother-in-law, *Ocepihk* (Root). *Ocepihk*, Big Bear's mother, was not only Little Bear's paternal grandmother, but also Bob Smallboy's paternal great-grandmother.[66]

Over the next year, and especially after the executions in November 1885, hundreds more Cree and Assiniboine Canadians fled into Montana in an exodus that Canadian and American authorities were powerless to quell.[67] Little Bear, Little Poplar, and their initial group of refugees continued to cling together as a band. In December 1885, the U.S. First Cavalry, stationed in what is now Montana, rounded up 137 Cree refugees—"62 bucks, 50 squaws, 25 children"—including Little Bear and "Chief Little Poplar, who proved refractory and was deposed, disarmed and tied to the wagon."[68] The Cavalry promptly turned the Canadian Cree over to the commanding officer at Fort Assinniboine (the spelling is peculiar to the fort) near Havre, sixty-five kilometres south of the Canadian border, a place that, thirty years later, would become their home.

In personally ordering their release in 1886, President Grover Cleveland in effect granted the Canadian Cree asylum, recognizing that their struggle with the Canadian government was of a political character. Ironically, three decades later the fort that was their first official "home" in America would become the permanent site of the Rocky Boy Reservation. Historian Thomas Wessel remarks:

> The Crees' expectancy to find a home in Montana was not unreasonable. In 1885, when Little Bear arrived in Montana, most of the area north of the Missouri River remained Indian land. In the western part of the state, the Flathead, Pend d'Oreille, and Kutenai still occupied portions of the Bitter Root Valley. That somewhere on that vast expanse of land the Cree and Chippewa might find a permanent home, did not require an exceptional imagination. But weather, politics and avarice intervened to deny both the Cree and the Chippewa.[69]

Also entering Montana as part of Little Bear's band were his twenty-one-year-old second wife, *Mâyihkwew* (Bad Face), and Rocky Boy's eighteen-year-old second wife, *Pekiskwewin* (Voice), both cousins of Isabelle. Suffice to say, Coyote's wife, *Kakokikanis*, and Isabelle Coyote and her cousins were among the fifty "squaws" identified by the Cavalry, just as Rocky Boy and Coyote were likely among the sixty-two "bucks" under the putative chieftainship of Little Poplar when the mixed band of Chippewa and Cree were first rounded up in December 1885 in Montana.[70]

Undoubtedly, the oldest of the refugees to accompany Little Bear on the arduous trek south was his grandmother *Ocepihk* (Root), then eighty—Big Bear's mother and Rocky Boy's mother-in-law. She was grandmother to both Little Bear and *Apitchitchiw* (who later came to be known as "Shorty" Young Boy in the U.S.; Small Boy in Canada). *Ocepihk*, Chief Bob Smallboy's great-grandmother, was an important link in the continuum between the pre-treaty Prairie Cree and the post-1885 Montana Cree.

Despite his rotten reputation in Canada, Little Bear was at first well liked and respected in Montana: "For the next two years, Little Bear and his band spent most of their time in the vicinity of Fort Assinniboine. The men cut woods for the fort and in general were supported by the military forces."[71] In the bitterly cold winters following the Riel Rebellion, the Cree and Chippewa camped together. There was safety in numbers, and companionship provided some warmth, even on the coldest of long nights. Over the next three decades, the Chippewa and Canadian Cree were to become a single united tribe, of whom Rocky Boy was often the spokesman, but Little Bear was always the true leader.

As we shall see in Chapter 4, Little Bear was returned to Canada by the U.S. Army against his will in 1896 and beat a Canadian murder charge laid in connection with the Frog Lake Massacre. Once liberated, he became first chief of the Montana Band at *Maskwachees* (Bear Hills, the Cree name for the land around Hobbema) in 1897. After once again forsaking Canada for the United States, he went on to become the first chief of the Rocky Boy Reservation near Havre, Montana, after it was officially opened in 1917. No wonder Bob Smallboy held Little Bear in such high esteem!

CHAPTER 3

The Grandfathers

Smallboy's direct ancestors included his great-grandfather Chief Bobtail and his grandfather Coyote on his mother's side, and his great-grandfather *Mukatai* and grandfather Chief Rocky Boy on his father's side. Both Bobtail and Rocky Boy had reservations named after them, having campaigned for land for their people. Bobtail was initially granted a reservation, but ten years later lost it when he criticized the Canadian government's treatment of the Indian, while Rocky Boy campaigned for fourteen years for his reservation and died within a year of it becoming a reality. Coyote, like Smallboy's father, *Apitchitchiw*, was in line to inherit the mantle of chief, but he had no political aspirations whatsoever. Like Little Bear, both Coyote and *Apitchitchiw* to a degree lived double lives in Canada and the United States. Eventually, Coyote established a reputation in Montana as an important Cree medicine man: "While others have claimed supernatural power and have demonstrated it to a certain degree, none has been as successful or as respected as was Poor Coyote."[1]

BOBTAIL

Chief *Keskayo* (Bobtail, also translated "Short Tail")—also known as Alexis Piché—was born in 1829, the son of Louis Piché, a Métis, and *Opihtaskiwis*, who was Cree.[2] He was the full brother of the original Chief Ermineskin (*Kosekosewuyanew*), one of the first signers of Treaty Six, whose band Bob Smallboy eventually came to lead. Bobtail's first wife was *Putchchun*, and there is some evidence that he took a Blackfoot wife as well.[3]

In the summer of 1871, Bobtail led Coyote and Little Poplar on the long trek to Rocky Boy's original home, the Turtle Mountain Reservation in North Dakota. They formed a significant part of a large band of Cree, Chippewa, and Assiniboine intent on concluding a multilateral peace treaty among most of the major Plains tribes. For Bobtail, these peace talks among the First Nations were of much greater importance than concurrent treaty negotiations with the Queen's representatives in Edmonton, led by Sweet Grass, the Cree chief whom the white negotiatiors regarded as most influential.[4] The climax of the peace talks in the Turtle Mountains came with the arrival at the Chippewa reservation of a large contingency of Blackfeet, including Peigan and Siksika families, along with representatives of the Cree, Assiniboine, Crow, and Sioux nations. The powwow hosted by the Chippewa Nation at Turtle Mountain resulted in a multilateral treaty still honoured to this day.[5]

For good reason, Chief Smallboy considered both the Battle of Belly River and the Turtle Mountain Treaty as being two of the most significant events in the oral history passed down to him by his grandparents and of even greater significance than Rocky Boy's later struggle for a reservation that, posthumously, was to bear his name.[6] As Bob Smallboy's grandniece Marie Smallboy, the granddaughter of Bob's younger brother, Johnny, explained in her testimony before the Standing Committee on Aboriginal Affairs in 2003:

> Our treaty in 1871 with the Blackfoot Confederacy continues today because:
>
> (1) The unwritten constitution, the law of the land, was internalized in each of our ways of life. It is reflected in our language, our beliefs, and our political, social, and economic systems. The many cultures that coexisted on Mihnstihk, Turtle Island [sic], shared the philosophy and values inherent in this unwritten constitution.
>
> (2) This way of life continues today. Its universal symbol is our pipe, containing a truth we all know in our hearts. Our treaty respects this truth.
>
> (3) We agreed to protect each of our respective territories. We knew what our responsibilities were. It was not within our jurisdiction to impose our laws on another's territory. Hence, it was not our place to make a law as to the form of government that the other should have.
>
> (4) The fact that we have internalized the law of the land in each of our ways of life enables us to maintain the spirit and intent of our treaty.[7]

Bob Smallboy passed on the oral history of the conflict of 1870 and the pact of 1871, told to him directly by his grandparents, as an explanation for the friendly relations between the Peigans and the Chippewa-Cree alliance following 1871. Both Bob and his brother, Johnny, in turn spoke of the pact with their children and grandchildren, who to this day put a lot of stock in the Turtle Mountain Treaty.

Accepting the arguments of Big Bear against signing away Indian rights to the land, Bobtail initially joined Big Bear in resisting the signing of Treaty Six in 1876. However, Bobtail had witnessed all too clearly the horror that Big Bear and his band eventually experienced—Canada's policy of starving its Indian population into compliance. Noticing a marked decline in the buffalo population, Bobtail agreed to sign an adhesion to Treaty Six at Blackfoot Crossing in 1877.

The highlights of that treaty are informative since they would come back to haunt the Department of Indian Affairs and the treaty commissioners. Treaty Six begins:

> The Plain and Wood Cree Tribes of Indians, and all the other Indians inhabiting the district hereinafter described and defined, do hereby cede, release, surrender and yield up to the Government of the Dominion of Canada for Her Majesty the Queen and her successors forever, all their rights, titles and privileges whatsoever, to the lands included within the following limits... .[8]

The northern boundary of the huge tract of land extended from the south shore of Red Deer Lake in eastern Manitoba "thence due west to the Athabaska River, thence up the said river, against the stream, to the Jasper House, in the Rocky Mountains; thence on a course south-eastwardly, *following the easterly range of the Mountains, to the source of the main branch of the Red Deer River.*"[9] The main branch of the Red Deer River was considerably farther east than the Bow or the Clearwater, but, more significantly, the "easterly range of the Mountains" was considerably farther east than the Continental Divide. It left out a panhandle of land extending from the Athabasca to the Red Deer that included the Kootenay Plains and what is now known as the Bighorn Wildland. It was in this panhandle, west of Mount Michener, that Smallboy first set up his camp.

Other provisions of the treaty to which Bobtail agreed concerned reserves supposedly dedicated to farming, one of which he himself was assigned:

> Her Majesty the Queen hereby agrees and undertakes to lay aside reserves for farming lands, due respect being had to lands at present cultivated by the said Indians, and other reserves for the benefit of the said Indians, to be administered and dealt with for them by Her Majesty's Government of the Dominion of Canada; provided, all such reserves shall not exceed in all

one square mile for each family of five, or in that proportion for larger or smaller families… .[10]

For their co-operation,

[e]ach Chief, duly recognized as such, shall receive an annual salary of twenty-five dollars per annum; and each subordinate officer, not exceeding four for each Band, shall receive fifteen dollars per annum; and each such Chief and subordinate officer, as aforesaid, shall also receive once every year, a suitable suit of clothing, and each Chief shall receive, in recognition of the closing of the treaty, a suitable flag and medal, and also as soon as convenient, one horse, harness and waggon.[11]

Isabelle Coyote told her great-granddaughter Marie Smallboy that she was *nisosâp* (twelve years old) when she witnessed the signing of the treaty at Blackfoot Crossing by her grandfather Chief Bobtail and her father, Coyote, one of the "subordinate officers." She said that Bobtail had agreed to sign the adhesions to Treaty Six on the understanding that the land reserved for Indian self-rule would incorporate four large lakes—Pigeon Lake, Gull Lake, Battle Lake, and Buffalo Lake—a significant portion of what is now central Alberta. However, according to Marie Smallboy, the Canadian government resorted almost immediately to deceit, by assigning to the elders of the band the task of walking around the boundaries of their new reserve. According to the oral tradition handed down from Bobtail to Isabelle to Marie, the elders simply ran out of steam. "They walked as far as they could in one day, and this became the boundary of the Reserve." Gone was Gull Lake, Buffalo Lake, and all the land in between that was rightfully Bobtail's to claim.[12]

In the wake of the Frog Lake Massacre, reports came back to the Peace Hills that Coyote had been killed and that Isabelle, Bobtail's eldest grandchild, had been taken captive by "Redcoats."[13] In protest, Coyote's brothers and cousins led the sacking of the Hudson's Bay Company trading post on the Battle River. Reports conflict as to Bobtail's role in that incident, the Smallboys contending that Bobtail tried to stop his sons and nephews, but was blamed by Hudson's Bay Company officials since he was present at the scene of the crime trying to stop the looting. As in the case of Big Bear, Canadian officials held the chief responsible for the actions of the warriors in his band. Geoffrey York puts the several incidents of confrontation in the Bear Hills area into perspective:

In 1885, the Indians of Bear Hills finally fought back by joining Louis Riel's rebellion, which was sweeping across the Prairies that year. They raided a farm, killed a number of cattle, gutted a Hudson's Bay trading post at Battle River, and forced almost all of the white settlers to abandon the region. When the Riel Rebellion collapsed, the Indians of Bear Hills gave up the fight, and white settlers soon returned to the area.[14]

The incident at the Hudson's Bay trading post was regarded as a blatant criminal act rather than political protest, and it cost Bobtail important points in terms of credibility. According to Marie Smallboy, citing oral history, when the North-West Mounted Police refused to give information on what had happened to his eldest son and his eldest granddaughter, Bobtail expressed regret for having trusted the white men and for signing away the rights of his people. He believed the whites were committing genocide, as demonstrated by the disappearance of Coyote and Isabelle.[15]

According to Marie Smallboy, the Canadian government was all too happy to strip Bobtail of his treaty status, and in an attempt to discredit him, it spread the story that he had accepted scrip, payment for land that was an option available for any who claimed to be Métis. Reserve No. 139 continued to bear his name on survey documents until 1909, when it officially became the Montana Reserve. The adjacent Ermineskin Reserve No. 138, which was surveyed in 1885 (but not approved until 1889), incorporated the Bobtail Band within its boundaries, and Bobtail and his sons were no longer able to claim chieftain status. Bobtail was banished to Calgary, along with his first wife, *Putchchun*. Later, Bobtail was allowed to move back to *Maskwachees* on the understanding that, along with his medal, he had given up his personal right to be chief.

COYOTE

Isabelle Coyote told her grandson Joe Smallboy the story of how her father, Coyote, came by his name, which was given to him by her grandfather Bobtail in 1870 after the Battle of Belly River. According to Joe, "After the plague of sores the Crees and Stoneys decided to get even with the Blackfoot for all the pain they had caused."[16] They followed the South Saskatchewan westward, upstream from the Forks right across what is now Alberta, but did not find a Blackfoot camp in all that space. Finally, they reached the Belly River, in the extreme southwest corner of the North-West Territories, and there found a Blood camp. They waited until dusk to encircle it, then, in the dark of night, attacked.

The Cree thought the camp would be easy pickings because the Bloods in the camp had obviously been drinking. They had no idea that Fort Whoop-Up was a mere five kilometres away and that the Peigans would come to the rescue of the Bloods with sophisticated repeater rifles. As Joe, citing his grandmother, Isabelle, explained it:

The Peigans fought well with new guns that Coyote had not seen before. They chased most of our guys back down the river. But my *omosômâw* and some other Cree in the raiding party got cut off and had to ride away through the hills towards the mountains. They were followed by the Peigans, who did not give up the chase. After days of riding to get there, the Crees' horses were all but spent, while the Peigans' horses were fresh.

Night come early but come slow, and they were stuck in this canyon. Coyote was not familiar with the country. They took to the cliffs on foot, climbing as high and fast as they could, but were corralled by the Peigans, who knew the land around there real well.

The Peigans rounded up the spent horses and rode off with them. But some did not pick horses. Some wanted to count coup. They had good rifles. They could pick things off from a distance. The fights were short. There was nowhere to hide.

My great-grandfather was real scared. He thought he was dead.

The dark of night brought a cloud down in a mountain fog. That would have been good for Coyote, except he had been seen by the Peigans. One of them ran up the sheep trails after him, so he ran higher. More than once, Coyote lost his feet on the narrow trail. Soon he could not see more than his own height ahead of him, then no distance at all. He felt his way through the fog in the dark. That next step could be his last—a long fall to his death.

Sounds were all mixed up. The Peigans were on every side of him, above and below and all around, even out in the air where he knew they could not be. He knew he would soon greet the steel knife in the gut, or fall to his death down the cliff. His teeth began to clatter from the cold and the fear. The clatter spoke into the night. He was fearful that his teeth would give his place away. He shut his teeth tight together, and held his breath, and listened, his body one big ear. But all he could hear was his heart beating in his head.

A rock fell from above him, a tiny rock. So he crawl back down the way he come, real slow, keeping real small, feeling his way along with his hands till the ledge got wider. He stood up. He took one step after another. He would step into the space he had made in the dark, then he would shift his weight into the step. He reached out with his hand in the dark—and touched something soft.

Someone had ahold of his hair. He saw a knife blade. He swung up with his own knife, but lost his balance. He hung there at the tip of the nose of the mountain's face. As he fell, he grabbed at the softness, grabbed the pants of his enemy. He pulled his leg off the ledge. The Peigan fell over him with a scream. He still hung on to Coyote's hair.

Coyote slid down the cliff face, following the Peigan as he fell. They come to rest in a heap against a big rock. The speech of the smaller rocks seemed to end nearby, then start up again far below. They both knew they was on the edge of the mountain, a long, long drop to the next rocks. This was no way to count coup!

They were slung across the rock like saddlebags on a horse's ass. They had such a thin grip on the rock that each guy depended on the other to live. So they kept ahold of each other still.

Coyote knew no one could win this battle. Nobody would win. He was scared, real scared! So scared he laughed aloud.

Up somewhere above them, a coyote laughed in reply. The canyon echoed with his laugh. Other coyotes joined in from across the way. And he laughed again, that first coyote. Laughed again.

That got the Peigan laughing, too. The coyotes laughed, the two men laughed, the whole damn canyon echoed with their laughter. Soon, they were hugging each other like brothers, them two men—and laughing like fools.

Coyote come awake with the first sun. They were on the edge of a clear drop, he knew that—but the Peigan's leg was broke, the bone sticking out through the flesh. Coyote tried to drag him up over the rocks as far as he could. The Peigan woke up and tried to crawl, dragging his bad leg, but he was in real pain. It took all morning to reach the trail.

From there, they could see the canyon below. The other Peigans had gone, taking all the horses with them.

And that was how my great-grandfather come to be called *Metacakan*— Coyote—by his father. Because whenever he was shit-ass scared, he laughed like a coyote. And that's what saved his life.[17]

Many summers later, said Joe, at a powwow at Fort McLeod, that same Peigan shouted out to Coyote, who recognized him by his limp. "The Peigan made a sound like a coyote laughing. Then he shouted that Coyote and his family could stay at his teepee that night or any night. And they become the best of friends."[18]

Coyote signed several adhesions to Treaty Six in which new names were added to the treaty rolls. His name appears second in the list, beside his "+," immediately below his father's name. Unlike Big Bear, who in 1882 'signed' his "+" symbolically by merely touching the pen, Bobtail and Coyote actually made their own "+" marks with the pen.

Before the Riel Rebellion, the Coyote family had lived with Bobtail in the Peace Hills near Hobbema, but Coyote made no secret of the fact that he sympathized with Big Bear in the "Riel Resistance" and in 1885 went off to join in the fight.[19] He took his wife, *Kakokikanis* (Hanger-On), and daughter, Isabelle, with him; they left the younger children, Baptiste and Francois, with Bobtail and his wives. It was standard practice for Cree warriors to take their adult women on the warpath with them, so that their food, shelter, and clothing were taken care of as they fought.

The Cree do not call the Riel uprising a "rebellion," but rather refer to that defining episode in their history as *Ka-mayahkamikahk*, literally, "When Bad Things Happened."[20] Certainly bad things happened to Coyote and to Smallboy's other grandparents and great-grandparents, on either side.

Although Bobtail did not take part directly in the conflicts at Frog Lake and Fort Pitt, remaining instead in the Peace Hills south of Edmonton, Coyote fought against the North-West Mounted Police and consequently felt sure he was wanted in Canada for treason or even for murder for his part in the resistance. Thus he joined Little Bear (*Imasees*), Kingbird, Little Poplar, and Rocky Boy in their zigzag flight across the North-West Territories to Montana, taking his wife and daughter with him.

Some years after arriving in Montana, Coyote took *Waskahte* ("Walking Alone" or "Walking-in-a-Circle") as his second wife. *Waskahte* eventually became *Apitchitchiw*'s step-mother-in-law, despite the fact that she was a year younger than he. Both *Waskahte* and *Apitchitchiw* would likely have been among the twenty-five "children" listed by the U.S. Cavalry as accompanying Little Bear and Little Poplar during the retreat into Montana in 1885. *Waskahte*, Smallboy's favourite "grandma," later became a "tribal historian," according to Smallboy, intent on preserving for posterity what her grandparents had told her about the days when buffalo abounded. By contrast, Smallboy's mother, Isabelle, became the *"family historian,"* preserving in her stories an account of what her father had told her about his struggles with the Peigans and Bloods and later with the white man.[21]

After his arrival in Montana in 1885, Coyote kept a low profile. In the Rocky Boy census roll of 1917, he was listed by the diminutive name "Poor Old Coyote," perhaps all too descriptive of his humbled station and impoverished situation after arriving in the United States. For the next ten years, he, Hanger-On, and Isabelle led a nomadic life, joining Rocky Boy and Little Bear in their travels around Montana. For Hanger-On, born in 1850 in Poplar Creek, Montana, to a Cree mother and Chippewa father, arriving in the comparative safety of the United States must have seemed like returning home.

Back at Bear Hills, the mystery of what had happened to Coyote and Isabelle continued. Virtually every branch of the Piché family named a daughter "Isabelle" after Bobtail's favourite granddaughter.[22] Afraid that he would be extradited back to Canada if his whereabouts were discovered, Coyote lay low, with the assistance of his immediate family. Most of the Indians at the Four Bands continued to believe that he had been killed in the confrontation with "Redcoats" near Fort Pitt. In 2005, Marie Smallboy still believed Coyote had been killed near Fort Pitt, until shown clear evidence that he had in fact survived, his name and that of his wives surfacing in the tentative census taken in Montana in 1917. This early roll of the Rocky Boy Indians in Montana clearly shows that "Poor Old Coyote" survived, with his two wives—their names mistranslated by Roger St. Pierre as "Hanger Owner" (from what could have been intended as "Hanger On-er") and "Walking Alone" (from what should have been "Walking-in-a-Circle").[23] By then, Coyote was a medicine man of some repute and had begun to turn his life around.

Hanger-On, Isabelle's mother and Smallboy's maternal grandmother, seems to have been kept out of the loop, where Smallboy was concerned, perhaps because *Waskahte*, his maternal step-grandmother, was such a dynamic personality. Hanger-On certainly appeared to be a comparatively dim bulb in Smallboy's life, outshone by the younger *Waskahte* and her storytelling skills. Hanger-On was the only member of the Coyote family who had the right to remain in Montana when all the others were rounded up for shipment back to Canada in 1896.[24] Because of her American birth, she and Coyote may have been allowed to stay in Montana in 1896, although it is more likely that they succeeded in evading capture. Isabelle and *Waskahte*, on the other hand, were caught in the sweep across the state designed to purge Montana of its Canadian Cree.

Despite, or perhaps because of, Isabelle being seven years older than her "step-mom," the two women got along famously for the next eighty years until *Waskahte*'s death in 1965. This could be another reason why Smallboy identified more with *Waskahte* and why she fit in so well as a member of the extended family. According to Smallboy, the two women regaled each other with stories about their past, the oral histories that were such an important part of Cree culture.

If Coyote visited his sons in Hobbema, it was on his own terms or not at all. Bob Smallboy recalled seeing his grandfather in the United States, but never in Canada. He vividly recalled Coyote hanging out with other members of his family at a remote Sun Dance, probably on the Arapaho Reservation in Wyoming.

After witnessing his father's disillusionment and Big Bear's ignominious defeat, Coyote had no political aspirations whatsoever. He had no time for the petty politics of the roving band. As an elder, people increasingly came to him for advice. Gradually, it became clear that his calling was of a different order, for he had powerful spirit helpers in the form of "Little People," Lilliputian beings, fully clothed and acculturated to a lifestyle approximating that of the North American Indian, who lived in a parallel world beneath the ground. Coyote claimed that he communicated with the Little People regularly.

The Cree regard medicine men who see the Little People as being exceptionally gifted, since traditionally the Little People reveal themselves to—and share their secrets with—only those medicine men privileged and skilled enough to receive their powers. Dianne Meili writes about Albert Lightning, another Cree medicine man who communicated with the Little People and who accompanied Chief Smallboy to Europe in 1982:

> I have heard stories and read about the May-may-quay-so-wuk, known to the Cree as little people who live far under the ground, among rocky places, and under the water in marshy areas… . Many people believe the little people still exist but remain in hiding because they no longer value the company of humans. Some say it was the task of the little people to record history and that their writings can be seen on rocks in the wilderness, yet no one can read them anymore. I could go on and on about the little people, but this is a story about Albert Lightning.[25]

As Eleanor Brass, a Cree author, wrote:

> Only Indians of good character are privileged to see them and, even then, only on rare occasions. Long ago, it was said these little people were crafters of arrowheads, flint knives and stone heads for hammers. These they traded with the Indians for buffalo meat, hides, porcupine quills, and other things they needed but couldn't get for themselves. These tiny people had mysterious powers and often played tricks on the Indians. Hence every time anything peculiar happened, they attributed it to the May-may-quay-so-wuk.[26]

Coyote's powers to heal and work magic were legendary. Eventually, he became for the Montana Cree "the man they consider to be their last great medicine man."[27]

ROCKY BOY

Apitchitchiw, Chief Smallboy said, was the son of Rocky Boy, in Cree, *Asinikosisan* (literally "Stoney's Son"), after whom the Rocky Boy Reservation near Havre, Montana, is named. *Asinikosisan* was originally translated "Rocky Boy" in the United States in typical diminutive fashion. Frank Linderman, who later talked at length with both Little Bear and

Rocky Boy, opines as to the evolution of the name in his description of the arrival of the group in Montana:

> In the spring of 1885 …, many of the Chippewas, under Stone-Child, whom belittling white men dubbed "Rocky Boy," returned to Montana, bringing with them a band of Crees led by Little Bear the young son of Big Bear, the Cree Chief…. Anyhow, because of their battles and their flight across the Canadian line into Montana these Chippewas and Crees under their two chiefs soon became known as "The Rocky Boy Renegades," having neither a home or a country.[28]

Of mixed Chippewa and Assiniboine ancestry, Rocky Boy likely received his name because his mother, *Nahkawewin* (Chippewa Speaker), was Assiniboine (Stoney). *Nahkawewin* was regarded with tremendous respect by the blind Isabelle, who in 1885 had travelled with her future husband's grandmother in the gruelling zigzag trek across much of present-day Saskatchewan, following Little Bear in his flight to the Land of the Long Knives. Isabelle later claimed that she visited *Nahkawewin* in the spirit world sometimes, and *Nahkawewin* was an inspiration to her. Indeed, according to Smallboy's grand-daughter Jessie Smallboy, when Jessie was presented to her great-grandmother Isabelle for naming shortly after she was born, Isabelle gave her a Stoney (Assiniboine) name, despite the fact that she was Cree. The oral history passed to Jessie by her parents is that Isabelle received a visit from her late husband's grandmother, a Stoney, who told her what to name the child. Jessie took her Stoney birth name sufficiently seriously that she eventually married a Stoney, and currently lives on the Stoney reserve on the Bighorn River in Alberta. She told me she has always been proud of the connection to her Assiniboine great-great-great-great grandmother, after whom she was named. This independent snippet of oral history serves to strengthen the fabric of the recorded history, and would seem to corroborate that Chippewa Speaker, the mother of Rocky Boy ("Stoney's Son"), was Assiniboine.[29]

Intermarriage between the Assiniboine and Cree was not uncommon in the nineteenth century. In fact, both Mandelbaum and Dusenberry called Big Bear and his band the "Cree-Assiniboine," because of the propensity of the Cree and Stoneys to live together and intermarry, despite the fact that the two tribes are of different linguistic ancestry. Big Bear made it clear to Alexander Morris that he represented both the Cree and the Stoneys hunting on the Great Plains: "He had been sent in by the Crees and by the Stonies or Assiniboines to speak for them."[30]

Dusenberry notes in his treatise on the religious practices of the Montana Cree that "the Cree have been allied with the Assiniboine for over three-hundred and fifty years."[31] This association continues because of the proximity of the Rocky Boy Reservation to the Fort Belknap Reservation, where several thousand Assiniboine live, and in Canada because of the proximity of the Stoney at the Bighorn Reserve and the Cree at the Sunchild-O'Chiese reserves west of Rocky Mountain House, both well within the territory of Treaty Six. The original splitting up of the Crees into Treaty Six and the Stoneys into Treaty Seven was no doubt designed to further fragment the "troublemakers." The odd men out were the Plains Chippewa, including Rocky Boy and his father, to whom Morris was downright hostile:

> The Lieutenant-Governor then met with the few Chippewas who came forward … and said, "If what I have heard is true I shall not be well pleased. I am told you are of a bad mind; you proposed to prevent me from crossing the [South Saskatchewan] River; if you did it was very foolish; you could no more stop me than you could the river itself. Then I am told you tried to prevent the other Indians from making the treaty. I tell you this to your faces so if it is not true you can say so; but whether it is or not it makes no difference in my duty… ."[32]

Rocky Boy's father, the spokesman for the Chippewa, admitted that he had told the Cree, "Do not be in a hurry in giving your assent …; all along the prices have been to one side, and we have had no say."[33] Everything in the treaties was for the white man's benefit, he told the Cree. Now he said to the lieutenant-governor: "I see dimly to-day what you are doing, and I find fault with a portion of it; that is why I stand back: Through what you have done you have cheated my kinsmen."[34] This accusation, levelled in public before the assembled multitude of chiefs, absolutely enraged Alexander Morris:

> GOVERNOR—"I will not sit here and hear such words from the Chippewas. Who are you? You come from my country and you tell me the Queen has cheated you; it is not so. You say we have the best of the bargains; you know it is not so. If you have any requests to make in a respectful manner I am ready to hear."[35]

Morris implied that the Chippewa should go back to Lake Superior where they belonged.

Later, in the United States, Rocky Boy claimed that he was Chippewa and that his family came from Wisconsin. He claimed Chippewa ancestry through his father, *Nawaswâtam* (The Chaser), while Little Bear claimed Chippewa ancestry through both his parents.[36] Rocky Boy had at least two brothers living in Montana, *Penneto* (The Fetcher) and *Akosipeya* (Full-of-Dew).[37]

Smallboy identified his paternal grandmother, Rocky Boy's wife, as being Big Bear's younger sister, *Miýweýihtakwan* (Pleasant One).[38] The marriage must have taken place following the Battle of Belly River in 1870, probably by arrangement between Pleasant One's father, *Mukatai*, and Rocky Boy's father, *Nawaswâtam*, in preparation for the peace talks in Chippewa country—the Turtle Mountains of North Dakota—planned for the following year. If so, Pleasant One probably accompanied Rocky Boy and *Nawaswâtam* to their tribal homeland for the peace talks with the Blackfoot and other Plains tribes in 1871 and then returned to what is now Saskatchewan later that year, where *Apitchitchiw* was born. They appear to have remained in Canada during the negotiations for Treaty Six, adhesions to which Bobtail signed in 1877 and Big Bear in 1882, once it was clear to the latter that, with the buffalo gone, his band would starve to death without government aid. Rocky Boy's loyalty to his brother-in-law apparently continued through the Riel Rebellion and the Frog Lake Massacre of 1885. Historian John C. Ewers noted:

> In the conference with Indians preceding the negotiation of the Qu'Appelle Treaty, or Number Four, with the Saulteaux [i.e., Chippewa], on September 8, 1874, "Saulteaux from the Cypress Hills entered the tent saying that they had no Chief, and did not want to go with the main body of the nation, that they had plenty of friends on the plains." Presumably these leaderless Chippewa from the Cypress Hills included Rocky Boy, and they were the Chippewa who cast their lot with Big Bear's Cree thereafter.[39]

In Montana, Rocky Boy's Chippewa were not distinguishable from Little Bear's "British Cree": "On the Saskatchewan plains it would appear that these Chippewa nomads became allied with and intermarried with the Prairie Cree, especially those of Big Bear's Band. As a minority Indian group they attracted little attention."[40] Until 1902, that is. Then, in a letter to the president of the United States dated 14 January 1902, Rocky Boy claimed to be an American-born Chippewa Indian. In that letter, which first brought him to the attention of the U.S. Indian Service, he complained of his plight and that of his wandering band.

In 1911, John B. Bottineau, solicitor for the Turtle Mountain Chippewa Indians of North Dakota, wrote a letter to the commissioner of Indian Affairs on behalf of his clients, in which he suggested that a significant number of Rocky Boy's band were from North Dakota:

> For the purpose of identification and completion of the rolls of my kinsmen, kindly give me access to the Roll of Chief Rock Boy's Band of Chippewa Indians, comprised of a great number of the Turtle Mountain and Pembina

Bands of Chippewa Indians of North Dakota and their descendants, who have wandered away from their old home with the Tribe, at different times since about 1870, and scattered; seeking a livelihood in the West and Northwest country, and now located under the leadership of Chief Rock Boy, upon the Blackfoot Reservation in Montana.[41]

Since Little Bear was widely believed to have fomented the Frog Lake Massacre, he had limited credibility as a peacemaker and treaty negotiator for the Chippewa-Cree. He recognized in Rocky Boy a personage that the Great White Father in Washington could respect. However, the fact that Rocky Boy was Little Bear's "uncle" by marriage meant that, although Rocky Boy was a year or two younger than Little Bear, he could "pull rank" on his titular nephew.[42] Once in a while he tried to do so, albeit unsuccessfully, and this caused a great deal of tension between the two men.[43] In a photograph taken at the time of the 1896 deportation, Little Bear drew attention to himself by standing on a chair, as if determined not to be upstaged.[44] By comparison, in the photo, Rocky Boy—though facing deportation to Canada in a cattle car—wore his best hat, with an eagle feather, and his wife, Voice, wore her best dress, fancily beaded moccasins, and multiple bead necklaces. This was a time, they seemed to say, to rise above the stress of the moment and act with dignity.

When Little Bear was prosecuted after his deportation from the United States to Canada in 1896, Rocky Boy and Voice, who had been shipped north with him and hundreds of other Chippewa-Cree, wasted no time returning south of the border. *Apitchitchiw* and Isabelle remained in Hobbema long enough to establish a home base on the Ermineskin Reserve, where Chief Bobtail embraced them, but soon they, too, were on the road again, heading back south.

The oral tradition preserved by the grandchildren and great-grandchildren of Big Bear, Little Bear, Bobtail, Coyote, and Rocky Boy is fortunately supplemented, and to a degree confirmed, by history books compiled by such scholars as Hugh Dempsey and Verne Dusenberry and by preservation of parallel oral traditions to be found in other sources, such as *Voices of the Plains Cree* by Edward Ahenakew.[45] It is also preserved by accounts of friends of Rocky Boy and Little Bear, who between 1902 and 1916 sought to promote a reservation in Rocky Boy's name.[46] For example, Frank Bird Linderman not only had talked at length to both Rocky Boy and Little Bear, but was "closely associated with Rocky Boy in his efforts to obtain a reservation for his band during the years 1908-1916, and was his white confidant and adviser during this period."[47] Senator William T. Cowan, "who knew Little Bear and Rocky Boy intimately well," affirmed in his manuscript pertaining to the establishment of the Rocky Boy Reservation "that Rocky Boy's wife was a sister of Big Bear, Little Bear's father."[48]

A second woman besides Isabelle is listed in the 1917 Rocky Boy rolls as part of *Apitchitchiw*'s household—"Chippewa Speaker," the mother of Rocky Boy. Since most of Rocky Boy's original band spoke Chippewa, it is likely that the name was not so much descriptive of her native language as descriptive of her talent: she must have been associated with some tribe other than Chippewa or Cree. Born in Saskatchewan in 1837, Chippewa Speaker was likely Assiniboine (Stoney). She was in her mid-teens when she gave birth to Rocky Boy.

Rocky Boy would have made sure that every member of his own family was on the roll when he first made a list of one hundred names in 1903 and also when he helped revise it in 1908. Even absentees associated with Rocky Boy's band were counted, especially if they had been present in Montana prior to 1889. One photograph of *Apitchitchiw* taken in 1910 depicts him standing beside a woman identified as his "mother" when she was 105 and he was about 40, suggesting that she was born in 1805. This would mean she gave birth at age sixty-six! It is more likely that the woman in the photograph was *Apitchitchiw*'s grandmother *Ocepihk*, rather than his mother.[49] If this analysis is correct, the photograph is likely the only one extant of Big Bear's mother.

CHAPTER 4

Montana

THE GOVERNOR'S SUN DANCE

Upon leaving Fort Assinniboine in 1886 after President Grover Cleveland so obligingly (and perhaps unwittingly) offered his band asylum, Little Bear assumed that he could go back to the huge tract of land north of the Missouri that had been reserved for Indians of every tribe. However, by then the people of Montana were clamouring for statehood, and as far as the settlers were concerned, it would not do for a quarter of the state to be reserved for Indian use. Accordingly, in 1887 and 1888, Washington ended the era of the joint reservation, confining the Blackfeet, Assiniboine, and Gros Ventre tribes (over their protest) to much smaller reservations.

Having made refugees out of the Canadian Cree by his order to release them from custody, President Cleveland authorized a mere one thousand dollar expenditure in distress aid for the Cree in February 1887 and a similar amount the following winter.[1] Little Bear's request to be allowed to join the Flathead in the Bitter Root Valley in 1887 was met with apathy and disdain.[2] The Cree therefore remained in the Fort Assinniboine area in the winter months, but in the summer roamed the territory in search of work and pasture for their horses. Although the secretary of the Interior, William F. Vilas, recommended on humanitarian grounds that Congress allow the Indian Office to establish a new reservation for Little Bear's Cree, Congress did not even respond to the recommendation, being all too aware that, as Montana approached statehood, the agitation for removal of the Cree had mounted. "Why is it that we cannot get rid of those Cree Indians?" asked

Thomas O. Miles of Silver Bow, an immigrant from Canada. Montana's first governor, Joseph K. Toole, and U.S. Secretary of State James G. Blaine sought the assistance of the U.S. Army to remove the Cree.[3]

Little Bear and Rocky Boy made every attempt to secure land of their own, trying to negotiate with the Flathead, Pend d'Oreille, Kootenay, and Blackfeet. In October 1887, however, the commissioner of Indian Affairs decided "that the Indian Department can make no promises in regards to land for British Cree refugees."[4] Less than six months later, the commissioner wrote to Vilas (apparently preaching to the converted, given Vilas's earlier humanitarian stand): "I am aware that these refugees are not native Indians of the United States nor that they have rights on any of our Indian reservations, but as a simple act of humanity, I think they should be given a chance to earn their bread when that is all they ask. They have been wandering about from place to place ... homeless and helpless."[5] As late as 1892, the commanding general of the Department of Dakota reported to Governor Toole:

> Since 1885 there have been in our territory about 200 Cree Indians who were political refugees who took part in the Riel Rebellion. These have been permitted to remain and have been up to 1887 fed and clothed through the intervention of the Army. At the present time these Cree men and women in Montana and North Dakota are employed by citizens in wood chopping and laundry and other work, which shows that they are very useful, are well conducted and would be greatly missed in the industries of the country were they now removed. This information comes from citizens.[6]

Three years later, under Governor John E. Rickarts, the attitude of the citizens towards Little Bear's band suddenly changed. The *Anaconda Standard* referred to them in headlines as "These Dirty Crees," alluding to them as "renegades" and "Canadian beggars."[7] For a decade, the homeless Chippewa-Cree band had wandered northern Montana from Fort Benton to Browning and as far south as the Big Horn Reservation on the Wyoming border, keeping the peace, according to all accounts. But in 1895, barely a decade after their arrival, Congress appropriated monies "to remove from the State of Montana and to deliver at the International boundary line the refugee Canadian Cree Indians."[8] What had gone wrong?

The answer is simple: Little Bear had once again thumbed his nose at the establishment. In 1894, he sought and received the endorsement of the Great Falls Chamber of Commerce to hold a Sun Dance, then banned as "heathen," on the fair grounds, as a theatrical "act" that would be incorporated into the county fair. This incurred the wrath of the Great Falls Ministerial Association, which wrote to Governor Rickarts:

To permit this performance would hurt the reputation of the city. The Sun Dance if tolerated would in other parts of the country be regarded as an index not merely of Indian barbarism and superstition, but of degraded taste and low public sentiment in a community that could encourage such orgies.... The bad effect on our prosperity would be felt at once. It turns loose several hundred idle, lazy, shiftless barbarians in the city and is a queer way of promoting prosperity. We ought not to make Great Falls a pleasant or attractive place for these people. We have enough respectable poor of our own to attend to.[9]

Rickarts overreacted. Without consulting Little Bear, the governor issued a proclamation prohibiting the Sun Dance at Cascade County Fair in Great Falls—a proclamation printed in its entirety, including preamble, in the *Great Falls Tribune*:

Investigation ... convinces me that [the Sun Dance] is not only inhuman and brutalizing, unnatural and indecent, and therefore abhorrent to Christian civilization, but that its aims and purposes are a menace to the peace and welfare of communities. My information ... leads me to regard the proposed exhibition as wholly inconsistent with Christian civilization.... The Cree Indians are refugees from Canada and therefore do not come within the restrictions imposed by the authorities on reservations. Whatever steps taken to prevent the Crees from requesting the Sun Dance must be by direction of the authorities of Montana....

Therefore, I, John E. Rickarts, by virtue of the authority vested in me as governor of the state of Montana do hereby prohibit within the limits of the state the festival known as the Sun Dance and the local authorities of the several counties are directed to take such steps as may be necessary in their respective communities to enforce this inhibition.[10]

Little Bear's response was as eloquent and diplomatic as anything ever publicly uttered by his father. It was reported by the *Havre Plaindealer* the next day:

We are here today to worship the Great Spirit. He brought us into the world and has taken care of us. My people take this method of expressing our gratitude. God put us here to love each other. Every day I and my people ask mercy of God and thank him for feeding us and keeping us healthy.

For two days and two nights I do not eat. Ever since I was born I have worshipped my God at this season of the year.

I do not think it right for the white people to stop me from holding the

Sun Dance. It is my method of devotion and my people want it. We mean no harm to anyone, but want to save our souls.

My people cut their skin in the shoulders. Christ was put on the Cross and had nails driven through his feet and hands the same as my people do. But if the white man objects we will not do this.

We do not want trouble with the white race. They are good to us and when we get through with our devotion those Indians who came here to dance will scatter as the birds to pick up a crumb here and crumb there on which to live.

My people are good people and we will do no wrong. The light, the air, the water and the birds are free and we also want to be free and be good so that the Great Spirit will smile with gladness and call us his children.[11]

When he said, "But if the white man objects we will not do this," Little Bear was referring only to the cutting of the skin. At no time did he intend to dispense with the Sun Dance altogether. When objections continued to mount, Little Bear moved the venue of the Sun Dance to Havre, only to find that the Ministerial Association there was just as active. When state authorities threatened to shut down the celebration yet again, Little Bear did the unthinkable—he moved the venue of the Sun Dance to Helena, as part of the fourth of July celebrations at the state capitol itself, performing the Sun Dance on the governor's front lawn.

CATTLE CARS FOR THE CREE

This expression of contempt for the authority of the governor on the part of Little Bear led the governor to pull rank in a most despicable manner. Rickarts demanded that U.S. Secretary of State Richard Olney negotiate with Canada for the removal of the "Canadian Cree" on the grounds that "they have become an intolerable nuisance constantly violating our game laws, foraging upon our herds, and not infrequently looting our cabins"—this despite the fact that not one Cree had ever been charged or tried, let alone convicted, of a crime since their arrival in Montana.[12] This statement by the governor was later parroted in an editorial in the *Anaconda Standard* almost word for word:

These Indians are wards of the British government and generally referred to as refugees of the Riel Rebellion. In default of a reservation and the restrictions of the Federal government, they become an intolerable nuisance constantly violating our game laws, foraging our herds, and not infrequently looting isolated cabins. The patience of our people has been sorely tried.[13]

Anticipating expulsion to Canada, several members of Little Bear's band enlisted the assistance of Great Falls attorney John Hoffman to obtain from the clerk of the federal court declarations of intent to apply for U.S. citizenship. Although four such declarations were issued, U.S. Attorney E. D. Weed, who had originally endorsed the applications, reversed himself and instructed the clerk not to issue any more declaration forms to Indians.

The Canadian government reached an agreement with the U.S. government to accept any Canadian Cree Indians delivered to the border, but wanted to redefine "Indian" to exclude any Métis. In the summer of 1896, Canadian Commissioner of Indian Affairs A. E. Forget travelled to Great Falls to assure the Cree—and Little Bear in particular—that there was nothing to fear upon their return. He gave Little Bear a copy of the general amnesty order, suggesting that Little Bear could depend upon it. As a direct response to this assurance, Little Bear agreed not to resist removal and to prepare his followers to move peacefully back across the border into Canada.

Some of his followers, including Coyote, smelled a rat and went into hiding.

Lieutenant John J. Pershing, the troop commander at Fort Assinniboine, began the roundup, targeting not just the Cree but any mixed bloods that seemed to fit the description of Canadian Indian.

In clear contravention of the agreement with the Canadian government, Governor Rickarts wrote to General Joseph P. Poe, the Assistant Secretary of War, insisting that "all Crees whether they hold certificates or not should be deported from the State of Montana." Only Forget's promise and assurance from United States officials prevented Little Bear and many of his followers from leaving Montana for other States before the Army could proceed with the deportation. Trusting official promises, Little Bear toured the State urging the Cree to remain in Montana until the Army was ready to move them to Canada.[14]

But this was only the beginning of the deception practised on both sides of the border. Unbeknownst to Little Bear, Forget fully intended to have him and his subchief Lucky Man arrested at the border and charged with murder. Once again, the top Canadian government representative had lied—not only to Little Bear, but to the United States.

Canada told the United States that it had granted a general amnesty to all Cree who had been involved in the 1885 conflict. To the extent that he relied upon this assurance, there was some truth to Pershing's declaration that Queen Victoria had pardoned the Cree for their role in the Riel

Rebellion and that they need fear no punishment. Pershing's 10th Cavalry surrounded and arrested the entire camp near Great Falls, and despite legal arguments to forestall the deportation, a "dragnet" operation across the state late in June 1896 saw anyone of Canadian Cree or Chippewa descent herded towards the Canadian border by train and wagon, including Little Bear, Rocky Boy, and their wives.

Some 537 Chippewa and Cree nomads were shipped in cattle cars to the Canadian border at the Coutts border crossing, along with 1,259 ponies, 159 wagons, and all their personal effects. Linderman later remarked: "United States soldiers rounded them up—Chippewas and Cree alike, and escorting them across the line, permitted them to go free on Canadian soil."[15] From there, they were on their own. They could either catch a Canadian train for passage north to their new home on Bobtail's reserve at Hobbema (which would soon be renamed the "Montana" Reserve in deference to their point of origin), fifty kilometres south of Edmonton, or ride or walk the several hundred kilometres to their home reserves. Most of them went to Hobbema.

Both *Apitchitchiw* and Isabelle were deported back to Canada in 1896, along with any Indian caught in the dragnet who did not have a home reservation. Whether Cree or Chippewa, they were all deemed to have come into Montana from Canada.

THE ARREST OF LITTLE BEAR

Despite the general amnesty and Lieutenant Pershing's assurance that they would not be punished upon their return to Canada, Little Bear and Lucky Man were promptly arrested at the border and sent to Regina for trial for allegedly having taken part in the Frog Lake Massacre. The *Great Falls Tribune* called the treatment of Little Bear "an outrageous breach of faith" and called the roundup "a trap which had been treacherously laid for them."[16] By "secret proclamation," a blatant oxymoron, the Canadian government had excluded Little Bear and Lucky Man (among others) from the general amnesty.

One of those present at Little Bear's preliminary hearing was A. M. Hamilton, secretary of the Saskatchewan Historical Society:

> Preparations were made to bring them to trial, but eleven years had passed since the Rebellion and it was difficult to obtain witnesses. All the white people had been killed, except for two women and the boy Cameron, and they were in such a state of fear and excitement that the two women at least had no definite recollection of the circumstances. Cameron had been in his store at the time and apparently did not see the actual killing.

It was, therefore, very difficult to get witnesses who could convict these two men. It was decided to send to Fort McLeod for the Cree woman who was Quinn's widow.... If she identified Aimiceese (Little Bear) and Lucky Man, they would be committed for trial, otherwise proceedings would be abandoned.

I was present in the office of the Indian Commissioner at Regina when Mrs. Quinn was brought there to identify or repudiate the killers of her husband. It was a dramatic scene and one that I will never forget. Mr. A. E. Forget, the Indian Commissioner, sat behind his big desk, looking as always, very dignified. Beside him sat Major Perry of the Northwest Mounted Police.... The two prisoners were brought in manacled. Aimiceese sat in a chair facing the Commissioner and the police officer, while Lucky Man sat on the floor shrouded in his blanket. Aimiceese was a striking looking man, and I should judge about forty years old or more. He was much stouter than the Crees usually are and powerfully built. He had a predatory falcon face and he looked around the room with a bold and insolent air. His handcuffs he concealed in the folds of his belted blanket. Lucky Man was a dreadful looking rascal, thin and emaciated, with his face seamed by a thousand wrinkles.... Two Red Coats, with side arms and open holsters, stood beside the prisoners as guards. Johnny Pritchard, a young half-breed, the son and brother of the two men who had saved the lives of Mrs. Delaney and Mrs. Gowenlock, stood between the prisoners and the Commissioner, in the traditional attitude of an Indian interpreter, with his hat held in both hands across his breast.

When all were in place, Forget said, "Pritchard, bring in the woman." Johnny went out and returned with Mrs. Quinn. She was a large and bulky Cree woman of the pure blood and had no English. Mr. Forget said, "Tell her, Pritchard, to look at these two men and say if she has ever seen them before." Pritchard rendered this into Cree and Mrs. Quinn, despite her great bulk, walking in moccasined feet as lightly as a cat, walked up to the two prisoners and gave them careful scrutiny. It was a tense moment. There is no doubt that both men knew that what the woman said meant their freedom or shameful death, but neither gave the slightest sign. Aimiceese continued to boldly stare about the room.... Lucky Man paid no attention.

There was a silence for a moment, broken only by the metallic clink of the handcuffs on Lucky Man's wrists. Then the woman came to a pause and spoke in Cree to the interpreter. "What does she say, Pritchard?" said Forget. "She says, Sir," said Johnny, "she has never seen either of these two men before." "By Gad!" said Mr. Forget. "I might have known. These are her own people and it was only her husband that they murdered."

Subsequently they were both released. I think Lucky Man died not long afterwards, but Aimiceese, who afterwards was assigned to the Hobbema

Agency in Alberta, arose to the position of a minor chief and gave no more trouble to the authorities.[17]

Mrs. Quinn's claim that she did not recognize Little Bear was an obvious untruth, for he had been trading at the Frog Lake Trading Post for months, if not years, before the uprising. Nonetheless, Little Bear and Lucky Man were discharged for lack of evidence, Forget no doubt taking into account the hornet's nest he had stirred up in the United States by his sleight of hand in giving assurance to the U.S. government (an assurance repeated to Little Bear in person) that the general amnesty applied to all Canadian Cree. It did not seem to occur to Forget that he was acting as both prosecutor and judge in the action against Little Bear, as well as deceitful bureaucrat.

Little Bear was allowed to rejoin the rest of his band that had formed the new Montana Reserve on land originally assigned to Chief Bobtail. Bobtail, having spurned his treaty status "because of the way the Indians were treated," had allegedly chosen to take scrip—land and money—rather than treaty status, although his descendants deny this.[18] Baptiste and Francois, Coyote's sons, still lived on the Maskwachees Reserve. Along with the Ermineskin, the Samson, and the Louis Bull bands, the Montana Band (rather than the "Bobtail" Band) is to this day one of the "Four Bands" of the Maskwachees Reserve at Hobbema.

It is not clear when *Apitchitchiw* and Isabelle took up residence together: whether before the "roundup" of 1896 or immediately after. Isabelle appears to have had two children before the roundup, and given the names that Isabelle chose for them, it is likely that *Apitchitchiw* was the young father. Little Boy (*Apisisiw*) was born in Havre in 1886, when *Apitchitchiw* was fifteen and Isabelle was twenty-one. She may have become pregnant during the great trek south, and she appears to have given birth while the band was at Fort Assinniboine. Little Girl (*Apisisisiw*) was born in Browning, Montana, in 1888. Thus Little Boy and Little Girl would have been ten and eight years old when their parents were deported back to Canada in 1896. Since they were American born, they arguably would not have been subject to deportation and likely continued residing in the United States after 1896 with their American-born grandmother Hanger-On and her husband, Coyote (who typically would have adopted them). A photograph of the Smallboy family taken in Montana in 1906 shows Isabelle standing with her children, including Bobtail Smallboy, Maggie, and Johnny, along with an unidentified young woman who could have been Little Girl, then eighteen.[19]

After their deportation, *Apitchitchiw* and Isabelle appear to have made a complete break from Montana for a few years. While they made *Maskwachees* (Hobbema) their "home base," it was never quite "home."

According to Bob Smallboy, resources were stretched too thin to support so many people, and *Apitchitchiw* found it difficult to make a living there: food was in short supply and work nonexistent. Accordingly, *Apitchitchiw* took Isabelle to the city—to Calgary, at first, which at that time was booming with incoming settlers with money enough to buy firewood. Bobtail had maintained a home in Calgary since virtually abandoning the Bobtail Reserve, and Bob Smallboy's sister, Margaret, was born there.

Once the demand for firewood waned in the spring of 1898, *Apitchitchiw* and Isabelle moved even farther south—to Fort McLeod. *Apitchitchiw* was particularly drawn to the Peigan Reserve near Cardston, where Isabelle's father had a close friend. "My parents lived with the Peigans and were friends with them," said Chief Smallboy. "They were living in that area when I was born. They lived in that area for some time.... The Peigan Indians helped my parents in many ways while we lived with them on their reserve."[20] But their real ties were always still farther south—to the camps of Rocky Boy and Little Bear as they and their bands continued roving from city to city, entrepreneurs hoping to sell their handicrafts even as they sought to preserve their freedom.

By then, Rocky Boy and Little Bear had already returned to the United States, both claiming they had American connections by virtue of their Chippewa ancestry. This argument figured prominently in their being able to stay in the United States and eventually in their being able to secure a reservation there. However, where Little Bear was concerned,

> [h]is actions, which had created a tragedy for his father's leadership, made his own chieftainship a continuing ordeal. Instead of being welcomed in Montana, *Imasees* and his followers were reviled and rejected, forced to wander from the garbage dumps of Helena to the unfriendly confines of the Blackfeet Reservation, any place where they could eke out a living. *Imasees* used his other name of Little Bear and constantly emphasized that his people were as much American as they were Canadian, but few people would listen.[21]

In Canada, the Department of Indian Affairs had a policy of discouraging new chiefs from establishing themselves. Bureaucrats were ordered to dispense with chiefs if they could get away with it. In fact, in 1897, the assistant secretary of the department circulated this policy to Indian agents and farmers-in-charge in the North-West Territories, which included what is now Alberta:

> The policy of the Department is to reduce, rather than increase the number of Chiefs and head men, and when vacancies occur they should not be filled

unless the Department is compelled by Treaty stipulations to consent to the same being done, as past experience has taught the Department, that the Indians get along much better without Chiefs or Head men and there is less difficulty in dealing with the Indians when there are no Chiefs or Head men to raise objections and place obstacles in the way of the Department and its officers.[22]

THE "BAPTISM" OF BOBTAIL SMALLBOY

In 1898, as the fall turned into winter, *Apitchitchiw* and Isabelle, with one-year-old Maggie in tow and Bobtail on the way, gathered firewood in the foothills and sold it to settlers at Fort McLeod. Already heavy with child, Isabelle thought of returning home to Hobbema, about 320 kilometres to the north, but *Apitchitchiw* was a practical man and knew there was no work for him there. It was best to stay the winter in a place where they could make a little money. They pitched their tent on the Peigan Reserve near the Oldman River, next to the teepee of Coyote's old friend. And so it was that Bob Smallboy came to be born in the land of the traditional enemies of the Cree.[23]

After a year on the Peigan Reserve, *Apitchitchiw* and Isabelle finally returned to Hobbema. Isabelle wanted her ailing grandfather to grant her young son a name. Accordingly, when Smallboy was a year old, she arranged for a naming ceremony, a feast to which all the elders were invited. Bobtail held his one-year-old grandson in his arms and sang a sacred song, accompanying his song by shaking a rattle in time. Then he smoked a pipe and blessed his grandson, at which point Isabelle announced that she wished to name the child *Keskayo* after her grandfather. All the people there agreed that the choice was a good one. Chief Bobtail then passed his grandson to his brother, Ermineskin, who also blessed the child and repeated his name, *Keskayo*, over and over. From there the baby was passed clockwise around the teepee, from elder to elder, each of them giving his blessing and calling out his name. Finally, the time came for the feast, including a dessert of ripe saskatoon berries.

Chief Bobtail knew that he did not have long to live. Therefore, before the evening was out, he conducted a ritual of his own in which he gave his chief's pipe stem power bundle to Isabelle, declaring that through her, his power as a chief would be revived. He told Isabelle that although she would only be a keeper of the bundle, her young son, *Keskayo*, would some day inherit it and become chief.[24] Later, Isabelle passed on the bundle to her son, as Bobtail had requested, and this was the basis for Bob Smallboy's claim that he was a hereditary chief, as well as an elected one.[25]

While Isabelle and *Apitchitchiw* were at Hobbema, Johnny was born in

January 1900, and six months later was baptized in Our Lady of the Seven Sorrows Church. Eighteen years later, when Bob Smallboy's fiancée, Louisa Headman, wanted a Roman Catholic wedding, Bob had to prove that he was a baptized Catholic. He did so by appropriating his brother's name and calling himself "Johnny Bob Smallboy," the name that appears on his certificate of marriage.

Bob Smallboy later claimed to have been baptized at Our Lady of the Seven Sorrows Church in Hobbema on 10 July 1900, along with Johnny, but the only evidence of this is a copy of a certificate of baptism made in 1964 bearing both his and Johnny's name.[26] Since *Apitchitchiw*, Isabelle, and their growing family were so mobile, July 1900 was probably the first opportunity they had, or the first time they were so inclined, to baptize either of the boys. However, there is no evidence to show that Bob was ever actually baptized.

During their stay near Billings, Montana, in 1902, when he was "four winters old," *Keskayo* Smallboy experienced a second baptism (or perhaps his first)—one that almost cost him his life. *Apitchitchiw* had pitched the family tent at the edge of the Crow Camp on the Little Big Horn River. A thick plank had been placed over the narrowest part of the river as a footbridge, but the plank tended to wobble and bounce as people walked across it. As the four-year-old *Keskayo* stood on the plank, the other children started jumping up and down on it, and *Keskayo* lost his balance and fell head first into the rushing torrent. Terrified by the prospect of parental retribution at the drowning death of one of their number, most of the children ran off, to distance themselves from this inevitable calamity. But Smallboy's sister, Maggie, then only five, ran along the bank of the river where her little brother was floating. *Keskayo* thrashed about frantically, trying to get air. His sister waded partway into the current and managed to grab his hand and fish him from the icy water. They both walked home together, wailing all the way. Chief Smallboy later recounted:

> The incident seems like a dream of something that happened a long, long time ago. I still remember the land and how it looked—the countryside and the trees along the way, the way they stood just so. I can remember it as if I can actually see the land before me, the land surrounding us on that day when I fell into the water.[27]

THE QUEST FOR STATUS

Apitchitchiw longed to seek his fortune back home in the south, in what is still called in Cree "the Land of the Long Knives"—America. "We moved to different places whenever we felt like going," Chief Smallboy recalled later. "Everyone was after the same thing—making a living. People had to work hard in those days. White men were not numerous, and jobs were scarce. That was long ago."[28] Undoubtedly, one of the bands of Cree families living near Browning, Montana, was that of Little Bear, who by then was eking out a living by salvaging bones and fat from a butcher shop.

"The Cavalry should cooperate with the agents in driving the Crees off every reservation," declared the *Anaconda Standard* on 1 August 1901, as vitriolic as ever. This admonition applied to the Smallboys as much as to anyone, as they moved from reservation to reservation, usually pitching their tent on the fringes of the host reservation so as not to incite violence from legitimate members of the band.

On 14 January 1902, Rocky Boy, through Anaconda attorney J. W. James, wrote a letter addressed to President Theodore Roosevelt in which he claimed to be an American Chippewa chief whose people had no land. He petitioned the president for a reservation for his people. James later admitted that he had "written certain letters for 'Rocky Boy,'" including this one:

Anaconda, Montana
14 January 1902
His Excellency Theodore Roosevelt,
President of the United States of America
Washington, D.C.

Dear Sir-,

I am the Chief of a band of Chippewa Indians that for years have been wandering through different parts of the United States without home or reservation. We now feel that if possible to secure it, we would like some home or reservation on which to live and have the privilege of sending our children to school.

I am known as an honest Indian and have credentials to show that my people have always been self supporting.

Can you arrange to send me the necessary transportation for myself and an interpreter, from this point to Washington, D.C. and give me a hearing when I arrive there. I believe the request of my people is a just one and if given the opportunity to present the matter to your Excellency, you will agree with me and we feel that you will use your influence toward the betterment of our conditions.

My entire tribe is composed of about one hundred and thirty souls, men women and children, all of whom are self supporting.

If given the opportunity we believe we can improve our present conditions.

The typed letter was signed "Rocky Boy his + mark."[29]

Rocky Boy's letter was referred by the White House to the secretary of the Interior and thence to the commissioner of Indian Affairs, who assigned U.S. Indian Agent W. H. Smead of the Flathead Reservation to ascertain the facts of the case. Smead contacted the Anaconda chief of police, William A. Taylor, and the attorney who had forwarded the letter to the president, J. W. James.

The *Anaconda Standard* was the first newspaper to report on the existence of Rocky Boy:

> Several weeks ago Rocky Boy, chief of the band, came to Anaconda and consulted a lawyer with reference to gaining permission from the department of the interior to settle down somewhere under the protection of the government, and in order that their children might be given an opportunity to receive some schooling. A letter was forwarded to President Roosevelt by Attorney J. W. James....
>
> According to the story told by Rocky Boy the fathers of this particular band were roaming about in the Dakotas when the Chippewa treaty was made. Consequently no provision was made for them by the government. For the past 12 years they have been roaming over Montana from place to place gaining a livelihood by selling polished horns and other Indian articles. It is now the desire of the band to remain in some place permanently so they and their children may be benefited. Though the band has been camped near Anaconda for several months the members are not particular as to what tract of land shall be given them. They like the country surrounding Anaconda, however, and would be content to remain here.[30]

The *Anaconda Standard's* story was based on an interview with Chief of Police Taylor, conducted on 10 February 1902, the date of Taylor's report to Smead. That police report read:

> I have made a very thorough investigation and am satisfied that the Indians now in this locality under Chief Rocky Boy are Chippewas whose ancestors left Chippewa Falls, Wis. And came to Montana some fifty years ago but were never allotted any land. There are now about one hundred in the band including children and they say they desire to get land to cultivate and teachers for their children.[31]

Attorney James clarified his clients' position in a letter to Smead dated 14 February 1902:

> Your letter of the 13th referred to "Rocky Boy" and today I went into detail with them about the matter.... Some of them claim to have been born in

Wisconsin, others in Michigan, some in the Dakotas, and all with one or two exceptions claim the United States as their birth place.… I also find that they have intermarried with several other tribes among whom are Crees and I think in all probability that is how you may have received the idea that they were Crees.[32]

Two weeks later, Smead reported to the Indian commissioner:

I had always supposed that the Indians referred to were part of the Cree tribe that has been in Montana for a long time, but from the correspondence from Chief of Police Taylor, and Attorney James of Anaconda where these Indians are now wintering, it appears that a part at least are Chippewas, American born, I am however satisfied that there are Crees mixed up with them, and I think it quite certain that some of these so called Chippewas are from the Canadian side.[33]

The commissioner of Indian Affairs considered Smead's findings unsatisfactory and instructed him to do a more thorough examination. Accordingly, on 27 March, Agent Smead conducted a personal interview with Rocky Boy and reported on 2 April:

I was advised by Rocky Boy that his people are at this time scattered about in the larger cities of the state, and that at the present time only a comparatively few were in Anaconda. This was true as there were only 17 male Indians at the meeting, of whom 6 were full bloods and 11 mixed bloods, some nearly white. These mixed bloods are Chippewas, American born Crees, Canadian born Crees, and one Snake. The full bloods were all as far as I could ascertain American born Indians and Chippewa descent.… Of those present at this meeting 14 favoured Rocky Boy and his plans, I however regret to say that 4 of the full bloods are opposed to Rocky Boy and object to being located upon any reservation, or for that matter, any place, permanently.

Rocky Boy claims to have a following of about 400 people, while from what I could learn his opponent, has not to exceed 10% of that number. Of this number however I am certain that there are a considerable number, if not a majority, of Canadian born Crees. In fact I am personally acquainted with a number of those present at this meeting, know them to be Crees and have had occasion to expel them from this reservation.[34]

He estimated the number of American-born Chippewa Indians to be under 200, "and probably not so many would be entitled to reservation privileges."[35]

In a letter dated 26 April 1902, Acting Commissioner of Indian Affairs A. C. Tonner frankly advised the secretary of the Interior:

> The policy of this Department is to break up tribal relations as soon as possible and cause the Indians to become self-supporting and self-reliant, and not to increase tribal membership or create new reservations unless the best of reasons exist therefore. In the present case it is shown that more than half, and probably a majority, of the Indians under consideration are Crees who belong in Canada, and have been for many years past self-supporting and who are capable of continuing to provide for themselves in the future. It is not therefore thought the circumstances in the case call for any further action.[36]

GOING PUBLIC

Upon the advice of his attorney, Rocky Boy went public. The lawyer wrote a letter to Senator Paris Gibson, dated 25 March 1903, asking for his intervention in helping Rocky Boy obtain a reservation for his band. James estimated that there were 130 members of the band ("at least eighty full blood Chippewas and fifty half breeds"); however, he admitted that "many of them are intermarried with Canadian Crees and other tribes."[37] The senator did his own calculations and, by July 1903, Rocky Boy's band of Chippewas had been whittled down to "twenty-five or thirty in number" who "can be quite easily identified through the aid of Rocky Boy." Special Agent Thomas Downs was assigned to the case.

In a report to the commissioner of Indian Affairs dated 3 October 1903, Special Agent Downs admitted that "owing to the migratory habits of these Indians it is very hard to get any definite information as to their identity...."

> Rocky Boy tells me that in the past they have been able to eke out an existence by making and selling bead work and polishing and selling horns, and doing odd jobs as they were offered, but that within the last few years they have been unable to find a market for their work, and as a consequence came near perishing from hunger during the past two or three winters.[38]

Downs supplied the commissioner with a list of ninety members of Rocky Boy's band, contained in a sworn schedule dated 1 October 1903, and an additional list of twenty-six members who were absent from the camp when Downs conducted his inquiry. Despite Rocky Boy's co-operation, Downs could positively identify only twenty-eight members of the band. The remaining sixty-two refused to give their names or any other information leading to their identity: "Some of them when questioned refused to answer. Others stated that they did not wish to settle down at any place for permanent residence, nor did they wish to have their children educated."[39] Ewers concluded from Downs's report: "We know only that some of them were conservatives who did not want to give up their nomadic life for settlement on a reservation, and did not want their children placed in schools."[40]

The editorial sentiments of newspapers in Montana against the wandering Indians had not changed much by 1904, when the *Helena Daily Independent* commented: "Some years ago the Crees were rounded up in Montana and taken across into Canada where they belong, but they soon drifted back and some months ago they were so much of a nuisance that an appeal was made to the state authorities for relief from their presence."[41]

For the citizenry of Helena, birthplace still made all the difference: those born in Canada were "Canadian Cree," while those born in the United States were "Chippewa." Thus the negotiations to give Rocky Boy's band of 110 "wandering American-born Indians" some space on the Flathead Reservation west of the Rocky Mountains in 1904 did not include the Canadian Cree, despite the fact that Rocky Boy had lived for years in Canada and had spent all his life virtually straddling the border. Even American-born Cree were denied land or rights on a reservation. The wandering bands of Indians under Rocky Boy and Little Bear were *persona non grata*. They had virtually no means of earning a living, yet their every effort to survive was criticized.

That year, a Senate bill that would have given Rocky Boy and his band space on the Flathead Reservation was defeated, leaving the closely allied Cree and Chippewa to continue scrounging dumps at the edges of cities for enough to eat. Following Downs's recommendation that room be found for Rocky Boy's band on the Flathead Reservation, Senator Gibson had introduced a bill into the Senate in 1904, providing for expenditure of under nineteen thousand dollars to move Rocky Boy and his band to that reservation. Although the bill passed in the Senate, it stalled in the House of Representatives, partly because the Flathead "were very much opposed" to sharing their reservation with Rocky Boy's group.

Eventually, the Smallboys arrived back at the Crow Indian Reservation south of Billings, Montana, famous for its Custer Battlefield at the Little Big Horn, and where, in the Little Big Horn River, the young Bobtail had almost drowned. But the Crows were equally opposed to sharing their reservation.[42] It seemed that nobody, but nobody, wanted to provide a home for *Apitchitchiw* and his family—or for any of the Canadian Cree.

CHAPTER 5

The Nomadic Life

THE ENTREPRENEUR

Apitchitchiw and Isabelle worked incredibly hard to make a meagre living during the lean years at the beginning of the twentieth century. Though blind, Isabelle sewed moccasins and purses made from rawhide and beads, and tooled leather belts for white men in nearby villages to buy. *Apitchitchiw* made furniture from horn, especially from old buffalo horns salvaged from mass graves or sites of old buffalo jumps. He would scrape and mould the outer surface of the horns with knives, smooth them down with files, and polish them with sandpaper and damp ash until they shone. Sometimes the horns would be nailed to boards as clothes' hooks. A master craftsman, *Apitchitchiw* applied himself to creating elaborate buffalo-horn chairs worthy of any chief, which would fetch as much as sixty dollars—a lot of money in those days. In the winter, there was always a demand in the towns for firewood, which *Apitchitchiw* supplied for eight dollars a cord.[1]

The family took advantage of the free transportation offered to Indians in the United States to reach new markets. "Wherever Indians desired to go they could and did go," Smallboy recalled. "Wherever they happened to be in the late fall—that is where they would spend the winter."[2] Usually, however, they would overwinter on the Blackfeet Reservation near Browning: "There were several families there besides ours," said Smallboy of these early memories. Although they were not officially assigned to any American reservation, they stayed on the Blackfeet and the Crow reservations in Montana, until finally moving farther north to the vicinity of Fort Assinniboine, south of Havre.[3]

Intertribal powwows and sun dances were of especial interest to the young *Keskayo*, and one particular Sun Dance at the Wind River Arapaho Reservation in Wyoming drew Indians of all tribes from all over the west, including Isabelle's parents, Coyote and *Kakokikanis* (Hanger-On). The Sun Dance rites were sacred, and children were not allowed to witness the opening ceremonies. So rigidly was this rule enforced, said Smallboy, that an elder would walk around the inner perimeter of the camp warning parents to keep their children inside their lodges. Still, from the very fact of its exclusivity, Smallboy derived a deep respect for the ceremony.

From Wyoming, the Smallboys moved northward back into Montana, where *Apitchitchiw*, ever flexible, trapped and hunted wolves for a living. Although the U.S. government was intent on curtailing the freedom of movement of the Canadian Cree, the young couple soon discovered that, in general, the attitude of the public towards nontreaty Indians in Montana was softening. In April 1908, in an amendment to the Indian Appropriations Bill, Congress approved thirty thousand dollars to move the Chippewa to a permanent location and provide them with support. Rocky Boy tried to co-operate with the Flathead Reservation agent, Samuel Bellow, who reported:

> Rocky Boy states to me that he is a Chippewa Indian, born on the American side of the Canadian line, and that he is the recognized chief of the Chippewas in Montana, that to the best of his knowledge there are about 200 of his people now in the State, living around Butte, Anaconda, and Garrison, and a small portion working on the Flathead, Blackfeet and Crow reservations; that about 85 members are full blood Chippewas and the remainder are mixed bloods, principally Crees.... .
>
> There is no means of verifying Rocky Boy's statements though I do not doubt that upon close investigation many of his band would be found to be Canadian Crees.[4]

U.S. Indian Office Inspector Frank C. Churchill interviewed Rocky Boy at Anaconda and reported on 29 July 1908, "He said there are about 50 persons in the vicinity of Garrison, Montana where he is now camped, 10 near Billings, Montana, 5 near Havre, Montana, and 6 on the Flathead Reservation."[5] Churchill reported in November that many Montana residents regarded the Montana Cree "as a lot of roving gypsies many if not most of whom came from Canada and they are looked upon by the citizens of certain sections of Montana as being very much in the way." He added: "Where they can be made to stay permanently is a problem that may not have been fully worked out."[6]

The camp near Garrison seemed particularly idyllic for the ten-year-old Bob Smallboy. As he later recounted, "The main thing is that the people were involved in life, and were making money to survive, doing many different things, different types of work to earn money, to earn a living."[7] Primarily, they serviced the tourist trade by making beaded purses, moccasins, belts of all sizes, and anything else "Indian" that the white man would buy, either as utilitarian objects or as souvenirs, by then as often made from cow horns as from buffalo horns salvaged from buffalo jumps.

In 1908, *Apitchitchiw*, Little Bear, and many other Canadian Cree got decent jobs gathering lodgepole pine cones for the Forest Service. But the *Helena Daily Independent* resented this gainful employment of Canadian Cree: "About 50 Indians have been gathering cones and now have 500 bushels of pine tree fruit which has netted the squaws and papooses 40 cents a bushel and is a bonanza to the natives.... The stores of the pine tree squirrels aided the Indians, who robbed them with impunity and it is likely that many a squirrel family will go hungry this winter."[8]

LAND FOR THE TAKING

In late 1908, Andy Bole and artist Charles Russell, who both knew Rocky Boy personally, started a campaign designed to shame the government into providing some form of assistance to Rocky Boy's band. A subscription list and petition were drawn up, and eventually enough pressure was brought to bear on the secretary of the Interior in Washington—mostly by another sympathizer, Judge James Hunt of Helena—that the secretary ordered the General Land Office to set aside 1,400,000 acres of land in Valley County, Montana, thenceforth to be known as the "Rocky Boy Indians Lands."

The commissioner of Indian Affairs sent T. W. Wheat, a land allotment clerk, to check on the condition of Rocky Boy's band in the Helena area—although neither the commissioner nor Wheat informed Rocky Boy or any of his band that such a vast tract of land had been set aside in northeastern Montana specifically for their use. As Andy Bole commented in a *Great Falls Tribune* editorial on 8 January 1909, "[Rocky Boy's] annually starved women and children get kicked around from pillar to post, enmeshed with department red tape, and nothing is done about it."[9] Charles Russell added:

It doesn't look very good for the people of Montana if they will sit and see a lot of women and children starve to death in this kind of weather. Lots of people seem to think that the Indians are not human beings at all and have no feelings. These kind of people would be the first to yell for help if their grub pile was running short and they didn't have enough clothes to keep out the cold, and yet because it is Rocky Boy and his bunch of Indians they are perfectly willing to let them die of hunger and cold without lifting a hand.[10]

This began a campaign to bring into focus the plight of the Chippewa Cree living at the fringes of Helena and to shame the government into providing some form of assistance to Rocky Boy's band. Bole, editor of the *Tribune*, had been consistently sympathetic with the landless Indians. The callous remark in the *Helena Daily Independent* accusing the starving Indians of depriving the squirrels of their pine seeds generated a reaction that eventually moved even Helena residents to pity the plight of the landless Indians and come to their aid.[11] Led by Judge Hunt, they arranged for food and clothing to be deposited with Rocky Boy's band, along with a supply of blankets.[12] On 10 January 1909, the *Daily Independent* reported: "With tears streaming down his cheeks while resting in the snow on his knees, and with his hands lifted in supplication, Chief Rocky Boy ... offered thanks to the people of Helena ... saying God would bless them."[13] Bole, Russell, and the *Great Falls Tribune* sent a cheque to Helena, intending it to reach Rocky Boy's band. "It was returned with the information that the government was at last awake to its responsibility and ... that Rocky Boy and his band would be fed and cared for and located on land in the spring."[14]

However, the secret Rocky Boy land allocation in Valley County was not politically popular, and there was mounting pressure on the government, especially by such influential developers as J. J. Hill, the president of Great Northern Railway, to shelve the resettlement plan. Given that most of the pressure to forsake the Indian and develop the land came from the railway company, there is a certain irony to Chief Smallboy's fond memories of what in 1982 he was still calling "the fire wagon," which he regarded as an addition to rather than a subtraction from the freedom of movement of the Indian. "If an Indian had to travel a long distance, he would ride the fire wagon or train, and it was free, for the Indian could go anywhere he wanted to go on the train without paying for his fare," Smallboy recalled.[15]

Thanks to the intervention of his distant cousin Chief Yellowface, Smallboy and his family were spared the humiliation of near-starvation in the winter of 1909, which led to a reversal of attitudes on the part of the citizens and press of Helena and to intervention by sympathetic Mormons north of the border. With mounting protest from white sympathizers, the commissioner of Indian Affairs once more became involved, directing

Wheat to conduct a yet more thorough investigation. Wheat reported on 20 April 1909:

> I have found Chief Rocky Boy and a portion of his band camped near the slaughter houses about one mile east of Helena. From Rocky Boy I learned that his band of Indians was scattered over the western part of Montana.... It may be stated here that there are a great many Canadian Crees roaming over the entire state of Montana, but very few are affiliated with Rocky Boy's band of Chippewas.... I found that the Indians belonging to this band are very poor. Nearly all of them are camped in the neighbourhood of slaughter houses near the towns and cities, and their food is limited to bread and refuse that they receive from these slaughter houses. They obtain their flour, clothing, bedding, camping equipage, etc., by selling bead work and polished cow horns made into hat racks. A few of the men work on ranches and at cutting wood. They seem to be willing to work after they receive employment, but they are backward about looking for work. These Indians know no home except ragged filthy tents. From Helena, it is about 400 miles, as the crow flies, to the lands on which it is proposed to locate these Indians.... It is impossible for the Indians to make this journey by their own efforts. Their horses are not equal to the task of making the trip, and the Indians have absolutely no means of subsistence on the way. In view of the long journey, the conditions of the Indians' horses and the utter lack of any means of subsistence, I would respectfully suggest that the Indians, their horses, wagons, and camp equipage be loaded on a freight train and taken to the lands on which they are to be located.[16]

Apitchitchiw, Isabelle, and the children had rejoined Rocky Boy in Montana for the summer of 1909, having heard that a decent deal was in the offing. But as winter approached, it became necessary to split up once more, to try to seek lodging and shelter from the winter by the good graces of Indians already assigned to reservations.

Following Wheat's suggestion, the band was loaded into boxcars in the fall of 1909 and shipped to the Blackfeet Reservation near Browning, where each person was allotted eighty acres, a quarter of the acreage held by their Blackfoot counterparts. Dusenberry writes:

> Little Bear was the outspoken critic of their location, for he was dissatisfied with the small acreage given to the new-comers in contrast to the amount allotted to the Blackfeet. Also, the Chippewa and Cree were made to feel inferior and unwanted by their Blackfeet neighbours. This further incensed Little Bear, who realized, though, that the feeling against him was too strong for him to secure a place for his people; so while he was the most

powerful speaker for the group, he enlisted Rocky Boy's aid and started Rocky Boy agitating again for another refuge. Talk was beginning to be heard about the plans the army had for abandoning Fort Assinniboine, and Little Bear—through the kindly and better liked Rocky Boy—saw a chance to secure a portion for the merged bands.[17]

The *Great Falls Tribune* reported that "the princely sum of $100 was forwarded to relieve the necessities of 125 people during the winter. Then Rocky Boy's band scattered again. They deemed it safer to trust to the tender mercies of a Montana winter than to the Great White Father which had so often proved a broken reed to pierce their hand."[18]

Despite the clear expression of dissatisfaction by Little Bear, Superintendent William N. Logan of the Fort Belknap Agency wrote to the commissioner of Indian Affairs: "Rocky Boy and his entire band are well pleased with their new location and the Blackfeet are perfectly satisfied to have the band settled there. The change from the location in Valley County to the Blackfeet Reservation is a happy one; they can easily make a living by farming and working out."[19]

This was an utter lie. However, the reason for the deception quickly became apparent. Within days, the Department of the Interior announced the opening for settlement of the Valley County area hitherto reserved for Rocky Boy's band.[20] Despite the assurances that a vast tract of land had been set aside for the Indians, in January 1910 the secretary of the Interior, Richard A. Ballinger, ordered the Rocky Boy Indian lands to be "thrown open to white settlers March 1, 1910," with settlement to commence at the end of that month.[21]

Instead of being shipped east to land set aside for them barely a year earlier—land that Rocky Boy had never been told had been allocated for his band's use—the Chippewa Cree, including the Smallboys, found themselves being loaded onto boxcars for a trip northwest to the Blackfeet Reservation at Browning. According to James Kipp of Lodgepole, who watched the Cree and all their possessions (including dogs, horses, and teepees) being unloaded at Browning, "When spring came, they disappeared into the four winds like the birds, and they didn't come back."[22]

A STIFF UPPER LIP

At first, the roster of Rocky Boy's band did not include Little Bear or his band, but gradually Rocky Boy saw the wisdom of including the names of "half-breeds and Canadian Crees," the better to compel government action. U.S. Indian Office Inspector Churchill remarked that it was "common understanding that chief Little Bear and some fifty persons are a part of this group of roving Indians that for many years have been camping near the larger towns in the state, particularly Garrison, Anaconda, Butte, Helena, Great Falls, Havre, and Cut Bank."[23] Dusenberry notes, "Little Bear's personality emerges during the next few years; still undaunted by every rebuff possible for almost thirty years, he became the definite leader of the homeless Indians of Montana."[24]

Smallboy recalled the way the Rocky Boy camp was set up. "The chief's teepee was at the centre of the camp, and in a circle at the centre, surrounding the chief's teepee, were the teepees of the warrior class—those men who had proven or distinguished themselves as brave men."[25] He said there was a circular walkway between the inner teepees and those of the rest of the camp, and the elders usually walked this inner circle at dawn to give their advice. But most of the conveyance of history and legend, in the form of storytelling, would take place at night. "There was often a serious side to the stories they told, such as fables, morals or parables—or true stories about the exploits of their warriors. Through this custom, people derived good thoughts and were able to go to sleep in a good frame of mind."[26]

In this way, the history of the tribe was preserved. But the system had a practical purpose, as well. Smallboy recalled that each morning, the elders would go around the camp making announcements and waking the people, telling them to give thanks to the Creator. They would circle the camp, giving advice to the young; sometimes they would visit families that were having domestic problems and give counsel.

Much of the advice of the elders concerned manners and appearance. Despite their destitute condition, personal cleanliness and neatness would bring goodness to the soul, the elders told Smallboy. Similarly, lots of exercise was good for the body and would lead to a long life. Vigorous exercise led to a pleasant state of mind, which in turn put body and soul in harmony. Survival, said Chief Smallboy, was not easy in those days. The people had to be strong. There was no room for sickness.

Some of the advice given by the elders at the Little Bear and Rocky Boy camps was of the "thou shalt not" variety. This kind of guidance tended to alienate many youths, but Chief Smallboy saw it as the ultimate salvation of the Indian. Although not all of the young men took time to listen to the elders and to learn about the ways of their forefathers, later it was upon them that the responsibility for the preservation of their way of life was to fall. Smallboy took the time to listen and to learn and to pass these things on to his children and grandchildren.[27] Like Rocky Boy and Little Bear before him, Chief Smallboy called upon his people to adopt their traditional ways as far as possible before the sacred institutions of the Indian vanished forever.

THE "CANADIAN CREE"

From the beginning, the *Helena Daily Independent* had tried to distinguish between the "Canadian Cree" and the "real Chippewas who never have been confined to any reservation but have been camp followers and hangers-on about the Assiniboine and Gros Ventre camps since the memory of man runneth not to the contrary."[28] However, by 1909, the Chippewa and Cree had become indistinguishable. The Indians themselves regarded it as an artificial distinction. *Apitchitchiw* regarded himself as Cree, as did Chief Smallboy to his dying day. In fact, Smallboy is regarded in many circles as being quintessentially Cree, yet he spoke the language with a marked Chippewa or "Old Cree" pronunciation, according to his interpreters. To compensate, he talked very slowly and gestured constantly as he spoke. His slow and distinct "precise" speech only served to emphasize a guttural and glottal inflexion and use of "w" endings more than modern Cree allows.

To this day, the U.S. government formally lists the descendants of "Rocky Boy's Chippewa" (the name under which they were originally incorporated as a tribe) as "Chippewa-Cree," but only because the constitution and charter of the Rocky Boy Reservation use this term. Today, however, the band universally self-identifies as Cree, simpliciter.

> Young men of that tribe now are "Cree" when they are asked to state their tribal affiliation. "They're going to make a Cree Indian out of you," they say to a white participant in the sweat lodge ceremony, the Sun Dance, or any other tribal function that a white man may share. Older men too refer to themselves as "Cree": even though they may tell one of the Blackfoot ancestor or Assiniboine heritage. Likewise, men and women will point out areas where Chippewa ceremonies such as the Great Medicine Lodge once took place. "It's all gone now," they will say. "We're all Crees here." … Cree [is] a designation they have developed for themselves out of their checkered and wandering past.[29]

Perhaps because he himself was not responsible for making a living in those idyllic childhood days, and therefore was insulated by *Apitchitchiw*, Isabelle, and *Waskahte* from the hostility and poverty that surrounded him, Bobtail Smallboy saw life through rose-coloured glasses. "The Indian always found a way to make a living, even in winter. That was why there was not much hunger for the people," he said. "The people got along well with the white man. There was nothing to hinder their relationships."[30]

If this was the case, the feeling was not mutual. Over the next six years, the wandering Chippewa-Cree and their request for Fort Assinniboine as a home reservation was the subject of much debate both in Montana and in Washington, DC. Initially, residents of nearby Havre were the most vocal about keeping the old fort "out of the hands of the Indians," especially after the buildings had been signed over to the State of Montana. The *Havre Plaindealer* remained the most outspoken of all the newspapers against "Rocky Boy and his band of trifling lazy renegade Chippewa Indians."[31] Andy Bole and the *Great Falls Tribune* remained sympathetic:

> These Indians have no powerful friends, they have no money, they have no property. They have nothing to commend themselves to the favour of any white man, but a claim that has justice and equity back of it. We hope they will get a reserve of land assigned to them … and with this land we hope they will get houses and stock and tools and food and everything they need to give them a start on the road to independence and self-support. And when they do get this they will get nothing more than long delayed justice.…. The condition of Rocky Boy and his band is dark with dishonor to every member of the white race.[32]

Following his visit to Rocky Boy's camp west of Bozeman in southern Montana in March of 1913, Frank Linderman suggested that the government should act quickly to grant the land around Fort Assinniboine to the Indians before "jealous boomers" and landgrabbers could get their hands on it. The *Plaindealer* responded in a vitriolic editorial: "Frank Linderman … has become interested in Chief Rocky Boy and his tribe of human scavengers and has determined to find for them a haven upon the Assinniboine military reservation." The editorial claimed that Linderman, a retired trapper, "has gained his knowledge from a too faithful reading of Leatherstocking Tales in which Pathfinder and Deerslayer, Indian heroes, had been exalted for their fidelity to principle and to whom faculties of reasoning almost superhuman were given by the author."[33]

In fact, the Montana Cree were applauded by many more citizens than Frank Linderman. Some residents of southern Alberta and northern Montana were deeply impressed by the Cree who wandered their territory. Joseph Y. Card wrote of the Cree wanderers, "They are of higher moral character than the average in that part of the country," and described them as "industrious and capable, despite many hardships."[34]

Apitchitchiw and Isabelle used horses to haul lodge poles and their possessions on travois. Margaret, Bobtail, Johnny, and Billy usually rode two to a pony as they moved from place to place. According to Chief Smallboy, "The horses were one factor in how long we would stay in a given camp. When the horses had eaten all the grass around the camp, then we would move camp to a place where the grass was longer so the horses could eat."[35]

In general, the Cree stayed in the rangelands west of the homesteads. There were no reports of problems with the law, and the people were counselled firmly by the elders not to trespass on land claimed by the settlers, Chief Smallboy recalled. The young men were counselled not to offend one another, and peace prevailed in the camp. "There were no problems with the police. They knew there were no problems. They knew everybody and how they were."[36]

THE PUSH FOR A RESERVATION

By 1913, Little Bear had become the leader of the homeless Indians, including the Smallboy family. *Apitchitchiw* and Isabelle were united with Little Bear and Rocky Boy's band on the unofficial Rocky Boy Reservation, but there was still no security: the status of the reservation was very much up in the air. Technically, *Apitchitchiw* and Isabelle (and by extension, Coyote) could at any time activate their treaty status at the Ermineskin Band in Alberta, so they had a fallback position. However, once they committed to a reserve, leaving it on any pretext would become increasingly difficult, as in Canada it was illegal for Indians to be off their reserves without written permission. To the extent that people of the First Nations could not go anywhere without a formal pass, they were prisoners on their reserves, at the mercy of the local Indian agent. This did not suit *Apitchitchiw*'s lifestyle at all. If freedom was to be found, it would have to be in the United States. Returning to Canada entailed taking a circuitous route to avoid villages, towns, and cities, where even walking down the street without a pass could land him in jail until transportation to his home reserve could be arranged. Once there, obtaining a pass would be all the more difficult because of the infraction.

In 1913, the *Cut Bank Pioneer Press* reported a confrontation between Little Bear and Secretary of the Interior Franklin K. Lane:

[Little Bear] stalked into the lobby of the Placer Hotel at Helena and had a conference with the representative of the White Father.

"God was taking care of us all right until the white man came and took the responsibility off His hands. Last winter our wives and our children lived on dogs and the carcasses of frozen horses to keep from starving."

"God ordained," said the Secretary, "that man must work to live and nobody gets the land who does not use it. The white man took the Indian land to raise wheat and corn and oats and cattle. The land produces nothing. It is the man who produces things."

"That's what we're after," responded the sombre old chief."[37]

Subsequently, the debate over obtaining a reservation for the roving Cree was taken, quite literally, to Washington, DC, where Bole campaigned in favour of granting Rocky Boy the military reserve. In late 1913, Rocky Boy and Little Bear received permission to camp on the grounds at Fort Assinniboine—as *Apitchitchiw* had been doing for some time.[38] However, a delegation from Havre complained to Cato Sells, the commissioner of Indian Affairs, that most of the Indians were Canadian Cree, "a shiftless vagabond band infected with disease," who were "notoriously improvident" and "a constant menace."[39] In fact, they were close to starvation much of the time, and they had few creature comforts. "The band arrived at Fort Assiniboine with little more than the clothes on their backs and ragged tents for housing," remarked historian Thomas Wessel.

> Few of the Chippewa-Cree had adequate clothing or blankets to survive the cold, snow-bound conditions that could last in the Bear Paw Mountains from November through April. Makeshift stoves made from inverted wash tubs or oil drums provided the only heat. Without more substantial housing, the winter months could wreak disaster on Little Bear's and Rocky Boy's people.[40]

A year later, the Cree were ordered off the Fort Belknap Agency and were not allowed to camp on the Missouri River near Great Falls.[41] The general perception was that they refused to work, although Bole and Linderman pointed out to Sells that this was far from the truth. White employers, Bole pointed out, would only hire an Indian who possessed a team of cart horses. Indian ponies hardly qualified as cart horses. Furthermore, those few Indians who did own cart horses had to belong to labour unions to be eligible for work. However, the labour unions in Montana declared Indians ineligible for membership[42]—a classic case of Catch-22.

In a brash move, Senator Henry L. Myers promised to relocate Rocky Boy's band back to the Blackfeet Reservation near Browning. This time the *Cut Bank Pioneer Press* became Rocky Boy's advocate: "The Havre papers are very peevish over the efforts made to set aside the Assinniboine reservation as a home for Rocky Boy.... It is a ridiculous assumption and a brazen affront to the residents of the Blackfeet to assert in one breath that the Assinniboine is too good for the Rocky Crees and that the proper place for them is on the Blackfeet reservation."[43]

Most of the Cree continued to camp at Fort Assinniboine. In January 1914, the Hill County Board of Commissioners cut off their food supply, so that H. H. Miller, the superintendent at Fort Belknap, had to arrange for food shipments to be made from the Blackfeet Reservation. With that charity, the Indian Office wanted control over their actions and insisted that the Cree at Fort Assinniboine put their hand to farming. Assistant Commissioner of Indian Affairs Edgar B. Merritt supplied seed, two ploughs, and a harrow for their use. Then he had the gall to declare that the Indians were in debt. The Indian Office suggested that the Indians, including *Apitchitchiw*, sell off their horses to liquidate the debt. Naturally, the Cree community objected to this insensitive incursion onto their traditional way of life.[44]

In May 1915, the Indian Office hired Roger St. Pierre as a government farmer to show the Cree how to make the land productive. "The change in status of the Chippewa-Cree from wandering nomads to settled reservation Indians exacerbated internal frictions and introduced new ones," said Wessel. "The apparent rivalry between Rocky Boy and Little Bear intensified the difficulty of transition... . Rocky Boy complained that Roger St. Pierre ignored him and spoke only to his rival. Indian Office officials generally approached the problem by ignoring both men."[45] The situation was aggravated when the Indian Office shipped several of the Cree children off to residential school in Oregon and ordered all men and boys to cut their hair. The Indian Office also required couples to legalize their marriages.

Once again, the question was raised as to whether the Cree could sponsor a Sun Dance. Little Bear had hosted them every summer since 1913:

> The Sun Dance was a time of renewal, a cleansing of the spirit. It linked the Plains Indians with the Past, prepared them for the future, and provided solace in the present. It was a time for seekers of dreams and for those who had found theirs. The Sun Dance lent itself to a variety of interpretations and the Indian's tenacity in holding onto the tradition spoke of its importance to them... .
>
> The observance of the Sun Dance unquestionably added to the Indian Office's burden. Aside from the association with barbarism and self-mutilation the government saw in the ceremonial, its performance was a costly affair. Many days of preparation, days taken from work on the reservation, accompanied the Sun Dance. In addition, the traditional gift giving, a part of the celebration, often left individual members of the band destitute and at the charity of the Indian Office for food and clothing. Government issued blankets, rations, and Indian ponies often diminished in copious quantities during the week-long festivities.[46]

The government sought to regulate the behaviour of the Indians by controlling their rations, which were already austere, and applying inane rules that in the circumstances made no sense. The manipulation of rations was sometimes blatantly criminal. The ration for beef, for example, amounted to two ounces per day. The May 1916 shipment of beef rations was not only 250 pounds short, it consisted entirely of front leg bones, liver, and fat, someone somewhere along the way having absconded with the meat. Yet the government farmer was informed he was being too generous with the rations.

A rule that the Indians could not cut wood for construction—not even for firewood—left the Cree freezing in the dark in their tents. As a demonstration of their true industriousness, once given permission to use the wood in late September, the Cree constructed forty-five houses by Christmas.[47]

Although he knew the Rocky Boy Reservation was on its way, Rocky Boy died still waiting—formal recognition of "his" reservation did not come until more than a year after his death in April 1916. After Rocky Boy's death, Little Bear became the unquestionable leader of the Indians living at Fort Assinniboine.

With the inclusion of Little Bear's band, the list of Indians on the Tentative Roll of Rocky Boy Indians dated 30 May 1917 reached 451, about 200 fewer than Little Bear angled for. These 451 souls were declared by the secretary of the Interior to be entitled to membership in Rocky Boy's band and to the benefits of the new reservation established in his name.[48] Of these, more than two-thirds were born in Canada, including the parents and grandparents of Bobtail Smallboy.

CHAPTER 6

Yellowface

A SUMMONING

Tuberculosis and pneumonia took their toll on the wandering Cree of Montana. By the time he was ten, Bobtail Smallboy had already lost a baby brother to the twin afflictions, as well as several friends. Many of the Cree were too ill or elderly to travel far, and in any case, few wished to return to Canada—the repressive country they had fled in 1885 at the time of the *Ka-mayahkamikahk* (When Bad Things Happened). In the wake of the Riel Resistance, Indians found off their reserves without passes were subject to instant arrest. It was safer to stay in Montana.

Little Bear and Rocky Boy still believed that the salvation of the Chippewa-Cree lay with the authorities in Washington, DC. However, pressures of a different order altogether led *Apitchitchiw* and Isabelle to move back north across the forty-ninth parallel with their children. Both Bobtail and Johnny would be profoundly affected by the prophecies and workings of magic that would emerge as their parents rubbed shoulders with the most revered prophet of the day: Yellowface (*Osâwahtihkwêyo*).[1] Yellowface was one of the most enigmatic figures of western Indian lore—a Cree-cum-Crow seer who was respected by virtually every Indian tribe in the west country for his words of wisdom.

The Smallboys were living with Rocky Boy near Great Falls when Isabelle and *Apitchitchiw* were approached by a distraught woman, the widow of Little Poplar, who told them that her son, who everyone in the camp knew was in the advanced stages of tuberculosis, had only a few days to live. In his delirium, he was calling for his father. When she told him that his father was dead, he cried out the name "Yellowface!"

In 1887, Chief Little Poplar had been shot by a man named Ward for alleged horse theft in western Montana.[2] His widow and son had moved in with Little Poplar's brother, Yellowface, who had adopted the boy as his own. Although Yellowface lived on the Crow Reservation in southern Montana, the boy's mother gravitated towards Little Bear's band, as some of its members were her relatives and she could speak Cree. Now on his deathbed, the young man urged his mother to send for Yellowface, his adoptive father.

Yellowface was a long day's ride away on the Crow Reservation. *Apitchitchiw* knew that he would not reach the shaman before the young man died, let alone ride all the way back. The medicine man's nephew was resigned to the fact that he might be dead before Yellowface arrived, but he had a message for his uncle, and for him alone, from the spirit world. He pleaded with his mother that if he should die before Yellowface arrived, she was not to bury him until Yellowface got there: he believed the shaman's medicine was powerful enough even to raise the dead. And he knew his mother believed it, too: she had told him many times the story of how Yellowface, once considered an idiot, had redeemed himself by saving her life when she had a high fever. Now, as they waited anxiously for *Apitchitchiw* to return with the medicine man, she repeated the story to Isabelle, who later repeated it to her children and grandchildren.

THE IDIOT

Ever since his own youth, Yellowface had reputedly been a thinker rather than a doer. In other words, he daydreamed.[3] While his flamboyant older brother, Little Poplar, rode with the young men of Big Bear's band hunting buffalo and counting coup, Yellowface stayed at home with his mother. In the Cree camp he earned the name *Kihtimikan* (Lazy Boy). He refused to do men's work, and yet he looked down on women's work with contempt. He did not even join the hunt for rabbits, let alone count coup. Instead, he hung around the camp listening to the tales of the old people, especially the women. He was particularly interested in what they said about herbs—which plants could be used for which afflictions. Women, he learned, had particularly interesting afflictions that they never generally discussed with the men. But they discussed these things in front of Yellowface because he was regarded as *mohcowiw*, an idiot. Why else would he stay at home when all the young men were out hunting?

Since his mother was a midwife, women of all ages came to her for advice and herbal remedies for "women's problems"—mostly menstrual difficulties, vaginal irritation, contraception, childbirth, and postnatal

Big Bear while in prison in 1886. GLENBOW ARCHIVES. NA-1315-17

Chief Little Bear, son of Big Bear, formerly known in Canada as *Imasees* (Little Bad Man). Widely but erroneously regarded as being the fomenter of the Frog Lake Massacre of 1885, he led a band of men, women, and children on a zigzag route across what is now Saskatchewan, taking two weeks to get to Montana. A nephew of Rocky Boy by marriage, he was the first chief of the Rocky Boy Reservation in Havre, Montana.

WILLIAM JAMES TOPLEY, LIBRARY AND ARCHIVES CANADA, PA-025886

Chief *Keskayo* (Bobtail), Bobtail Smallboy's maternal grandfather and namesake.

Chief Smallboy's paternal grandfather, *Asinikosisan* (Rocky Boy), after whom the Rocky Boy Reservation in Havre, Montana, is named. GLENBOW ARCHIVES, NA-1270-5

A Peigan camp along the Belly River, similar to the one the Cree attacked in 1870, precipitating the bloodiest confrontation between Indian tribes in Canadian history. GLENBOW ARCHIVES, NA-1463-1

Yellowface, Cree-cum-Crow Chief, whom Chief Smallboy admired as a prophet (1942).

The Medicine Man, 1908, oil on canvas, by Charles M. Russell. Here Russell may be portraying Yellowface in 1908. AMON CARTER MUSEUM, FORT WORTH, TEXAS

Witnesses to a Sun Dance sit on the ground inside a brush-fenced compound. GLENBOW ARCHIVES, NA-1223-14

Little Bear stands on a chair in this posed photograph of Canadian Cree rounded up in Montana for deportation to Canada in 1896. The well-dressed personages seated on chairs in the foreground are believed to be Chief Rocky Boy and his second wife, Voice. FROM HUGH A. DEMPSEY, *BIG BEAR: THE LOSS OF FREEDOM*, CREDIT: TED BRASSER

A large camp near Browning, Montana, showing the layout. The chief's teepee is in the centre. Families tended to cluster together. GLENBOW ARCHIVES, NA-1461-1

Alexander Morris, the lieutenant-governor of the North-West Territories, who negotiated Treaty Six. ARCHIVES OF MANITOBA, MORRIS, ALEXANDER 3 (N21821)

The highlighted territory of Treaty Six shows the way it interfaces with Treaties Seven and Eight. The "Panhandle" of Treaty Eight extends from the headwaters of the Red Deer River to the town of Jasper on the Athabasca River and includes most of Jasper and Banff National Parks. Jasper cuts off the rest of Treaty Eight land from the territory claimed by Smallboy as "Indian Land," including the Kootenay Plains and the Big Horn Wilderness area. ADAPTED FROM GEOGRAPHIC BOARD OF CANADA, *HANDBOOK OF INDIANS OF CANADA*, OTTAWA: KING'S PRINTER, 1913

A log "death lodge" built over Rocky Boy's grave on the Rocky Boy Reservation. GLENBOW ARCHIVES, NA-1410-3

The Crow reservation in Montana where Smallboy grew up and the river into which he fell. PHOTOGRAPH BY FRED E. MILLER (1868–1936), COPYRIGHT NANCY F. O'CONNOR, 1984

Chief Smallboy's great-grandmother, *Ocepihk* (Root), the mother of Big Bear, poses with her grandson, Smallboy's father, *Apitchitchiw* ("Shorty" Young Boy, known in Canada as Small Boy), age 40, in 1910. GLENBOW ARCHIVES, NA-1431-8

Isabelle Coyote *Apitchitchiw*, age 41, poses with her children (left to right): Margaret, 10; Little Girl, 18; Jenny, 4; Johnny, 6; Billy, 1; and Bobtail, 8 (1906). GLENBOW ARCHIVES, NA-1431-9

Keskayo (Bobtail) Smallboy, age 8, in 1906. Glenbow Archives, NA-1431-4

care. She kept many medicines in her teepee. He learned, for example, that tansy, snakeroot, catnip, and prairie sage were as useful for regulating periods as they were for reducing fever.

It happened that while most of the men of the camp were away following a small herd of buffalo, the fiancée of Little Poplar came down with pneumonia. Her fever was very high, so high that she had fits. Afraid she might die, her father paid Yellowface's mother a visit and described the symptoms: the girl had been hot to the touch for days, yet could not get warm, shivering all the time. Just that day she had coughed up blood and had gone into convulsions, labouring to breathe.

The camp's medicine man had gone hunting with the younger men, helping them track the buffalo he had seen in a dream, the father explained. The camp midwife was the only person he could turn to.

Yellowface's mother did not know what to do. She was a midwife, not a medicine man. The girl needed stronger medicine than she could provide. He would have to wait until the other men returned to the camp. Then they could conduct prayers and sing, fast, and sweat. Her medicine was good for women's problems, not for a fever like he had described. She remained solemn, so as not to give false hope, and all the time she talked she sadly shook her head, realizing from what the man had told her that his daughter did not have long to live.

The man turned in despair towards the open flap of the teepee. As he turned, he saw Yellowface staring at the flames of an open fire, over which a steaming pot of water hung suspended. The boy had said something to him that he had not quite heard. The boy's mother had heard, though, and quickly made excuses for her son.

"*Keskwew!*" she said to Yellowface. "Fool! He is *mohcowiw*. Please—do not listen to him!"

"Why, what did he say?" asked the man.

"Nothing! He said nothing!"

"What did you say?" he demanded of Yellowface.

The boy shrugged. "All I said was, 'Don't worry.'"

"Yes, he said that, but he did not mean it!" said his mother. "He does not know what he is saying! He is *mohcowiw*—a lazy, ignorant fool who does nothing but sit about the teepee all day, always underfoot. His words mean nothing, nothing!"

But the man seized upon Yellowface's unguarded remark as if it were a rich gift. Perhaps he believed Yellowface and his mother were holding out on him. Perhaps he thought they knew some remedy so rare and unusual, so difficult to concoct, that they could not afford to share it without compensation. He took the remark, "Don't worry," as assurance that Yellowface and his mother would do something—for a price. Quickly he went to his own teepee to put together a package that Yellowface would find hard to refuse.

As soon as the man had gone, Yellowface had to contend with his mother's wrath.

"Go over there right now and apologize for your lie!" she cried.

"What lie?"

"He believes that you have told him you can save her!"

"All I said was that it's no use to worry. If the Great Spirit wills that she live, she will live. If the Great Spirit wills that she die, she will die. That's all I meant."

"*I* may know that is what you meant, but he does not! When you tell a man who is about to lose his child not to worry, he will think you know a cure. He will think that we are holding back. If we do not have a cure, he will kill us both if she dies! This is a terrible thing that you have done!"

They argued back and forth for many minutes, until they were interrupted by the sick girl's father, who had returned with four fine horses, one of them piled high with blankets—all that the man could afford to give. The top blanket was particularly colourful. He tethered the horses to the base of a teepee pole and left without a word of explanation. None was needed.

"You see how your loose tongue gets you into trouble!" cried Yellowface's mother. "This time you can answer for it with your own scalp! You are the one he asks for. You must go over there and see this girl and do what you can to cure her. If she is still alive when your father returns, perhaps he can talk better than I to explain to him and to you this terrible thing that you have done!"

Nonetheless, she helped Yellowface use the boiling water to brew the most powerful medicine she knew, which, along with the colourful blanket, he carried with him as he walked through the camp to the teepee of Little Poplar's intended bride.

Already it was clear that the girl's father had spread the word. Women and children and older men still in the camp watched as Yellowface approached. Some followed at a distance. Was he even more of an idiot than they had assumed?

Outside the girl's teepee, the father greeted Yellowface and invited him inside, where the girl's mother and aunts wailed and burned sprigs of wormwood in a vain attempt to chase away the fever.

"They must come out," Yellowface said. He did not want any witnesses to what he was about to do.

"Out! Out!" cried the father. "Hurry! The boy has come with *maskihkiy*."

"What medicine would *that* be?" asked one of the girl's sisters sarcastically, as she obeyed her father. She knew Yellowface's reputation as a lazy idiot and held him in contempt.

Yellowface ignored her—ignored them all. Solemnly, he smudged the entranceway to the teepee with sweet grass. Camp drummers took up position beside the teepee and started beating their drum and singing—wailing for the Great Spirit's intercession. Nervously, Yellowface entered the teepee backwards, closing the entrance flap behind him.

He approached the girl and tried to wake her, but she was still delirious. He sat her up and forced her to drink the medicine his mother had made until she gasped for air, choking on the bitter brew. She shook even more. Her teeth chattered. Uncovering her body, he dipped his fingers in the medicine and splashed it on her chest and abdomen as he had seen his mother do to her patients, then he sang songs along with the drummers seated in a circle outside the tepee, songs appealing to the Great Spirit to remove the malady.

He scooped the tansy and sage and other herbal leaves out of the pot onto her chest as a poultice, then covered the girl with a buffalo robe. Then he lay full length on top of the buffalo robe, praying for the disease to enter his own body rather than stay within hers. He covered his own body with his fancy new blanket. He chanted and chanted along with the drums and rattles, and at last, still in this unusual position stretched out upon her supine form, he fell asleep. Some say he entered a trance-like state in order that his spirit could travel to meet hers in another place and fetch her back.

Hours later, he was awakened by his outraged brother, who pushed through the small crowd anxiously waiting outside. Having talked to his mother, Little Poplar entered the teepee with murder on his mind. The hunting party had returned empty-handed, only to be informed that the idiot was performing as a medicine man—without any apparent training in this field. When their mother explained the offhand remark that had led to the embarrassment of riches tethered to their teepee, Little Poplar had flown into a rage. Knife drawn, he ran through the camp, his parents rushing in pursuit to discourage him from taking his young brother's life.

The girl's father fully believed in the boy's apparent claims. He alone forestalled the intended assault. He knew, or believed, that the youth had exerted himself all through the night on behalf of the girl. Nonetheless, he was as shocked as Little Poplar to find Yellowface stretched out on top of his unconscious daughter, only a buffalo robe between them.

Yellowface was groggy with sleep as Little Poplar hurled abuse on his young brother's head, threats of imminent torture followed by death. Yellowface sheepishly scrambled off the girl, then stared at the out-thrust knife in his brother's hand. He huddled terrified in his new blanket.

Their parents entered the teepee. Their mother begged Little Poplar to stand back—Yellowface after all was barely fourteen snows, not yet a man. And he was an idiot. Anyone could see that.

Little Poplar was not convinced. Holding his knife to his brother's throat, he warned him to run on foot as far away from the camp as he could in the time left until dawn. "In the morning, I and my friends will track you down and kill you for the shame you have caused me and my family!" As for the horses, they would be returned to the man who properly owned them—his girlfriend's father.

Yellowface looked around him but saw only stern faces. Those faces followed him all the way to the edge of the camp. They watched him walk northward into the darkness. He had no weapons, only the clothes on his back and the fancy blanket. He knew he was a total outcast from his camp, his band, possibly his tribe. But he also knew that the punishment was just. He knew he had no right to do what he had done. Had he not just looked upon the nakedness of his brother's intended? Had he not touched, indeed massaged, her naked body? Had he not lain upon her? Had he not *slept* with her? Yet at another level, he knew he was innocent. He had intended to take the sickness into himself, that was all.

He realized then that he should have minded his own business. His mother had been right: he'd had no right to say what he had said. He should not have made the remark he did about not worrying, even though he had not intended to suggest that he could effect a cure.

He was not a medicine man. He knew no magic. He had merely done what seemed at the time the most sensible thing to do.

He moved swiftly, running in the grass. He knew dew would not form where he ran, so there would be a clear trail through the grass in the morning. He hoped the warming sun would soon rise, yet that would mean his death when the young men caught up with him.

Once he was out of sight of the camp, he walked to the edge of a creek bank, then backtracked, wading down the creek to where the woods approached it on the other side. Keeping both creek and woods between him and the camp, he circled around it, heading steadily south.

Most of the people back at the camp had gone to sleep. The men were exhausted from the long, fruitless hunt. There was little that could be done for the girl now that she had been subjected to Yellowface's amateurish "bad medicine." The girl's parents and aunts stood vigil, wailing disconsolately, waiting for her inevitable death.

So they were quite amazed when, as the sun rose, the girl awoke and looked around her. Perhaps due to the Great Spirit, or perhaps thanks to Yellowface lying on top of her for most of the night drawing out the evil spirit that had inhabited her, her fever had broken.

Her father ran rejoicing through the camp, giving praise to both the Great Spirit and to Yellowface, demanding that he be sent for and forgiven. The girl had recovered, was even now sitting up, sipping soup—polishing off the rest of the idiot's tansy-and-sage decoction. Where was the boy, that he might reward him in accordance with their agreement?

Swallowing his pride, Little Poplar and his friends rode after the youth, crying out that the girl had pulled through, that all was forgiven. Had they been hunting for him in earnest, they might have noticed that his trail ended not that far north of the camp. Their own tracks obscured his, so they did not find him to deliver the message.

CREE MEETS CROW

For days Yellowface wandered aimlessly southward, and on the fourth day he saw in a coulee a single teepee with Crow markings. Two horses grazed not far away, tethered to saskatoon bushes. An argument was in progress, but a one-sided fight it proved to be, the man hurling abuse at his young wife's head as she sat outside the teepee waiting for a pot of water to boil on the puny fire. The man had a stick, and he was not above using it: the woman winced as it sung through the air towards her and cracked against the flesh of her arms, raising welts. She cried out and picked up a burning brand, hurling it at her husband. He knocked it away, but burned himself in the process, and beat her again, pausing only to take a drink from a flask that he propped against the entrance to the teepee. So preoccupied was he that he did not notice Yellowface creeping nearer.

This was the first opportunity Yellowface had ever had to count coup. Up until now, he had not been violent once in his life. But what he had seen—the way the man had beaten his wife—demanded action. He seized a rock in both hands and crept to the edge of the clearing. He was aware that the man outweighed him—and had a knife.

Seizing the man's whisky flask, the woman poured some of the contents into the fire. The flames flared. Her husband howled with rage and the stick once again descended. She tossed the flask back towards the bushes, hardly a metre away from where Yellowface crouched. The Crow warrior stumbled over to retrieve it, eager to assess how much whisky was left. He stooped to scoop up the flask, and in that instant, Yellowface was upon him. He smashed in the Crow's skull, then used the Crow's own knife to slit his throat.

The young Crow woman looked at the Cree youth with fear, expecting him to treat her in similar fashion. Instead, Yellowknife sat down beside her before the fire. He handed her the knife. She wiped it off on the grass, dipped it in the now-boiling water, and handed it back to him. He gestured that he had not eaten for many days. Soon he was munching on flakes of pemmican and dried venison, fresh saskatoon berries, and rush roots.

From that day forth, Yellowface and *Pisiskapumew* (She Who Sees) lived together as man and wife. She taught him to speak Crow; he taught her Cree.

The Crow had co-operated with the white man perhaps more than any other tribe in the western plains and, in return, had reached a generous settlement in the form of the Big Horn Reservation in southern Montana.

Yellowface and She Who Sees settled there for a time, but her former husband's relatives asked too many questions about the fate of her first husband. Fearing reprisals, they left the reservation and for years remained on the move, following the buffalo north and south across the prairies, becoming at one with the many Native groups that had been dispossessed of their land and livelihood.

In time, Yellowface became chief of the Crow Indians not content to live on the huge reservation in southern Montana. Their hunting expeditions took them from the Dakotas to the Rockies, from Wyoming to Canada. The less there was to eat, the more they travelled, sometimes far out of their traditional hunting grounds. There were no more buffalo.

In 1886, Yellowface led a hunting party up to the base of Table Mountain, a huge mesa just south of the Canadian border, to look for signs of game for his small band. They had not ridden very far before they saw a small hunting party of Cree warriors who had the same idea. The younger men immediately talked of counting coup, but Yellowface reminded them that in the wake of the difficult times in Canada, the Cree had lost their taste for war. It was for this reason that he had brought the peace lance, a spear bedecked with eagle feathers down along its whole length. He now held it high from the crest of the hill.

Almost immediately, the Cree waved back with a similar lance and, in accordance with custom, the headman and lance-bearer of each group cantered down to a central neutral zone to talk while their followers looked on from afar. Only when he was a few metres away did Yellowface recognize the Cree chief as none other than his older brother, Little Poplar!

The reunion was emotional. Quickly, Little Poplar explained how their father had died, although their mother still lived and was a medicine woman at Little Bear's camp. He described his involvement in the events at Fort Pitt, how he had baited the Redcoats there by riding back and forth within firing range, thereby gaining points for bravery on either side. For years he had been married to the girl Yellowface had saved—yes, she was still alive, very much a woman, probably soon in need of their mother's services as a midwife. Little Poplar's wife did not remember what Yellowface had done the night he had chased away the fever, but their mother had told them both in detail, over and over, not letting them forget that whatever

Yellowface had done, it had worked, with the help of the Great Spirit. Little Poplar told Yellowface that his wife, more than anyone, had become his advocate, proclaiming that Yellowface had been wronged.

"You are welcome to join us at any time, my Brother," said Little Poplar. Then, noticing his brother's beadwork, he added, "From this time on, the Crow and the Cree are as one!" And from that time forth, the Crow and the Cree nations lived in peace.

The two bands joined forces in the hunt for pronghorns, then returned to Little Bear's camp. The following year, Little Poplar was killed by a white man after allegedly stealing a horse. Yellowface remained as chief of a mixed band of Crow and Cree, although he continued to be regarded as a Crow chief.

THE LAND OF ANSWERS

The day after *Apitchitchiw* left to ride across Montana to fetch Yellowface, the young man, twenty-one years old, breathed his last. In accordance with her son's last expressed wish, when he stopped breathing, his mother had his body placed in a death lodge apart from the rest of the camp. Three days later, *Apitchitchiw* and Yellowface arrived at the camp near Great Falls with a large band of mixed Cree and Crow followers they had gathered along the way. As was his custom, Yellowface brought his two daughters along for the ride.

Immediately upon his arrival, Yellowface entered the death lodge to pray over his nephew. He gently probed the body with his fingertips until he found what he was looking for—a warm spot under the young man's heart. He placed an oil tincture there and on his nephew's lips and tongue, then went away to pray. On the following day, after more fervent praying, his nephew revived enough to give his uncle a message, according to Yellowface, "from the Spirit world." For the next three days, the young man chattered away nonstop, saying that the hope of the future of his people lay in a "Land of Answers" to the north.

He described the land in detail and gave a description of the man who, he said, could reveal much about their past and future, their heritage and destiny. They would recognize the Land of Answers, he said, because they would feel no threat: they would be made to feel welcome and would be offered food without the need to ask for it. They would be allowed to set up their camp in a well-protected place, and they and their women would be safe.[4] These words Yellowface conveyed with great solemnity to all those assembled, including the impressionable Bobtail and Johnny Smallboy.

At Rocky Boy's camp at the outskirts of Great Falls, Yellowface invited Crow and Cree alike—both from his own band and from Rocky Boy's—

to follow him to the Land of Answers that his deceased nephew had described. Anyone from among the boy's friends who wished to travel with them would be welcome. *Apitchitchiw*, who had fetched Yellowface and appears to have been (at least at that time) among the medicine man's inner circle, was among those answering the invitation with a whoop of approval. Bobtail and Johnny would travel with him.

They travelled northward from Great Falls with a sense of purpose, only to encounter even more hostility on the road north. They left in late August 1908 with some two hundred people in tow. But there was no rush. Yellowface took his time, avoiding roads and built-up areas. Each night they would pitch their tents and teepees, sometimes after hiking only twenty-five to thirty kilometres. Even with these precautions, everywhere they went, they encountered hostility from white settlers and surveyors, who were in the process of marking out their land for homesteading.

During their journey, they also encountered a singular artist, Charles Russell, who sketched and later painted the trek of Yellowface for posterity, calling the painting *The Medicine Man* (1908).[5] Yellowface must have worked his magic with the artist, because Russell later became one of the primary advocates for the Chippewa-Cree receiving a reservation in Montana.

The women gathered firewood as they needed it. The men formed a hunting party that knocked down a deer and an errant steer owned by some unsuspecting rancher, who, Yellowface rationalized, deserved to lose it, having had the temerity to squat upon their land. At least for now, they didn't have to eat rabbit or prairie chicken or gopher meat on the trek north.

They did not seem aware that they had crossed the forty-ninth parallel into Canada. This land—the very land of his birth—seemed to the young Bobtail Smallboy to be very much like Montana, with its ring of mountains to the west and south. But the cowboys who came across them on the day after their arrival, rather than running them off the land as most American ranchers would have, were polite and courteous. They invited Yellowface to their ranch house for a chat.

To Yellowface, the four cowboys seemed friendly enough, but just to confirm their motives, he sent his two attractive daughters to the ranch house, where they were received with friendship by the foreman and his wife. The girls told her that their father had a very important message to give them. The kindly woman said they should wait to give the message directly to "the Boss." The young women did not ask for food, but the woman gave them meat, bread, and dried fruit enough to go around. Yellowface then sought permission to set up a more permanent camp until such time as he could speak to "the Boss."

At the foreman's suggestion, Yellowface moved the camp a kilometre farther away from the ranch house, where they patiently awaited the arrival of the Boss. These English words, repeated like an incantation, seemed to electrify the camp whenever they were repeated.

Time passed until it was Bob Smallboy's tenth birthday, and a blizzard struck their Cardston camp, coating every tent and teepee with dense snow that in some places formed drifts metres deep. Predictably, two fur traders from Cardston rode out to the camp the next day to barter for furs. Yellowface gave the traders an audience, but his heart was not in it. Then he saw the foreman riding up with a man whom he later claimed to have recognized immediately from his late nephew's description. Turning from the fur traders, he greeted the two newcomers, shaking hands with both men, and then he let out a joyful whoop that alerted the whole camp to the arrival of the Boss.

As others in the camp ran here and there in their excitement, Yellowface led the way to his own big teepee in the middle of the camp, which was already astir as his wife and two daughters purged the lodge of dogs and dust. The Boss was given a seat of honour on a buffalo-horn chair covered with a cougar pelt. Then all the members of the band crowded in and around the chief's teepee. One of the young men who had been away at school translated the words of the visitor into a lilting Cree that seemed to the listening Smallboy to be far more beautiful than the monotones of English.

For five hours the assembled company sat listening to the dialogue between Chief Yellowface and the Boss as they hypothesized about the origins of the Indian and the white man in terms of Mormon theology.

THE MORMON VERSION

This encounter between Yellowface and "the Boss" (who was Bishop James S. Parker of the Church of Jesus Christ of Latter-Day Saints) was, naturally enough, documented by the Mormons in attendance, in particular by Joseph Y. Card, then twenty-three, who wrote the following account.[6]

THE STORY OF YELLOWFACE
Joseph Y. Card

It was late September, 1908, in southwestern Alberta. Already the autumn tints had begun to show in the foothills and along the Belly River. The hill tops were brown, the atmosphere hazy with the calm, restful quiet of the Indian Summer days.

Toward evening a band of Cree Indians pitched camp on the banks of the river. They were tired and anxious, for they had journeyed far, and had met with much abuse from white settlers who had driven them from their camping grounds with curses and with insults to their wives and daughters. Four hundred miles they had traveled from the north in search of a people whom the Great Spirit had shown in a vision to one of the young men of their tribe—a people who would tell them of their forefathers and of the Great White Spirit, whom they had learned of in their legends told by the old men of the tribe when they were peacefully gathered around their campfire at night, who, they said, would come again some day and bring happiness and freedom. These would be the signs by which they would know when they had found this people: The men would be honorable and would not seek to destroy the virtue of their wives and daughters. They would be made welcome to the homes and camping grounds of these people and would be given food.

It had taken many days to make the journey and much faith to push on under the trying circumstances. Now winter would soon be upon them and they were quite unprepared. Little wonder that hope began to fail and a feeling of sadness was upon them. Hurriedly they prepared for night and for rest, for when morning came might they not be ordered on to find new camping grounds?

While they sleep, let us draw near the camp and learn a little more of who they are and where their journey has taken them.

The Crees are a tribe of Indians of higher intelligence and higher moral character than the average in that part of the country. At the time when the different tribes were placed on reserves, the Crees refused to be confined to a reservation and as a result they are free to rove about from place to place. But they have no home and no help from the government as the others do, so they must make their own living, which makes them more industrious and capable. As the white people settle more thickly, times become harder for them, hunting grounds more scarce, and they have many hardships.

There was only part of the tribe camped on the river bank that night— about sixty teepees and possibly 200 of the tribe. The rest were back in their camping grounds in the northern wilderness, east of Edmonton, Alberta, Canada. Yellow-Face, chief of the tribe, had come with his family and others because of a strange incident that had occurred back in their summer home to one of the young men of their tribe, the son of Chief Yellow-Face, who, during a severe illness, realizing he was about to die, begged his people not to bury him until every spot on his body was cold. His father was then away on a hunting trip. Then he apparently died, and for three days they kept him in the wigwam. The weather was hot and his body became swollen and began to spoil. But under his left arm, over the heart, there remained a spot of warmth and they hesitated to bury him, for they had given their word that they would not. His father finally returned to camp. He viewed his son's body and placed a kind of oil on his lips and tongue and evidently prayed over him. At last, on the fourth day, he revived again, and told his people that he had been to the Spirit World and had been given a message for them that there was a people in the south who had a record of their forefathers and they must go and find them. He gave them a description of the man to whom they must go, and to none other, and told them many things about the spirit world and the Great Spirit. After a few days he died and was buried. But the message had been delivered to his people.

Then the Indians proceeded as soon as they could get ready, to do as they had been bidden. They had traveled south to what is known as the Church Ranch in Southern Alberta, Canada, a beautiful stretch of prairie land from three to seven miles wide and some thirty miles in length, in all 66,000 acres, bounded on the west by the Waterton River, on the south by the Rocky Mountains and on the east by the Belly River, running from one to three thousand head of cattle and belonging to the L.D.S. Church. Bishop James S. Parker of the Mountain View Ward was the manager of the ranch. The Indian camp was on the Belly River within a short distance of the ranch house.

On the following morning three or four of the cowboys riding from the ranch spied the camp of the Indians and out of curiosity rode down among them. The Indians were afraid that they had come to order them to move on, but the boys were friendly. They bought some moccasins, gloves, etc. from them, paid no undue attention to the women, and, on leaving, invited them to come up to the house. Among these cowboys were George and James Anderson, Olaf A. Olsen and Roy Draper.

Here with joy they witnessed the first sign fulfilled. Had not these young men manifested a spirit of kindness and honour? Their faith was renewed, a council was held, and two of the women were sent over to the house, one named Buckskin, apparently on a friendly visit, but possibly to further make sure that the sign was certain.

There was a man and his wife, Mr. and Mrs. Olaf A. Olsen, living on the ranch, who had charge while Bishop Parker was absent, which was often, for with his own wife and family and ward duties he had to be absent for days at a time when work was not pressing.

The squaws were made welcome by Mrs. Olsen, who talked with them as best she could with their limited knowledge of English. But she liked their way and noticed the difference between these squaws and the squaws of the nearby reservations. These squaws did not beg, but now [sic] knowing why she did it, she gave them food—meat, bread and dried fruit—when they were leaving. Oh how great was the joy of the tribe on their return! The second sign was fulfilled, and they were fed by the hands of these people.

It was necessary then to make an effort to find the man to whom they were to go for the information they were seeking, telling her the story in trusting confidence with a warning not to treat it lightly nor to repeat it to others who may be unappreciative.

On the following day the chief himself and some of his men with an interpreter went to the ranch house. On seeing Mr. Olsen they knew at once that he was not the man they were looking for; but they asked permission to camp on the river. He told them they had permission to camp until the boss came to see about it. "What does the boss look like?" they inquired. And upon getting a description, they knew at once that their search was ended; for they had to wait only until the Boss came. Surely that would not be long. But disappointment was once more to try their faith and patience, for Bishop Parker's visits were always hurried ones. The ward and home were seven miles from the ranch and the fastest means of going and coming was horseback, so, although he had been told the Indians were very anxious to see him, he had supposed they were only wanting permission to hunt and trap, or some other of the many favors that the other Indians were always asking, and he had made no special effort to see them. They had moved their camp up the river a mile away from the ranch house, and when they came to the house he was not there, for, while at the ranch, he did not stay at the house but was out on the range with the cattle. At last they made known to Mrs. Olsen that they had a very important message for him. Several weeks passed, and it was November.

One day there was a blizzard so severe that to ride the range was useless. The snow fell so thick and fast that only a few feet around could any object be discerned. Bishop Parker was at the ranch, and after lunch he proposed to Mr. Olsen that they go down and see what it was that the Indians wanted. Mr. Olsen was only too glad to go, for he and Mrs. Olsen had witnessed the anxiety of the Crees and had been curious to know what it could mean.

The two men arrived at the camp. Smoke was rising from the teepees. These people, too, were not venturing far from shelter. Outside one of the teepees two fur buyers were bartering with Yellow Face and the men for some furs and hides, and no one noticed the approach of the visitors until Mr. Olsen spoke, telling Yellow Face that he had brought the Boss. Yellow Face turned; an expression of joy covered his face and he shook hands with the man. He then gave two shrill yells which startled his visitors. He dismissed the fur buyers without ceremony and led the men to his own big tent in the centre of the enclosure. They noticed, as they went towards the tent, that everybody was hurrying in the same direction. At the tent door they noticed quite a commotion going on inside. Several dogs which had been enjoying the shelter and warmth of the tent were being driven out by the Chief's squaw with a big stick, and so much force behind it that they were losing no time in making their getaway. The Chief's two daughters were cleaning up the tent and they arranged the seat by spreading a robe on the floor and placing a box upon it, then spread over this a beautiful robe of mountain lion skin. When all was ready, Yellow Face took Bishop Parker by the arm and seated him upon the seat, placing his interpreter at one side of the tent, standing, and he himself standing opposite where he could see the faces of both. Mr. Olsen squatted down by the side of Brother Parker, and at a signal all of the others crowded into the tent and sat upon the floor. The two daughters of Yellow Face sat directly in front of Bishop Parker with their needle work. All was done with wonderful order, and then all was still. Yellow Face spoke, nodding to Brother Parker: "You talk," he said. Brother Parker had not dreamed of the nature of their mission and he had felt a peculiar feeling all during the time they had been gathering themselves about him. What did it mean? Why all this honour? Then he answered, "No. I came to hear you, to see what you want. They said you had a message for me." "No," said Yellow Face. "You have a message for us—about our forefathers."

Bishop Parker was so surprised and so thrilled at the experience that he hardly knew what to say or where to begin. His work and life had been in the frontier. He had never been a student of scripture nor given to study to a great extent of any books. He had read the Book of Mormon, knew its truthfulness and worth, and he studied it some in the classes at Sunday School, but to tell it as he was now expected to do, he felt wholly unable. But, offering a silent prayer to his Heavenly Father for help, he began the story of Lehi and his family leaving Jerusalem, speaking a few sentences, then waiting while the interpreter repeated the story to them in their own language. It was a never-to-be-forgotten sight—those dusky faces upturned to him, watching every movement of his lips, drinking in with oh such interest every word he spoke! No one moved. They seemed like statues. For five long hours they sat, listening to the story of their forefathers. Yellow Face stood raised to his full height. He was tall and straight as an arrow, his arms folded across his breast. He did not move, only asking a question now and then, or offering an explanation as he did to tell why they had come and of their trials and the signs which they had received. His daughter, with her needle in one hand and a bead in the other, sat for the whole five hours without so much as moving a muscle of her face, it seemed.

The story progressed with wonderful success, for the Lord did indeed help with His spirit and power to bring to the memory of the relator things long forgotten, to give him power when he had waited for the interpreter to repeat his words to the Indians in their own tongue, and his interest had been diverted in watching their expressions and interest, to take up the story again without hesitation and to make the story impressive to the ones to whom it meant so much—who they were, where they came from, why they were dark skinned and what the future held for them.

When Brother Parker had told his story, Yellow Face turned to his people and in their own tongue talked for half an hour in very serious tones, and although Brother Parker could not understand the words, he felt the spirit and knew he was teaching them and exhorting them to live good lives. Then, speaking again through the interpreter, he held his right hand up and said he knew what had been spoken was true. "For the Great Spirit has told me here," he said, laying his hand upon his breast. Then he told of experiences his own father had had with visitations from the spirit world, things which he considered so sacred that he begged him not to repeat them for fear they might not be told as they really were. Brother Parker has never revealed these things to anyone.

Night comes early in that country in November, and it was with regret that they had to stop and return to the routine of life. But they were happy, all of them, in the blessings of the day, and they met again many times.[7]

According to Chief Smallboy's account of this meeting, when at last Yellowface stood up, arms folded across his chest, he told his followers that Parker had told a story of their origins consistent with what he had heard from his grandparents. Their prophecies, Yellowface said, were to be fulfilled. He talked about his own encounters with the spirit world—and those of his father.

These tales of visiting the spirit world were to have a profound effect on several of the young men in attendance, not least upon the young Bob Smallboy, who to his dying day regarded Yellowface, the mentor of his youth, to be a prophet of the first order.[8]

CHAPTER 7

A Tug of War

HOBBEMA

With the outbreak of the First World War, Canadian officialdom clamped down on the free-roving tendencies of the Cree Indians and more than ever before insisted upon their staying on their reserves unless they had a pass from the Department of Indian Affairs signed by an Indian agent. After all, Canada had declared war, and many young men were either off fighting or in training, and concerns were expressed for the young women left behind. The political pressure from the settlers to keep the Indians off homestead land had never been greater, and the Indian agents acted with requisite haste to bring commensurate pressure to bear on the Indians to stay at home.

Nonetheless, in the summer of 1915, *Apitchitchiw* and Isabelle were on the road with Maggie, Bobtail, Johnny, and Billy, having decided to take the family back north to Hobbema at least for a visit. They had two horses, two dogs—and were back down to four children, two of the little ones having succumbed to pneumonia during the harsh winters of deprivation, as they scraped together an existence from garbage tossed out by the meat markets in Helena and Bozeman. Altogether, Isabelle was to give birth to twelve children, with only eight surviving infancy and only six surviving to adulthood.

They journeyed northwest into Alberta, keeping near the mountains where their movements would not be noticed by white settlers. However, while the police may have been on the prowl for stray Indians, the rest of the white population seemed preoccupied with events occurring overseas.

The Smallboys camped that summer on the Kootenay Plains west of Nordegg— Bob's introduction to the land he would eventually occupy on behalf of all Indians. Later, they visited Isabelle's sister, now an O'Chiese, who lived west of Rocky Mountain House. "In those days," said Chief Smallboy, "people lived in lodges that could be moved... . The Indians lived in this remote area east of the mountains for a long time; that is what I was told."[1]

From Rocky Mountain House, the Smallboys rode east to the Ermineskin Reserve, No. 138. There were no squabbles with the government over where they could live: the Indian Agency was committed to accommodating every Indian who sought a home. They received a land allotment near the Pichés and Coyotes, Bob's cousins. Their home was secure. It was with mixed feelings that they forsook the Land of the Long Knives, for now, to live more-or-less permanently in Canada. As Chief Smallboy remarked, "It was not until 1915 that I began to live on an Indian reservation. By then, many things had changed. It was a different way of life from how I had been taught to live."[2]

As in the United States, Indians in the reserve system in Canada had to grovel before the white man at every turn, whether in the course of obtaining treaty status, land, seed, stock, rations, or supplies. And as in the United States, Indian agents were obsessed with the bottom line. They were convinced that the Indians were primarily a workforce and that, with industry, they could be self-sustaining. Money therefore drove everything on the reserve.

In the reserve system, Smallboy was subjected to a litany of insults, especially insults to his intelligence, partly because he could not or would not speak English. The personal dignity of the individual Indian seemed to be a low priority. "We were taught not to use words that might cause insult to others," said Smallboy—yet at Hobbema, insults were the order of the day. "We grew up to respect the rights of others"—but at Hobbema, Indian agents showed no respect for Indians at all.[3] The Indian agents misunderstood Smallboy's retiring politeness as weakness. They relished in riding roughshod over the meek.

"To steal from your people is a wrong; it is against the law," said Smallboy. What sounds like a truism had a more profound context: he was talking expansively, having witnessed breach after breach of promise, including the withholding of rations and the redistribution of land promised to or belonging to the Indian. With the co-operation of the U.S. government, Montana had duped his grandfathers out of a vast tract of Indian land. Similarly, Canada had stolen from her people, the Indians who had put their trust in her, for had the Indian tribes not been deprived, illegally, of their land and freedom? Had the Crown not converted Indian lands to its own use? "This land that we are standing on, is this not now called 'Crown' land?" Chief Smallboy asked me rhetorically in August 1982 as we stood outside his cabin at the camp. "How did the Crown acquire this land, except by stealth?" He had made a similar argument in a speech he had given earlier that year in London, England:

> Long ago—over one hundred years have passed—my great-grandfather *Keskayo* (Bobtail) signed a treaty with Queen Victoria's representatives. In the Treaty our chiefs surrendered most of our lands, but only the topsoil which they had asked for. And the Rocky Mountains were never surrendered by treaty. In return for the surrender, the Queen's men promised certain things. It was agreed by our chiefs and the Queen's men that those agreements would last for as long as the sun would shine. Our chiefs were promised assistance towards survival for the Indian people. It was upon these assurances that our chiefs agreed to sign the treaty, and to surrender some of our lands.
>
> But now it has been made known to us that the Government wishes to put an end to all these things which they had promised to our grandfathers. The White man now desires to take those lands which we did not surrender. My mind is heavy with concern.....[4]

Obsessed with demonstrating that Indians could be self-sufficient, the Indian Office in the United States and the Indian Agency in Canada had imposed their values on the Indians, attempting to break their spirit and reduce them in a single generation from nomads to agriculturalists. "The Indian child is not given much to think about. He is not shown how to worship his Creator in the Indian way. He sees the white man's ways and is impressed by these. He sees the affluence of the white man and soon he learns to follow the paths of the white man."[5]

For Smallboy, the temptation to adopt the white man's values had never been stronger than during the First World War. Employment opportunities were up in Canada with so many men away at war, and the demand for fresh farm produce, including grain, was also up. Rationing extended not only to food, but also to seed grain, which was in great demand. Indian agents asserted their authority and clamped down on the Indian's freedom of movement as never before. Each family had to decide which reserve they wanted to belong to forever after; absenteeism from the reserve was simply not tolerated. At the same time, Indians caught without passes had to declare which reserve they belonged to, or they would be taken to one nearby—dealer's choice. Thenceforth, that reserve would become "home"—the Indian having no say in the matter.

THE CALL OF MONTANA

Isabelle was quite content to stay in Hobbema with her huge extended family, but *Apitchitchiw* had a far more difficult choice to make, partly because, with a new reservation in the offing back in Montana, the tensions between his father and Little Bear were heating up.

> The apparent rivalry between Rocky Boy and Little Bear intensified the difficulty of transition. Although the two bands lived and traveled together, the two old chiefs held tenaciously to what remaining authority they possessed. Little Bear was at a disadvantage in the contest. The years had not completely removed the stigma of his Canadian birth and whenever he behaved too independently, government officials were quick to remind him of his tentative status. At the same time, Rocky Boy complained that Roger St. Pierre ignored him and spoke only to his rival, although it was he who was supposed to receive the land and not Little Bear.[6]

St. Pierre's attitude seemed to be "a plague on both your houses!" However, there is little doubt he favoured the Chippewa over the Cree.

Apitchitchiw, himself caught in the middle, knew that divisive factions might try to thwart the natural and proper selection of a new leader, in the event of his father's death. At forty-five, he was favoured by Rocky Boy to lead the band, but the longer he was absent, the less likely it was that he would be selected. From among the Chippewa, *Apitchitchiw*'s brother-in-law Baptiste Samatte, the forty-six-year-old husband of Rocky Boy's daughter Front Sky Woman, had a high profile and could communicate in English, but, like Coyote, he was regarded as more of a mystic than a potential chief. Most of the potential leaders were solidly in Little Bear's camp, especially Little Bear's son Four Souls and Little Bear's long-term subchief Pete Kanawa.

Apitchitchiw knew his father's wishes in this respect, but also knew that Little Bear, more than anyone else, had currency as chief. A chief, he believed, should be selected the traditional way—by reputation rather than by election. As Smallboy explained in an interview conducted on 9 January 1983, days before he sustained the frostbite to his legs that would ultimately prove fatal: "Only courageous men could earn the right to become chief. The more courageous, the better equipped [a person] was to be leader. His reputation would precede him. A chief had to prove his capability over a period of years. A body of legend would build up around him."[7] A chief was selected rather than elected and accordingly had to be a natural leader: "There was nothing artificial about his selection. A man became chief based on what he had already done, not on what he was going to do. Today, the system of elections is based on promises for the future. In the past, selection of the chief was based on what he had already done."[8]

The rigid attitudes of the government farmer at Fort Assinniboine didn't help ease tensions between Rocky Boy and Little Bear, who both "found it difficult to relinquish their authority to a Chippewa mixed-blood," especially one like Roger St. Pierre:

> Rocky Boy insisted that the government send rations for the band directly to him where he could oversee its distribution. In the meantime, Little Bear wrote directly to the Commissioner of Indian Affairs insisting that the Commissioner authorize an increased supply of rations for his people.... When tensions reached a breaking point, Rocky Boy frequently left Assinniboine and solicited aid from his traditional friends in Great Falls and Helena.[9]

The Indian Office ignored both men, regarding the rival chieftains as an irrelevance. "They are not going to be a hard bunch to lead," Superintendent Jewell D. Martin wrote to the commissioner of Indian Affairs in late 1915, reflecting his contempt for the group. "They are transgressors and have found their way proverbially 'hard' so long, that they are about ready to listen to advice, and I anticipate phenomenal progress on their part in the immediate future."[10] It was this kind of attitude on the part of U.S. Indian Office and Canadian Indian Affairs branch administrators—revisited later on at Hobbema—that eventually led Smallboy to abandon reserve life altogether.

THE HOMESTEAD

While *Apitchitchiw* travelled to Havre, Montana, to determine the band's political future, Bob Smallboy stayed on at Hobbema with his mother and brothers (Margaret having married by then), for now enjoying the relative stability of the Ermineskin Reserve. That was probably a wise decision, because it would be another year before the Rocky Boy Reservation would be established, and it would go through teething pains for many years thereafter. There were teething pains of a different order at Ermineskin, where in their father's absence the Smallboy brothers had 640 acres of farmland to homestead, that is, to clear and cultivate. That proved a more daunting task than they had anticipated; it would take not years, but decades.

With many men gone to war, there was a need as never before to market-garden as well as farm. If vegetables and beef were what sold, *Apitchitchiw* told his family, then that is what they should turn their hand to. Thus it was in 1915 that, for the first time, the Smallboy family settled down on the land allotted to them, taking up more-or-less permanent residence on the Ermineskin Reserve, alongside their uncles, aunts, and cousins, in particular the Pichés, the Coyotes, and the Ermineskins.

Bob worked with horses and cattle and quickly learned the basics of farm management. "I did not receive any education," he said in 1982. "I did not go to school. I can't read; I do not speak English. But a person can learn by observing how certain things are made useful by some people. By observing how things are done, a person will soon know how to do those things."[11] In applying his native intelligence to farm management, Smallboy recognized his own innate "capacity to understand, to have respect for these things, to understand how things should work."[12]

Although *Apitchitchiw* was frequently absent for long periods of time from the Ermineskin Reserve, Bob and Johnny developed a great deal of respect for him. Often, elders came to their parents' cabin, and the boys learned to listen to what they had to say without interruption. "It was considered a sign of disrespect to walk in front of an elder, or to talk when an elder is talking," Smallboy said, with a twinge of nostalgia. "Such disrespect would be punished. Children who would not behave were told to play outside, thus missing out on the elders' counsel. As a teenager, I was taught other ways to show respect for adults. This included being open to advice, and respecting the advice of an elder when it was given."[13]

In the year after their arrival in Hobbema, the Smallboys lived in tents, as they cleared tracts of land and added to a makeshift log cabin and poplar log outbuildings on their allotted land. *Apitchitchiw* continued to be torn between Montana and Alberta. He used any excuse to visit his father and grandmothers in Montana, especially to go to the Sun Dances (more properly, Thirst Dances) that were held annually on the insistence of Little Bear.

Sun Dances had been banned in Canada since 1895 by an amendment to the Indian Act. Therefore, any Indian who believed that this was an essential part of his existence had to travel once a year to Montana for spiritual sustenance. "The Catholic missionaries at Hobbema helped to stamp out the tradition, warning the Indian Affairs Department whenever they heard of plans for a dance.... . They demanded suppression of the ritual."[14] The spiritual dance was soon replaced by a grotesque parody: "By the early years of the twentieth century, the Hobbema Indians had become figures of amusement for the white settlers. The Cree women were invited to participate in cart races in the annual agricultural fairs, and Chief Ermineskin was reduced to giving demonstrations of Indian war dancing at the agricultural fairs."[15] Furthermore, in Canada, the residential schools were doing their best to destroy not only the spiritual beliefs and traditions of the Cree people, but also their language.

Apitchitchiw would have none of this. His children were going to be brought up in accordance with Cree tradition, speaking the Cree language. They would learn to get by with no English whatsoever, if necessary.

Besides Smallboy's immediate family, among other relatives waiting for the new Rocky Boy Reservation to open were Smallboy's two grand-fathers, Coyote and Rocky Boy; his maternal grandmother, *Kakokikanis* (Hanger-On); his great-grandmother Chippewa Speaker; and his two step-grandmothers, *Waskahte* and *Pekiskwewin* (Voice). Having agreed to wait for the promised reservation, they were all trapped at Havre, subject-ing themselves to the rigid requirements of the Indian Office, which now, harkening back to Big Bear, had a rope around their neck.

THE DEATH OF ROCKY BOY

In 1916, Senator Henry L. Myers, who had initially tried to get the band to move to the Blackfeet Reservation just west of the Rocky Mountains, introduced a bill to create a reservation of 30,900 acres in the vicin-ity of Fort Assinniboine. The bequest was expanded to 56,035 acres by Congress.[16] This time, the legislation passed, resulting in the Montana Cree at last receiving a home where they could settle, after thirty-one years of wandering in the wilderness.

Rocky Boy's untimely death shortly after the legislation went through Congress, and a year before the reservation was actually established in his name, has often been attributed to "bad medicine": "It is also reported that through the use of an evil medicine bundle, on the part of others less prominent on the reservation, Rocky Boy met his death just as the reservation was opening—a time when his advice was most needed."[17] The most powerful medicine man in the camp was Coyote, who was solidly behind Little Bear in the race to determine who would be the first chief of the Rocky Boy Reservation once it was established.

Rocky Boy, probably suffering from tuberculosis, complained bitterly that, in his illness, he was being manipulated by Little Bear. "Little Bear and Pete Kanawa ... are trying hard to get the half breeds in this reserva-tion," he wrote to Frank Linderman, an old refrain. "The half-breeds took homesteads like the white man. Some of them sold their rights, their land. Then Little Bear trys to get them in here although he has no right to do this. I am the one that have to let them on if my tribe of Indians want them." He added: "I am very sick. I don't know if I shall ever see you again."[18]

Although both Roger St. Pierre and Superintendent Martin noted that Rocky Boy was seriously ill as early as December 1915, they did not summon a doctor. After all, at this juncture there was no official reservation, so it was not their responsibility to do so. A physician did not visit the camp until 1 April 1916. By then, there was not much he could do.

When the news came of Rocky Boy's failing health later that month, *Apitchitchiw* and Isabelle travelled back to Havre with the children, stopping in Calgary long enough to buy clay marbles for the younger ones to play with. The cheap marbles, though colourful, were defective and often broke on contact—a symbol used by Smallboy in later years to show how things always seemed to turn out when an Indian traded with the white man.

By the time Smallboy and his father arrived at Fort Assinniboine, Rocky Boy was already on his deathbed. All his relatives and friends had gathered around to keep vigil. Conspicuous in their absence were Coyote and Little Bear. There is no evidence at all that Coyote treated Rocky Boy for his illness, despite the fact that he was by then an accomplished medicine man.

The ailing chief died on 18 April.[19] The *Great Falls Tribune* reported on 23 April 1916:

> Rocky Boy is dead. The chief of the nomadic band of Chippewa Indians passed to the "Happy Hunting Ground" on Tuesday, April 18, on the reservation near Box Elder.... In that passing, one of the most picturesque of the Indian characters in the last third of a century of Montana history disappears from the stage and the passing marks the closing of a unique chapter in Montana Indian history.[20]

That same day, the newspaper published a letter written by Bob Smallboy's uncle Baptiste Samatte:

> My Dear Sir:
>   Today I am writing this letter to you to tell you a sad news. On the 18th inst. At 9 o'clock a.m. our leader of the Chippewas passed away to eternity. When he received letters from you [i.e, Gibson] he was glad and he wished very much to see you all, who have labored so long in his behalf, and gave you his ideas....
>   But these are his last words on his last breath. Never forget what I have tried to do for the homeless people in Montana toward the government and also, he said, never forget Mr. William Bole, Theodore Gibson and his father, and Frank Linderman who done and taken pains to get us a home from our government. And he told all the people to strive and labor hard so that the government may see that we are ambitious to get a home and land and also he told his people to be kind to one another and help one another.
>   He died so peacefully, just like he was going to some place for a time. I wish you would tell Mr. Bole and Frank Linderman about the death of

our chief, Rocky Boy. We have lost a valuable man. We are sorrowing and mourning for him. I am sending my best regard to you and also to the old man. May Almighty bless us until we meet again.[21]

Rocky Boy was buried, ironically enough, not far from Coyote's cabin on a hilltop overlooking Parker Canyon, five kilometres from the Indian Agency Office. A small log hut was built over the grave as a memorial.

In the end, there was little doubt as to who would be the next chief. It would fall to Little Bear to lead his people onto the formal reservation of "Chippewas and other homeless Indians," approved in the spring of 1917.[22] However, in preparing his nest, Little Bear was determined to eject one particularly obnoxious cowbird that had taken up residence there: the government farmer St. Pierre, who had married one of the Chippewa women from Rocky Boy's band. "Almost from the beginning, St. Pierre became an uncomfortable man in the middle, unable to please either his superiors at Fort Belknap or the Indians at Fort Assinniboine."[23]

WORK FOR FOOD—OR JAIL

St. Pierre was not popular with the Chippewa-Cree because he had been ordered to withhold food from anyone suspected of infringing the rules, and he used this power arbitrarily to enforce compliance. He was also responsible for implementing the reimbursement plan, by which Indians had to pay for expensive machinery purchased by the Indian Office. The Cree at Fort Assinniboine were expected to pay not only for expensive farm machinery, but also for expensive mistakes. For example, farm superintendent John B. Parker at one point purchased a herd of cows so that the malnourished children at the camp could have milk—only to find that the cows were culls that no longer produced milk. The superintendent charged the band for his mistake, taking it out of their ration money. The Indians had no say in the purchase, just as they had no say in what equipment was to be purchased on their behalf. In the spring of 1916, the Indian Office purchased two seed drills and five sets of harrows, financing for which the Indians had to secure, several members of the band being required to "sign" for the equipment if they wanted to use it.

Converting virgin land to gardens was back-breaking work, and it took all the efforts of the band members to plough and plant a total of two hundred acres of the reservation land to grain and vegetables. Nonetheless, Superintendent C. W. Rastall wrote, "I found a rather indolent spirit among many of the younger men." He added, "I hope to soon introduce a plan which will prove efficacious in getting these young men to go to work."[24] That "plan" was to cut off rations to those who refused to work (the same food-for-work ploy that had failed so abysmally for Tom Quinn at Frog Lake in April 1885). Rastall tried to prevent younger men, including teenagers Bob and Johnny Smallboy, from leaving the reservation, with threats of incarceration.[25]

To this end, Roger St. Pierre, now farmer-in-charge, received fast approval for construction of a two-cell jail on the reservation, even though the members of the band refused to help him build one.[26] A later policy of indiscriminate jailing appeared to come from the top, with directions from Assistant Commissioner of Indian Affairs Edgar B. Merritt encouraging the superintendent "to prosecute and jail malcontents at Rocky Boy's."[27] The farm superintendent required members of the band to sign an agreement that stipulated: "Should I use these rations and not farm my place, I accept sentence in the agency jail for a term of 30 days at hard labor."[28] At least one woman was jailed for "contumacy," and one young man was jailed for giving his rations to his uncle, an octogenarian to whom the superintendent had not issued grant rations because the old man had found it too difficult to work in the fields.[29] In a special retrospective investigation conducted before a subcommittee on Indian Affairs, "it was disclosed that Indians either worked on their land, raised their prescribed gardens, and performed other duties assigned them or else they were jailed."[30]

Although these strictures were eventually removed, it is little wonder that *Apitchitchiw* and his sons decided to move back north more-or-less permanently. Certainly such unanticipated rigidity on the part of the white overseers of the "slaves" (as Smallboy described their status) militated against retaining their 160-acre family "assignment" on the reservation in Montana, as opposed to the "allotment" at Ermineskin four times that size.

RESIDENTIAL SCHOOLS

Another reason to prefer settling permanently on a reserve in Alberta rather than a reservation in Montana was the attitude of the U.S. Indian Office towards education. *Apitchitchiw* was perfectly happy with the way Smallboy had turned out, even though he could speak no English. If they went to Hobbema, the younger children would attend the residential school—but at least it was located right on the reserve. If they stayed in Montana, the children would be shipped off to a residential school in Oregon for months at a time. In Montana, more than in Alberta, Indian parents were deemed to be a "bad influence" on the children.

At the Rocky Boy Reservation, parents would not see their children from September to June of the following year. If the children ran away from a school in, say, Oregon (where most of them were sent), they were returned to the school to make up for the time skipped and thus were prevented from returning home over the summer as well. This became firm policy in cases where children had run away from school and made their way home, there to be sheltered by their parents. Malcolm McDowell, of the Board of Indian Commissioners, went even further, opining in a letter to all superintendents that Indian children should be removed from their parents and forbidden to return once their education was complete because "all the good learned in school evaporated when the children returned home."[31]

If the school at Hobbema was better, it was only marginally so, for "the residential school was continuing its efforts to destroy the Indian language and spiritual beliefs.... The residential school brought the Hobbema Indians dangerously close to losing their traditions and their language forever."[32] Both in the United States and in Canada, Indian children would be punished for speaking Cree. Parents, including *Apitchitchiw*, were concerned that their children learning to talk in a foreign language would create a rift between the generations. Later, Smallboy was adamant that white education harmed Indian children to the extent that it caused them to adopt white values and forsake Indian values. "They are not taught anything of benefit to them in the future," he said. "It seems there is nothing good left of our Indian ways, as far as they are concerned.... They do not recognize their own relatives. The white man's education has created this confusion."[33]

NAMES

Much of the dispute between Little Bear and Roger St. Pierre was over who would be "assigned" (rather than allotted, as in Canada) quarter-section parcels of land to work. Each assignment was to be for a two-year period, renewable only if it was demonstrated that the land had been improved. However, given the harsh climate and the impoverished soil, who could be sure that the land could be improved? Since there was no guarantee that the lease would be renewed, there was no incentive for individuals to invest their labour in their assigned property.[34] Names identified by Rocky Boy nine years earlier were already on the roll of names used by Roger St. Pierre to identify legitimate members of the band—names he rather arbitrarily translated and sometimes invented out of whole cloth.

A few months after Rocky Boy's death, Little Bear submitted a list of more than six hundred names, which St. Pierre proceeded to whittle down with the blessing of the superintendent of the Fort Belknap Agency, Charles Rastall.[35] Friction between Little Bear and St. Pierre had existed since St. Pierre's arrival at Fort Assinniboine in May 1915, although until the formal opening of the reservation two years later, the government farmer prevailed in virtually every argument. He was also held responsible when anything went wrong. When Rastall underestimated the cost of fencing part of the reservation, he sent a negative report to Cato Sells, blaming the government farmer-in-charge: "I found St. Pierre, as in many other instances, wholly deficient in the knowledge which he claimed to have about these matters."[36]

Little Bear got his wish to rid the reservation of St. Pierre when the position of government farmer was upgraded in February 1917 to require agricultural college certification. St. Pierre no longer qualified for the post and in May was replaced by John B. Parker. St. Pierre was demoted from farmer-in-charge to assistant foreman of the fence-building crew, the very duties for which Rastall had castigated him in his letter to Cato Sells.

Parker sympathized with St. Pierre and kept him on staff during the transition period in his much-diminished role as they attempted to reconstruct a list, using Rocky Boy's roll of 1908 and Little Bear's much longer list submitted in 1916:[37]

> After his arrival at the Rocky Boy's Reservation, Parker's first assignment was to establish an official enrolment list for the reservation. The act establishing the reservation specified that the land was for "Rocky Boy's band of Chippewa and such other homeless Indians in the State of Montana as the Secretary of the Interior may see fit to locate thereon." Immediately the old question of "Canadian Indians" arose.[38]

Knowing the propensity of politicians to flip-flop when it came to whether Canadian Cree would be included in the Rocky Boy Reservation, St. Pierre assigned ages arbitrarily, so that a disproportionately high number of Canadian Cree on the 1917 roll were said to be fifty years old or younger, that is to say, were born in Canada in 1867 (the year of Canadian Confederation) or later. That way, should policy change, these people would appear to be truly Canadian, leaving more land for American-born people of Chippewa ancestry—including St. Pierre and his wife. His actions were somewhat supported by Rastall, who "questioned whether some of the Indians living at Rocky Boy's in 1917 were entitled to remain."[39]

As mentioned earlier, St. Pierre's resentment against Little Bear and his band shows through his derogatory translations of their names. If he had an axe to grind with the male leaders of the band, he had taken it out on the names of their women, probably without their being any the wiser.[40] Whether it was St. Pierre's bizarre sense of humour or a genuine mean streak, how was John Parker, who could speak no Cree, to know which names were genuine translations and which were thinly veiled insults? As Front Sky Woman told Verne Dusenberry, perhaps with a touch of resentment:

> Indian names given to the children are not the ones by which they are enrolled at the agency nor the ones by which they are called by their parents or siblings when speaking to the child in the presence of a white person. Thus each child has an Indian name, one that was bestowed upon him in a traditional Cree fashion, plus one or two names drawn from the Anglo-American tradition. On the Rocky Boy reservation, very few of the older men have followed the latter practice and are known only by their Indian names.[41]

Smallboy thought that abandoning the Indian way of naming had contributed to the loss of direction experienced by people of the First Nations:

> Long ago, everyone had Indian names. As a child, one would receive a name, and by that name he was known. If you heard a child's name, no matter how many years later, you were able to recall knowledge of him. If you saw him later as an adult, you would recognize him by his name, where he came from and his family ties—even his grandparents. It was a way that was good.
>
> But as it is in the present, a name is used by numerous persons; they do not use Indian names. If you heard a child's name and you met him later as an adult, there is nothing you would recall about him. If you met him five years later, you would not recognize anything about him.[42]

Chief Smallboy also talked about the loss of the naming tradition in a speech he made in London, England, in 1981:

> Much has been lost in that we do not retain our Indian names anymore. Long ago, every Indian was named after certain things. Rarely would you hear of two persons having the same name—each name was different. From a name, you could tell something about a person and why he had received the name as a child. He could gain recognition from his name anywhere he went. That is one thing we have lost. And now we have white man's names and there are many who lose recognition. We cannot tell anything from the names of the young people, or anything about the young person's parents. It is that which we have lost: we have lost our names.[43]

The Cree tradition of giving unique names to each individual was abandoned in Canada with the establishment of reserves in the wake of the signing of Treaty Six in 1876. Similarly, the tradition of unique naming was retained in the English language in the United States only until each Indian band was confined to its reservation, in the case of the Rocky Boy Reservation, until 30 May 1917.

Once affiliated with a reservation in the United States or a reserve in Canada, the given name of the head of the family became the fixed surname of all his descendants. Thus in the United States *Apitchitchiw* was translated as "Short Young Boy" and he came to be known as "Shorty," while in Canada his name was translated as "Small Boy." In each case, the name stuck—as Jessie Smallboy found out during her first visit to Montana in the 1970s, when her parents, Joe and Dorothy, took the children to visit relatives on the Rocky Boy Reservation. Her relatives referred to her great-grandfather as Young Boy and to her grandfather as *Keskayo* or "Bobtail." "That was the first time I heard that," she said.[44] In the United States, Smallboy's "illegitimate" older brother and sister (whether half or full remains a mystery) retained their unique names: Little Boy and Little Girl.[45]

THE LIST

Little Bear was incensed that the fencing foreman, at Parker's behest, would deign to shorten his roll list. He could not abide Roger St. Pierre making recommendations as to who was "in" and who was "out" of the reservation even before it officially opened. He made his feelings known in Washington, DC, and finally, "in June, the Indian Office sent an experienced officer, James McLaughlin, to Rocky Boy's to complete an enrolment list. Over 650 people made claim to membership in Rocky Boy's band in 1917."[46]

The initial list submitted to Washington contained precisely 658 names. Consulting with Parker, who in turn depended on St. Pierre, McLaughlin narrowed down the enrolment list to 425 people. "He included all of the Chippewa living at Fort Assinniboine in the previous three years and those Cree who could demonstrate their association with Little Bear. The elimination of so many people from the enrolment list created the base of a large floating landless Indian population in Montana that plagued the Indian Office over the next years."[47] When the final roll was published on 16 July 1917, 452 names were on it, including many of Bob Smallboy's relatives.[48]

Following this project, St. Pierre took a year's leave of absence for a protracted honeymoon, but feelings ran so high among the Cree, especially

Little Bear, that when St. Pierre and his wife returned to Havre, he was prohibited from dealing in tribal business. He was allowed to return to Rocky Boy's only as the husband of a member of the reservation—and therefore as a tribal member himself.[49]

Bob Smallboy was not interested in claiming his share of the new reservation. After witnessing the internecine politics in reservation life south of the border in the wake of his grandfather's death, he was quite content to return north to develop his parents' allotment of land at Hobbema. He had seen enough of the white man's world in Montana to know that American society itself was full of prejudice directed against Indians. Canada was only marginally better, but at least he was left to his own devices and was more likely to be treated like a human being.[50] For him, the potential to earn a decent living was one more step towards freedom.

CHAPTER 8

Family and the Farm

MARRIAGE

By the time the First World War was over, hay was selling for eighteen to twenty dollars a ton and wheat for more than two dollars a bushel—artificially high because of the prolonged drought, which had not parched central Alberta as much as it had points farther south. Making the family farm profitable was of great interest to the twenty-year-old Smallboy, especially now that his father had arranged for him to be married to Louisa Headman (Pymis). Bob eventually brought her father, David Headman, traditional gifts: moccasins beaded by his mother, a good horse, and a fancy blanket. In turn, knowing that Bob Smallboy and his father were traditionalists, Louisa had her father help her erect a small teepee beside their cabin. When Smallboy and Louisa moved into it together, the traditional marriage would be complete.

Aside from their traditional Cree marriage, Bob and Louisa were married in the Catholic Church by Father P. Moulin, witnessed by Louisa's aunt Minnie Headman and Joe Omeasoo. Omeasoo witnessing the marriage was the first evidence of a major bond that was to develop between the Smallboy and Omeasoo families, which, half a century later, was to throw them together in a manner that nobody could have anticipated. As a measure of their friendship with Joe Omeasoo, the young couple named their first child "Joe" after him.[1]

Part of the obligation incurred by Bob Smallboy was to work the Headmans' land as well as his own. This resulted in several difficulties for the young man, since he had been told by his mother and by the elders

that in-laws were to be kept at arm's length. "There are some old traditions which still are practiced in today's times," said Chief Smallboy, and
this was one of them. "I was brought up with the idea that I should never
speak to my mother-in-law. Even my father-in-law I was always reluctant
to speak to. Communication between my in-laws and myself was the role
of my wife."[2] So if Dave Headman had a message for Bob, he would tell
his wife, Suzanne, who would tell Louisa, who in turn would convey the
message to Bob. "My answer would then be conveyed through the same
process in reverse: I would tell my wife, who would then pass it on to her
mother—my mother-in-law—who would then convey my answer to her
husband—my father-in-law." If a man spoke to his mother-in-law by
accident, both would be horribly embarrassed—"I would probably have to
leave home for a few days until the effect of the embarrassment wore off!"[3]
Smallboy said this tradition was practised to keep in-laws from interfer-
ing in the lives of their married children. Where the man has taken up
residence with his in-laws, so that their house was his "home," a stony
silence is formally required of the Cree, even to this day.

ECONOMICS, NORTH AND SOUTH

Following the war, life as a provider meant hard work clearing and cultivating the portions of land for which they were responsible. However,
there was one event in Montana each year that Smallboy tried faithfully
to attend with his father—Little Bear's Sun Dance. Invariably, he and
Louisa took two or three weeks to travel down to Montana in June, once
the cows had safely calved and the crops were planted. Louisa was thus
introduced to and could see the contrast between the American and
Canadian systems. She much preferred the Canadian model. As for Bob,
he would have preferred no reserve whatsoever.

It grieved Smallboy to watch his grandparents and cousins suffer at the
hands of the surly new farmer-in-charge at the Rocky Boy Reservation.
It would have grieved him even more had he seen them coping with the
winter winds in tattered, uninsulated tents and drafty ten-foot-by-twelve-
foot poplar-log cabins.

Coyote and his wives were doing all right economically. Since his having
seen the Little People in the spring of 1916, his medicine had become
stronger than ever, and he received many gifts for his services. But most of
the inhabitants of the Rocky Boy Reservation lived in abject poverty. The
young men could be cut off from rations if they were found "simply loaf-
ing about the agency and seemingly doing little to help themselves."[4]

Smallboy had no use for the ration system, which had put him at the
mercy of the Indian Office. His father had taught him, and he earnestly

believed, that by dint of hard work, he could grow all the meat and pota-toes his family could eat. However, at that point he was not farming for the money, but for subsistence. "The Indian's main concern is survival, and as long as he has enough to survive, he is satisfied. All he asks is the will and health and satisfaction to do things for himself. He is not afraid of hardship as long as his survival is assured."[5]

Smallboy generally followed the advice of his father in agricultural matters, especially in animal husbandry, and certainly he followed *Apitchitchiw*'s example in the "hard work" department. But *Apitchitchiw* was still concerned with retaining his status on the reservation in Montana, where Little Bear was now de facto chief. Gambling and drink-ing threatened to become a problem on the reservation. Self-sufficiency was out of the question there, where the drought had hit hard. Rations had been reduced. Most of the Chippewa-Cree, trying to survive yet another winter in tattered tents exposed to the vicious northwest wind, were reduced to misery.

This hell on earth was compounded in 1919 by the advent of the Spanish flu. At least one-third of the population of the reservation came down with it, and four died, including *Kakokikanis* (Hanger-On), at sixty-eight. "Living conditions at Rocky Boy's remained abominable," wrote Thomas Wessel. "The situation was particularly difficult for the very old who were completely dependent on supplies issued at the agency office."[6] Parker was authorized to spend one thousand dollars on blankets and clothing for the elderly, but only "when their condition became desperate."[7] Usually, as in the case of Rocky Boy and *Kakokikanis*, that determination came too late to guarantee their survival.

The influenza pandemic swept through the Ermineskin Reserve, as well as the Rocky Boy Reservation. Then came tuberculosis and wide-spread pneumonia. That meant the men could not get out to work the land (which since 1917 had been in a deep drought). Many starved or succumbed to hypothermia. Their generally poor health, deriving from malnourishment and exposure, meant that they were rendered more sus-ceptible to disease. It seemed that the cycle of hardship would never end.

When the drought finally broke in 1920, prices for farm produce became depressed from the sudden glut in the market of grains and vegetables. Smallboy had to use his wits to make the land pay for itself. Although the land in Hobbema was nowhere near as barren as that in Havre, he soon realized that success in farming in Alberta's unforgiving climate would require his cultivating the unused land of other members of the band. Since so much of the reserve was undeveloped and uncultivated, he ranged beef cattle on the land, which at that time remained largely unfenced all the way to Pigeon Lake to the west. He planted small grains that he could use himself, including barley (primarily used as greenfeed for his cattle), oats, and hay, and raised a few cows. Wheat was then about ninety cents a bushel and hay six dollars a ton. Soon he had an economic base to develop his farm to rival any other in Hobbema. He built sheds and granaries to provide shelter for the birthing animals and to protect the grain from the winter winds.

Every step of the way, the Indian Agency stuck its nose in Smallboy's business, wondering what in the world he was doing. His personal policy was noncommunication. Explain nothing. Let them figure it out. Because of this, a measure of tension developed between the Indian agent and Smallboy, a tension born of contempt on either side.

Yet this contempt for the authority of the staff of the Department of Indian Affairs did not for a moment translate into disrespect towards his parents or *their* authority. Despite his increased independence born of personal initiative, he always listened to the advice of his mother and father. "Even when I was married, my parents still maintained much control over me," Smallboy said, "and for that I have no regret today. They brought me into this world, and I saw how hard they worked to keep us alive. And while they were alive, I tried to repay them for all they did for me. I do not know if I repaid them. It could be I still owe them plenty!"[8]

LIFE AFTER LITTLE BEAR

When Little Bear died on the Rocky Boy Reservation in 1922, the factionalism there between full bloods and Métis—as well as the more artificial division between Cree and Chippewa—intensified briefly. "There occurred a minor scramble on the reservation to take over the authority Little Bear exercised, a fleeting authority at best that went unrecognized formally or informally within the Indian Service."[9] *Apitchitchiw* and Coyote were at the forefront of ensuring that Cree traditions be preserved:

> Why these Indians followed the Cree tradition rather than the Chippewa is a matter for speculation. The domineering influence of the Cree leader, Little Bear, may account in part for the Cree ascendancy. His lieutenants after his death, especially *Kennewash*, Young Boy, and Poor Coyote, were forceful and respected men who insisted that their tribal rites be continued. During these times of stress in the early years of the reservation, these men along with many of the others, regardless of previous tribal affiliation, could contemplate the supernatural together.[10]

The mutual contemplation did not last long, however, because *Apitchitchiw* was being drawn increasingly to his extended family in the north.

One reason for this was a new ready market for his wares right on the reserve in Hobbema. In 1923, the Department of Indian Affairs subdivided a prime strip of reserve land on Pigeon Lake and rapid construction followed of some forty cabins for white holidayers. Construction of the cabins employed Indian workers, including Smallboy, who earned considerable extra income that summer. More importantly, the Indians at Hobbema obtained permission to hold a Sun Dance. Even with the RCMP supervising the dance, the Catholic Church complained bitterly in a letter of protest addressed to the department "that the revival of the Sun Dance would allow 'the old paganism' to survive. They demanded the suppression of the ritual."[11]

On 14 December 1923, Bob and Louisa Smallboy received a Department of Indian Affairs pass framed as a "permit": "Bob Smallboy & Wife No. 181 of Ermineskin Band is permitted to be absent from his Reserve for Two Months from date hereof. Business: Visiting at Rocky Boy, Montana, and is not permitted to carry a gun."[12] They visited the ailing Coyote at the Rocky Boy Reservation and probably stayed at his cabin with Bob's parents and *Waskahte*, as Bob and his siblings had done years earlier after Rocky Boy's death. The fact that a permit was required to leave Hobbema, even in peacetime, was a measure of the extent to which restrictions still applied to Indians forty years after the pass system had been implemented in the wake of the Riel Resistance.[13]

By this time Bob and Louisa had two small children, yet there is no indication that they were permitted to take the kids with them to the United States. More than likely, the children stayed at home with their uncle Johnny.

Smallboy soon discovered that the reservation system instituted at the Rocky Boy Reservation was far from satisfactory. What Smallboy and Louisa saw that Christmas was not merely a great deal of unhappiness, but actual suffering. Some families still lived in tents. Parents were still up in arms over their children being taken away from them for a white man's education in far-away Oregon. There were no roads on the reservation, and all of its grassland, Smallboy was told, was being grazed by other peoples' sheep—twelve thousand white sheep, to be precise, owned by a single white man, J. S. Sprinkle. The sheep were not doing well in the bitterly cold weather. Smallboy knew that the revenue generated by leasing the land to white men was minimal compared to the money that could be made ranging their own cattle on the land.

Added to all this, six months earlier, a new tyrant had come to the reservation in the form of Superintendent John D. Keeley, a former school principal.

Keeley brought a prison warden's mentality to his new assignment. He demanded unquestioning loyalty, discipline, and obedience... . He was determined to bring the Chippewa-Cree to heel and conform with Indian Office regulations. The solution to problems at Rocky Boy's, Keeley proclaimed, was to end "government indulgence" and instill discipline in the camp.

Keeley moved swiftly to establish his authority at Rocky Boy's. The day he took over the administration of the reservation, he ordered the ration roll cut from 395 to 117. The new superintendent stated that he intended to eliminate the ration issue altogether except for the aging and infirm.[14]

Smallboy must have seen how awful the conditions were in comparison to the Ermineskin Reserve: "Little construction had taken place on the reservation since 1915. The log cabins built that fall had badly deteriorated and few additional cabins had been constructed. By 1924, as many as 10 people lived in 10' by 12' structures without floors or adequate ventilation."[15]

If the American system was simply not working, perhaps it was because of its underlying philosophy. According to Commissioner of Indian Affairs Charles H. Burke, "The primary object in establishing this reservation was merely to provide a home for the Indians and, thus, stop their former nomadic habits."[16] The primary object having been accomplished, there was no need to fund the Rocky Boy Band beyond the bare minimum. The Indians were expected to supplement their income with outside labour. As Wessel remarked, "The incongruity of such an idea apparently never disturbed the Commissioner's logic. The only time outside labor was available was during the months when the Chippewa-Cree needed to work their own farms."[17] What nobody ever seemed to factor in to this equation was the fact that the "nomadic habits" of the Cree were precisely the driving force behind the lifestyle that Smallboy and his parents most valued.

After Coyote's death the following year, *Apitchitchiw* and Isabelle temporarily moved in with *Waskahte*, sharing Coyote's old cabin. *Waskahte* was delighted to be reunited with Isabelle, her old friend and confidante. When the couple moved back north to Hobbema the following spring, more-or-less permanently, *Waskahte* went with them.

THE FARM

In June 1925, while in Hobbema, *Apitchitchiw* received word that the annual Sun Dance had been disallowed at the Rocky Boy Reservation, despite the fact that it had been held there without incident for the past ten years. It became imperative, once the crops were in, for as many of the

Smallboy clan as possible to go down to Montana to participate and show support:

> In July, 1925, the leaders of the Chippewa-Cree organized a movable feast and danced away most of the summer performing the annual ritual at Havre, on Beaver Creek, and at the reservation. Keeley ordered the dance leader, Day Child, and the other Chippewa-Cree back to the reservation, but few heeded his words. His threats to remove all of the participants from the rolls and prohibit them from living at Rocky Boy's had little effect.[18]

The dance leader, Day Child (called *Kîsikâw-okimow*, "Day Chief," by Bob Smallboy, who regarded him as a perspicacious prophet), was already getting on in years and was rendered prostrate by the dance, coupled with the unaccustomed confrontation with the forces of the establishment. His nephew Standing Rock built a cabin near the agency office so he could take care of the old man, but Keeley ordered the cabin torn down, saying that henceforth only families with children in the agency school would be allowed to live at the camp—and then only over the winter.[19] One member of the Board of Indian Commissioners threatened to deport all malcontents and anyone who was unco-operative back to Canada.[20] That did not seem much of a threat to Bob Smallboy, who was already happily ensconced there. It only made him want to get back to his farm on the relatively tranquil Maskwachees Reserve.

Part of Smallboy's farming technique was to save seed from his crops to plant the following year. Why pay through the nose for sowable seed from the Indian agent when you could hold back some of your own? It was just as well that he did hold some back for planting, because in 1926 the drought seemed to have returned. It was boom or bust, it seemed, although some economic stability was provided by Smallboy's growing herd of cattle that ranged the Hobbema grazing lands.

The only way to make a living at farming in Alberta, Smallboy realized, was to have access to at least a section of land. He was able to graze more than this, not because he had been allotted more, but because other members of the band showed no interest in using their land for farming, contenting themselves with receiving food rations through the Indian Agency. Since the Indian agent took note of whose land was being used for agricultural purposes, it was in the interests of band members to have their land worked for them, for a portion of the crop, and to allow cattle to graze on their pastures.

Public reaction to the attempted transfer of land out of Indian hands in New Mexico led to increased scrutiny of the Indian Office in the

United States and the Indian Agency in Canada. Both countries decided in 1928 to beef up their school and health services on reservations and reserves across the continent. By now, Smallboy had three children in school—Joe, Clara, and Elizabeth—so once again, pressure was mounting to conform to white values. He resented the fact that he could not teach his children anything while they were in the clutches of the white man. Besides their language, the children were losing their spiritual values, their whole way of life. Smallboy spent each summer desperately unravelling what the Church had ravelled.

Despite his own lack of education, he made things work on the farm. Once again, he had back-to-back bumper crops. Once again, he withheld seed so he could sow his own crops. When the drought returned in earnest in 1929, central Alberta was largely spared and Bob Smallboy and his clan did not suffer. In fact, there was widespread demand for Alberta crops, and prices were generally up, there being such a shortage of vegetables and feed across the continent. Still, on the advice of his father, Smallboy diversified and, through the band, was able to buy farm equipment from overextended farmers.

His farm began to look quite modern, in terms of technology. He had access to a threshing machine, tractor, reaper, binder, ploughs and harrows, tillers, hay wagons, and a manure spreader. He had horses large enough to pull a plough, and brothers numerous enough to help him cultivate some of the land and take off the crops; round up, brand, and castrate the calves in the spring; and round up the steers for market in the fall. And so it went, through the Depression years, with the cattle always there in the background to supply a source of income should the crops fail. Their cabin became a house, the sheds were replaced by a ramshackle barn—and all this without Smallboy ever uttering, or reading, a word of English.

Despite the fact that Smallboy could not read, write, or speak English, the Indian agent at Hobbema seemed to trust him more as he grew older. In 1935, *Apitchitchiw* was taken ill while visiting the Rocky Boy Reservation and hovered near death from pneumonia. Smallboy and Louisa embarked on a trip with two children to the Rocky Boy Reservation to "visit relatives." This time, Colonel R. A. Palmer, the Indian agent, allowed Smallboy to carry a gun. Nonetheless, they still had to get permission to leave the reserve, and this in itself Smallboy found annoying, if only because of his memories of a far more freewheeling existence before the First World War.

Waskahte's STORIES

Later, Smallboy claimed that his closest mentor between the wars was not his father or Yellowface, from whom he had already learned so much, but his maternal step-grandmother, *Waskahte*, a tribal historian who described to Smallboy in detail how things had been when she was a little girl. She remembered the last vestiges of a Plains Indian economy based on the buffalo, when there were only a few white men in the plains country. On 31 January 1982, while in London, England, campaigning for British recognition that Aboriginal rights should be included in the legislation that was to become the Canadian Constitution Act, 1982, Chief Smallboy spoke about the Cree tradition of storytelling—or more specifically "history-telling"—referring specifically to *Waskahte* and the accounts of the distant past that she had shared with him on the farm at Ermineskin.[21]

When Smallboy called *Waskahte* a tribal historian, he did not use the term loosely. Like Isabelle and Bob and Joe Smallboy, *Waskahte* could make a story come to life. But when she spoke, she conveyed the precise words of other elders to whom she had listened, especially the words of her late husband, the eccentric Coyote. She was a serious historian with a memory for detail, rather than a flamboyant storyteller like Joe.

Waskahte always made it clear to Bob Smallboy that she had not personally experienced all of the things that she was relating, but that these things had happened to the *tribe*. She was passing on the stories that had been told to her. Therefore, she described the last great buffalo chase, when the buffalo disappeared and the people starved, in the third, not the first, person.

When Big Bear's band had followed the elusive buffalo south in 1882 and failed to catch up with the last of the herd, the people, sick with hunger, turned back north towards Canada, scouring the hills for any sign of food. But everything had gone, even the gophers, even the mice. Skeletal women and children dropped from fatigue. Weeks before, they had killed off the dogs and most of the horses. Eventually, there was nothing to eat at all, so the people cooked up their moccasins and ate strips of leather and rawhide. Weeks later, the lucky ones reached a Hudson's Bay Company post, and the company, taking pity on them, fed them. "The Hudson's Bay post contributed to their survival," she told Smallboy. From there they went from company post to company post until they reached Edmonton, where eventually the Canadian government decided to feed them again—provided that Big Bear agree to place his "+" beside his name in an adhesion to Treaty Six.

Invariably, *Waskahte* would state the more universal moral of the story she was telling: "And that is why the elders have always advised us never to refuse food offered to us. We must never feel that we are too good to eat certain foods. To eat the food that is available to us and not to waste it—that is a cardinal principle with us."[22] *Waskahte* told Smallboy of a time when the Indians relied on the buffalo for clothing, including moccasins, loincloths, leggings, and shirts. Buffalo robes served as blankets; bowstrings and arrow thongs and quivers were also made of buffalo hide, not to mention the teepees themselves. Bones were used as tools, ranging from needles to knives. Spoons were made from horn, and cooking utensils from hide and bones. Storage containers for food were made of rawhide. Traditionally, women had been in charge of making such things, and they took delight in making them attractive with beadwork and quillwork.

"One could tell by going inside a person's home that she took pride in her work," *Waskahte* told Smallboy. She described Indian crafts such as beadwork and quillwork, and she showed Louisa how to dye porcupine quills. "Porcupine quills were used to make things attractive," she said, demonstrating how to apply them to clothing such as moccasins and leggings. Ermine skins were used for decoration and trim. She said the things Indians manufactured for themselves (as opposed to those made for the tourist trade) were well made and were taken care of, so they lasted through many seasons of use.

The sound of Smallboy chopping firewood or tending the stove triggered another story about the survival of her ancestors. They had used buffalo chips (dried-out buffalo manure) for their fires, she said. "The buffalo chips would burn all night, and the next morning the coals would still be glowing. The Indians would cover the fire with earth during the night to contain the heat."[23]

The scent of cattle or the sound of Smallboy pounding on rails to make a corral triggered yet another story about one of her favourite topics: hunting the buffalo. *Waskahte* told Smallboy that men did not learn to be hunters automatically; they had to learn hunting techniques, just as women learned sewing techniques and how to prepare the hides. The hunter had to be aware of the psychology and anatomy of the animal he was hunting. It was no good, for example, to shoot an animal where it was amply protected by ribs—a good hunter would study the skeletons of the animals he hunted to find out where they were most vulnerable.

Once the buffalo herd had been sighted, she said, the whole camp was involved in a flurry of activity. A hunting party of men would draw as close to the buffalo herd as possible, while the older men, women, and young boys would set to work building a buffalo pound of big poplars felled in a circle, one on top of another, to make a corral. They would build a ramp at one end of the pound up which the buffalo would run, then tumble or jump over the steep inner end of the ramp into the pound itself.

But it was never a matter of herding or chasing the buffalo into the pound, *Waskahte* said. Rather, a brave man with special spiritual gifts would entice the buffalo into following him into the pound. Approaching the buffalo, the "runner" would perform a sweet-grass ritual, burning a braid of sweet grass and singing a special prayer. He would continue to sing as he circled the herd, and then he would run in the direction of the camp and pound. The buffalo would follow the runner to the pound and then up and over the ramp into the enclosure. "The power to round up the buffalo herd was a blessing from the Creator, and the ability to perform the task was a gift," said *Waskahte*. "It may have been that a spirit being had observed the one to be chosen even when he was a child—had observed him with pity and granted him powers, had blessed him with this special gift. Not many people had this power to get the buffalo."[24]

Waskahte and other elders, to whom Smallboy must have listened attentively, were very explicit as to how to make a buffalo pound—and how to make it work. The oral account given by Smallboy was remarkably close to descriptions of buffalo pounds contained in history books and anthropological texts:

> The *pihtokahân*, or buffalo pound, was made of big trees that were cut and fallen in one direction, one on top of another in a circle, much like a round corral. Each tree was secured with the small end attached to the next fallen tree. The *pihtokahân* had to be strong and high so that the buffalo could not break it or jump over it. An entrance was made at the side from which the buffalo were expected to come. At the entrance, a platform was constructed between the two gate poles, designed so that it sloped into the *pihtokahân*. The inner end of the platform would be high enough so that the buffalo, once they were inside, would not be able to run out.... The *pihtokahân* was constructed so that the inner wall would have an incline inwards. Directly below the tip of the inclined inner wall, special railings of approximately a small arm's length from the ground were constructed on the inner perimeter of the pound.[25]

Waskahte told Smallboy that the runner, with the buffalo following closely behind, would run up the ramp and jump over the inside end of the platform. Once he had crawled under the platform to safety, he would make offerings of berries to the Great Spirit and to the Spirit of the Buffalo. "This ritual was performed to show gratitude to the Creator and to appease the spirit of the buffalo for his gift of food for the camp."[26]

Only after all the buffalo had been impounded and the ritual had been conducted would the men shoot at the buffalo with their obsidian-head arrows. Praise would be given to the men who were able to penetrate the buffalo the deepest, with only the arrow feathers protruding from the backs of the fallen animals, while scorn would be heaped on those whose arrows did not penetrate deep enough to kill.

Buffalo hunting was in some ways a blood sport, but more importantly, it was a serious occupation: the life of the meat-eating community depended upon it. An important aspect of the buffalo kill was exposing young ones to danger to help them build up courage for the hunt. "Some of the buffalo inside the *pihtokahân* would have been wounded by not having been shot at the proper spot. These buffalo would be sitting on the ground, wounded, but still quite capable of charging at would-be assailants." The boys of the band were responsible for retrieving these arrows from the wounded animals:

> It took some courage to accomplish this task! A boy would select a wounded buffalo. He would run in towards the fallen animal, grab the protruding arrow, wrangle it free, and run as fast as he could towards the wall of the *pihtokahân*. He would duck under the rails to safety. Often, wounded animals would give chase and on many occasions the buffalo would catch up with the running boy. Usually when that happened, the boy would be killed or badly crippled. There were many close calls! Some of the boys would barely make it to safety, with the buffalo in chase butting his head on the railings that had been constructed just for this purpose. It was a dangerous experience, but it was part of the manhood training that the young ones had to go through.[27]

DEVELOPING THE FARM

Smallboy brought up his own children to have respect for their parents and elders and for Indian values that, between the wars, seemed to become more and more elusive. The family worked as a unit to help develop the farm, and although farming was not a part of their heritage, they made a go of it. After all, they had a section of fertile land that could not be touched by creditors, and the government was committed to giving them subsidies as long as they lived on the reserve.

Yellowface had predicted a time when white men would be hungry, as the Indians had been before them. To Smallboy, this information had been grist for the mill: the Cree, he knew, could suffer no more than they already had. All through the 1930s, the Smallboy family farmed. Their land was mercifully north of the "dust bowl" and received more moisture than most homesteads to the south. Bob was able to diversify.

Each farming family was given a ration of seeds to plant each spring, and Smallboy began to turn even this small blessing to his advantage. Each year, he kept back enough seed grain for his own purposes the following spring, and by 1939, he was seeding 1,740 bushels of grain, including 967 bushels of oats, 752 bushels of wheat, and 21 bushels of barley. He often sold seed grain to his neighbours, thus undercutting the fixed price established by the Indian agent. Not only could he undermine the monopoly of the agent in terms of price, he could also get around the strict rationing that had been imposed on seed grain during the Depression years. Thus the Indian farms at *Maskwachees* became some of the most productive around, thanks to the efforts of Bob Smallboy and others like him, who supplied fellow Indians with seed grain year after year.

During the Second World War, Smallboy once again took advantage of demand for farm produce in a war economy, and once again thrived. Yet he recognized the perils of prosperity. He was the envy of many of his peers on the reserve. How could he do so well when he and his family cut across the grain of modern values? They developed a grudging respect for this man who refused to speak to the Indian agents in their language, insisting instead that they learn to speak *his,* if it was important for them to communicate with him at all. The other Indians could not deny that what he was doing worked, not realizing that the real key to his success was simply hard work.

Having gathered momentum during the war, Smallboy's farm continued to prosper afterwards, even as some fellow farmers despaired and turned to drink in the face of relaxed laws governing alcohol. As others lost interest in the land, Bob and his only son, Joe, grown up by now, took up the slack, buying better stock and more modern equipment to handle the increase in productivity. Joe became a horse wrangler and for a while worked the rodeo circuit—a true cowboy with few other aspirations.

It was clear to all on the reserve, including the Indian agent, that Bob Smallboy knew what he was doing. He could cope with the white man's world quite handily, as long as it remained over the next hill. By the white man's standards, he was more than merely successful. But the white man's standards were not his own. Increasingly, he saw Indians turning to drink, driving while impaired, killing themselves in increasing numbers. He saw an increase in domestic violence and the cycle of despair, even in the face of general prosperity.

Although Smallboy had sent Joe, Clara, and Elizabeth to school, where they learned the English language and were thoroughly indoctrinated in Catholicism, he insisted that they also speak Cree. Furthermore, he always spoke to them of getting back to the ways he had left behind in Montana. One ray of hope—a portent of what could come some day—was the lifting of the ban on the sacred Sun Dance, probably the most defining symbol of Cree culture outside the Cree language itself. "In 1951, after being banned for more than half a century, the Sun Dance was finally legalized, and in the 1960s and the 1970s the ceremonies were revived and strengthened."[28]

One of Smallboy's cousins, Peter O'Chiese, his mother's sister's son, had created what Smallboy regarded as a potentially idyllic community just west of Rocky Mountain House, which he had visited as a teenager. Sometime, he vowed, sometime before he died, he would move even farther into the west country to the foothills of the Rocky Mountains. After all, that was Indian land. Queen Victoria had bartered for the arable land, not for the mountains and foothills—and she had not included the Kootenay Plains in Treaty Six. As far as Smallboy was concerned, the foothills and mountains still belonged to the Indian. Someday, he would reclaim them for his people.

CHAPTER 9

Politics

RELIGION

Until the end of the Second World War, adult Canadian Indians were more-or-less left to their own devices on the reserves. As long as they were properly registered, they received monthly cheques to cover their food and clothing. Shelter in the form of substandard housing, usually bungalows or cabins, was provided through the band offices by the Department of Indian Affairs. Still, the Indian's life was regulated by officious Indian agents and pushy clerics intent on eradicating any "heathen" rituals that did not conform to the closed system of Christianity espoused in Rome or Canterbury.

Baptism, it seemed, was a prerequisite to survival. As Smallboy found out in 1918, it was certainly a prerequisite to marriage in the Church. It was probably a prerequisite for Christian burial, as well. The churches were anxious to educate all of the children in accordance with one religious view or another. Although even nominal Christians among the Cree did not include Christ or the Christian God among their deities, they did pay lip service to Christian dogma, thanks to the indoctrination techniques of the residential schools. Yet each year they lived for the moment when they could attend a powwow, play stick games, go to a sweat lodge, or, most importantly, attend a Sun Dance. These, not church services, were the important events of the Indian's calendar. Yet weddings continued to be conducted in the Catholic Church, even arranged marriages, like the one between Bob Smallboy's son, Joe, and Lazarus Roan's eldest daughter, Dorothy. "After she was given to her rancher husband in an arranged marriage in 1952, she often spent all day in the saddle rounding up cattle for branding. She took to the rugged lifestyle and hard physical work of Smallboy's."[1]

In Hobbema, Our Lady of the Seven Sorrows Church had some-thing of a monopoly on the population in the faith department. Unlike the Rocky Boy Reservation, Ermineskin had a day school, as well as a residential school. There were few complaints of abuse, other than the general abhorrence of the manipulation of children's lives in the name of Jesus. Most complaints centred around the notion that Cree was not to be spoken.[2]

Despite the hardships of Montana experienced by his parents and grandparents, Smallboy found life on the Ermineskin Reserve in Canada in the second half of the twentieth century both degrading and danger-ous to his people. The new threats of Christian education and mass media threatened to undermine not just traditional values, but the very identity of people of First Nations ancestry. This encroachment of white culture and values had led many Indians to drunkenness, moral decline, despair, and suicide.

On a macro level, the icons of traditional religious culture, including rituals from the Shaking Tent to the Thirst Dance, were systematically being strangled by a rival religious system that branded any departure from Christian ritual as "pagan" or "heathen"—in short, as devil worship. Worse yet, the distinctive Cree language, the language of "precise speech" that itself was the hallmark of a healthy culture, was widely regarded among priests and nuns as the devil's language. Educators and clerics felt threatened by anything they themselves could not understand. Therefore, they insisted that English should be the "Christian" lingua franca of the reserves. Cree—the agent of paganism—had to be purged from the lips of every student, and any pupil of a residential school who had the temerity to utter a single word in the forbidden language was punished.

Geoffrey York cites examples of several Cree men bewailing their loss. "There was a cut in the family," said one. "There was a loss of culture and language. In the classrooms, we weren't allowed to speak our language. A lot of our customs practically died out." Another remarked: "I took my grandchildren to the Kehewin reserve for Indian Days last year, and they couldn't understand any of it. It's really sad to see the Indian people losing their language." Said a third: "The nuns told us that our spiritual beliefs were a sin. So we lost that. I didn't believe any of those spiritual things until I had a family of my own."[3]

A good number of the members of the Four Bands took their Christian religion seriously, some of the women becoming nuns them-selves, yet they were determined to preserve their language despite the early attempts of other nuns to wipe it out. Sister Nancy LeClaire (1911–1986), for example, became a nun at an early age and remained one until her death. For the last twenty years of her life, she worked on her

Alberta Elders' Cree Dictionary, now one of the most accessible texts to the language. She used Maskwachees Cultural College as a home base, and in 1975, several of my English students worked for her. Every week, she would keep us posted on her methodical progress through the dictionary, as she collected Cree words like butterflies. At that point, she was at the Fs and Gs. Years later, in 1983, my wife and children lived at her former residence, by then a teacherage, and she would come to visit regularly, for old times' sake. She kept us informed of her progress through the alphabet. She was absolutely ecstatic when she hit the letter P.[4]

The word "Cree" is in fact a bastardization of the French-Canadian *Cris*, which in turn was an abbreviation for *Cristinaux*, descriptive of the affinity the original Ojibwa had with Christian missionaries. Nancy's older brother, Albert Lightning (1900–1991), our landlord in the early 1980s, was renowned as a Cree elder and medicine man, yet could never keep Christian vocabulary out of his speeches for long. In an interview with Dianne Meili on 15 April 1991, four days before his death, Albert told her "he wanted to talk some more about his visit 'upstairs' to see the Great Spirit, of which he had spoken to me many times before. He talked at length about the second coming of Christ. He explained that God had shown him all the spirits that Indians were given to live with on earth."[5]

In 1982, Albert travelled with Smallboy to London, England, and talked about the seven heavens of Cree belief (he had visited four of them personally, he said). At home, he talked to my former wife and me not only of going "upstairs" to consult with the Great Spirit, but of (literally) going "downstairs" to consult the Spirit of the White Buffalo that lived in the cellar of our house. The white buffalo was his personal symbol, and its spirit came to him when he pounded his drum and smudged himself with sweet grass. He also talked about the Little People, describing them much the way Coyote had before he died. Yet in virtually every conversation about these traditional Cree religious motifs, he would praise Jesus, claim that Christ had communicated with him, and talk about the Second Coming, which Jesus personally told him he would see.[6]

While many of his friends were caught up in the fervour of religiosity, Smallboy and his family managed to run the gauntlet of such external pressures, partly because he was not educated himself and took a skeptical (if not downright cynical) view of religious institutions and "white education," and what they had to offer.

MODERNITY

For forty years, Smallboy succeeded in "switching off" the modern world that swirled around the confines of the reserve, a world that threatened to suck the entire traditional Indian system into its gyre. The only times he had to deal with the modern world directly were those occasions in which he left the reserve to visit relatives or when he wanted to sell grain or buy new equipment for the farm. Most of the time, he chose to do business with other Indians. But after the Second World War—especially with the advent of fast cars and television—he discovered, to his chagrin, that the modern world could no longer be ignored. It would not stay away. Rather, its influence came to be felt within the heart of the reserve, especially after the prohibition on alcohol was lifted. Even the elected leaders began to drink, and Smallboy suspected members of the band council of "selling out" to government agents. As Chief John Snow remarked, the post-war era from 1945 to 1965 "was a period when the Indian people were forgotten because the dominant society became too involved with the economic development boom and its own growing affluence."[7]

The arrogance of non-Native employees of the Indian Agency filtered down through English-speaking Indian employees or Indian leaders who were assigned or elected to work with the Cree. Smallboy noticed that Cree leaders who ran for and were elected to office subsequently became spokespeople for the agency rather than for their Indian peers: "They were more inclined to stand side by side with the white administrators in an attempt to perform their duties. This kind of person works only to make a good name for himself." To do that, an Indian must first buy into the modern value system, which Smallboy equated with the value system of the white man. If an Indian defines respect in terms of those values, the tendency will be for the Indian to kowtow to the system and to bend over backwards to "try to find ways to please the white man in order to win his respect." That usually meant "adopting the white man's pride." But he recognized that this was not what the people expected of their chiefs and councillors. He believed that chiefs and councillors "must make an effort to fight for our people, and this is why they elect us to be their leaders." He believed strongly in leading by example, for to say one thing and do another was "fundamentally dishonest."[8]

Often the reserve system was so unforgiving that it created dishonesty just by following the rules. Smallboy had been exposed to bureaucratic hypocrisy in Montana, and now he saw it raising its ugly head in Hobbema as well. The councillors seconded into the system by Indian Affairs grew distant from the people they were meant to represent. "One of the problems is that the councillors and chiefs are not able to reach their people any longer, because of the nature of their association with white government agents." The government agents regarded the impoverished with contempt and the traditional Indian—one who refused to speak English, for example—as if he were beneath contempt. Instead of easing the plight of the poor or providing services to those who had refused to make the transition into the English-speaking world, they made things more difficult. "At certain times, the needy or the poor are unable to obtain any kind of assistance at all from the governments because of this kind of relationship."[9]

Smallboy objected to the lock the government had on the way Indian money was expended. Why could not the bands be entrusted to use band money in a coordinated way, every man and woman having a say as to how it should be spent? And why was there such an obsession on the part of the Indian Agency for people to work just for the sake of working? "A person who earns anything the hard way on the reserve is one who succeeds in developing pride for himself," he said. Why should the government be able to step in to reduce such a person's income, either through taxation or cuts in allowances? It was two-faced for the government to penalize productive farmers or entrepreneurs or artisans when the same government agents were obsessed with "success" in terms of money. "The white man knows this also, because he talks about it all the time. No one can deny it."[10]

Money, said Smallboy, was increasingly becoming an obsession for the Indian. "By the time they complete their schooling, the child already knows of many, many ways to have respect for money," he said. "It is the only thing that is important to him. It is as if it is their God. This does not appear to be a good way."[11]

The government system in place after the Second World War was based on the presupposition that Indians could be self-supporting, a presumption that in turn assumed that Indians were interested in making money. But, as Smallboy related, making money was not the most important thing to the Indian. A free lifestyle was more important. Working like *awahkan* (slaves) to earn money was counterproductive, not only because it detracted from the process of living itself, but also because preoccupation with money was an artificial standard not appropriate to the Indian way of life. "When our children are put in schools, this is the type of environment in which they are required to function."[12]

The temptation to follow the path of modernity was made even more appealing to the Indian by the advent of television. "The first thing the children do when they get home from the white man's school is to turn on the white man's television," he said. Television was often a babysitter, promoting a subculture that undermined Indian values. Indian values were thus destroyed and Indian children were, in Smallboy's opinion, "ruined for life."[13]

Throughout his married life, Smallboy had a running battle with Indian agents, who treated him contemptuously not only because he refused to learn English, but also because he did things in accordance with Indian tradition, rather than conforming to their values. It was humiliating to him to have to rely on Louisa or Joe to fight his administrative battles in a language he did not understand. Bureaucrats—and as far as he was concerned, Indian agents were at the bottom of the pile—wanted to control every economic decision of the Indian. An individual Indian entrepreneur like *Apitchitchiw* (or Smallboy or Lazarus Roan) could run rings around the Indian agent, yet were prevented from doing so by the agent's narrow, bureaucratic vision. The tiny bureaucratic mindset of administrators bent on enforcing rules and regulations had been an irritation at the Rocky Boy Reservation long before Bob Smallboy moved to Hobbema.

"It must be noted," Chief Smallboy said in a radio broadcast shortly after he moved to the Kootenay Plains, "that when the white man first negotiated with the Indian long ago, it wasn't intended for the Indian agent to control the Indian. Rather, the white agent's position, as I understand it, was to be an agent or assistant to the Indian people when they needed him."

> But what happened is that we have relied on these white agents to control our affairs. We let them set up our various programs and meetings, and this is why they are slowly taking full control of our lands and making decisions for us—and they decide how the money should be spent.[14]

If Indian agents were skilled enough to make life-altering decisions for the Indians on their watch, he said, they would be successful businessmen in their own community, rather than petty government administrators in the Indian community.

Looking inward, Smallboy the farmer suddenly discovered that for most of his life, he too had followed "the white man's tracks" and had lost much because of it. "We have lost our identity," he said reproachfully. "We felt disgraced by our Indianness. In public we were ashamed to use our language. Although our physical appearance told of our Indianness, we were persistent in our desire to become like the white man."[15] In matters of culture, of language, of religion, of fundamental values, the Indians on the reserve had sold out, Smallboy said.

> It is for this reason, I believe, that we are being punished for the desolation of our existence. We moan and make grumbling sounds that the white man's tracks have led in the wrong direction. With this, I say, let us return home to our own Indian ways! It is our only salvation in the distant future, to return to our own ways. We can see we have tried to be like white men and we have failed.[16]

GOVERNANCE

Smallboy implied that he had encountered bribery on the reserve. "In the past, money has been appropriated to assist certain individuals financially," he said. "I was approached and asked whether I wanted a share."[17] He claimed that he refused to accept even the suggestion of favours, since he believed that all of the money should be distributed to those who needed it. "I had always suggested to our council to distribute this kind of money to the people who needed it most, but this never happened," he said. By taking government bribes, councillors and chiefs undermined the trust that band members would have liked to give them. "I do not blame our Indian leaders," Smallboy hastened to add. "It's the system and the way things are carried out that gets me to say these things. I am hoping that my comments will be useful in reminding Indian leaders to run their own affairs on the reserves more carefully, so they can be respected as the true leaders of the people they serve."[18]

Smallboy was not impressed that, as part of the reserve system, successive governments could impose their will on his people. But he was also skeptical about the election system within the reserves. Chiefs and councillors were supposedly selected as spokespeople for their bands, as if they were municipal governments. However, in the 1950s, the titular chiefs had no real power; nor were they spokesmen of the people to the government. Rather, they were spokesmen of the government to the people.

Smallboy believed that chiefs should be either hereditary or distinguished by reputation—preferably both. As Chief John Snow explained, "The position was at least semi-hereditary, but a Chief whose leadership was not wise or generally accepted would not last long...."

> In the Indian tradition "Chief" was a meaningful, prestigious, and honorable title; it had always been held only by those with unique talents, skills, courage, and wisdom. Now, it was denigrated, made fun of, and abused by government officials who wanted to put in "progressive" leaders who agreed with the policy of assimilating the Indian people into European society.[19]

Lieutenant-Governor Alexander Morris had said in 1876, "Chiefs ought to be respected, they ought to be looked up to by their people; they ought to have good Councillors; the Chiefs and the Councillors should consult for the good of the people." However, he left no doubt where their loyalty should lie: "Once the Queen approves a Chief or Councillor he cannot be removed unless he behaves badly. The Chiefs and head men are not to be lightly put aside. When a treaty is made they become servants of the Queen; they are to try and keep order amongst their people."[20]

Smallboy had generally kept his own counsel over the years, rather than foisting his opinions on others. For all that, he came to be highly regarded in the Cree community as a man of integrity and a man who forced the government to operate according to *his* terms rather than the Queen's. His utter refusal to communicate in the Queen's or any other form of English came to be regarded as a symbol of his personal power, and this won him widespread respect, even from the most educated Indians on the reserve.

AN ELECTED AND HEREDITARY CHIEF

Although both Isabelle and *Waskahte* had told Smallboy years earlier that he could claim hereditary chieftainship from his great-grandfather Chief Bobtail, Smallboy at first had difficulty understanding how. Isabelle explained. Bobtail, not his brother Ermineskin, had received the medicine bundle from their father. Chief Bobtail had ritually transferred the bundle to her before his death in 1900, following Bobtail Smallboy's naming ceremony, when he received his grandfather's name, *Keskayo*. At that time, Chief Bobtail had told Isabelle that it was her son who would eventually inherit the bundle as chief.

In 1957, several high-ranking members of the Ermineskin Band began urging Bob Smallboy to run for office. It was at that juncture that his mother told him of his great-grandfather's wishes, and Bobtail's bundle was ritually transferred to him.[21]

Smallboy still fretted that this was not enough. A chief should prove his capability over a period of years, he believed. The title was earned. A body of legend should have built up around him. What had he done to deserve the honour? The answer was simple: time and time again, he had stood up to the establishment with his passive attitudes. He was an immovable object, adopting an opaque, unreachable stance. His refusal to speak English was widely admired; it took sagacity of the highest order to survive without that alien language. He had proven himself over and over in the farming game, through flood and drought, through famine and blight, through fair season and foul.

Undoubtedly, a major determining factor was the legend of his pedigree, in particular his claimed descent from Bobtail and Big Bear. But even more than that, the members of the Ermineskin Band were convinced that, once elected chief, he would represent the concerns and interests of the people—*their* interests—rather than the concerns and interests of the Department of Indian Affairs. "It was a two-way system," Smallboy explained, but not where allegiance to Indian Affairs was concerned. "A good chief had to be sensitive to the needs of his people despite his own demonstrated bravery and courage."[22] Thus the two competing interests were the people and individual personality.

Bob Smallboy was not one to play political games. If he was to become chief, it had to be because of what he was and what he had done. He knew that it was not in his nature to take the position lightly. "I was pursued for two years to accept this job," he said in an interview on Cree Radio in December 1968, "but knowing what this position entailed, I refused to accept it."[23]

A growing number of band members expressed support for his candidacy, declaring their trust in his judgment. He made it clear from the outset that he would work for the people of the reserve rather than follow his own inclinations or that of the government. "We must make an effort to fight for our people—this is why they elect us to be their leaders," he said.[24] He ran for office in 1959 against five other candidates—and won. From that time until his death a quarter of a century later, he was known as Chief Smallboy, or more affectionately on his home turf (and much farther afield in the 1980s) as "The Chief," or simply "Chief."

Upon taking office in 1959, one of the first concerns he expressed was the fact that Maskwachees Reserve, of which Hobbema was the hub, had become overpopulated. He called an open council meeting, during which he raised the subject of trying to acquire more land. "At one of those meetings," he said later, "only one councillor supported my idea to request land elsewhere for a reserve."[25]

His plan was simple: if the government would grant them relatively unarable land in the foothills of western Alberta, they could build a community there for older people and those not interested in farming, thus freeing up the arable land for young farmers.[26] Chief Smallboy had now plunged into the world of contemporary democratic politics, where his voice was only one of many. The transition was extremely stressful for both him and Louisa, who died in 1959 not long after his election.[27]

In the old days, Smallboy declared, "the people were respectful of their chiefs and were careful not to offend them."[28] Not any more. Although he believed he had been chosen as chief because of his past record of accomplishments, which implied astute leadership and decision-making capability, Smallboy could hardly conceive of the notion that his ideas, drawn from the long history of his grandfathers trying to negotiate reservations in both Canada and the United States, would be totally ignored by younger, less experienced, more arrogant councillors. This was not the traditional way of doing things at all. He saw for the first time the pitfalls of democracy.

"It has been nine years since I was elected to perform the duties of Chief of the Ermineskin Band in Hobbema," he said in the 1968 interview with Cree Radio. "Ever since that time, I have observed the chiefs and councillors and how they operate their business on the reserve for the people they serve."

As you know, an Indian who is chosen by his people to run the reserve and the welfare of his community, including the well-being of his children, is elected because the people have trust and confidence in him.... . I witnessed the situation the Indian leaders were in—those who were assigned to work for their people. They were more inclined to stand side by side with the white administrators in an attempt to perform their duties. This kind of person works only to make a good name for himself. As Indians, I see where we try to find ways to please the white man in order to win his respect. We continue to pursue this attitude in an attempt to adopt the white man's pride, and this is not expected of us, the chiefs and councillors, by our people. We must make an effort to fight for our people, and this is why they elect us to be their leaders. It is not good to create dishonesty among our poor Indian people.[29]

Smallboy was aware that elected leaders worked hand-in-fist with the Indian agents or, as they were later euphemistically called, the "farm instructors," who could at any time countermand the decisions of the council. The farm instructor had considerably more power and influence within the Department of Indian Affairs than any individual chief or council. Smallboy intended to change this. He remembered the way Rocky Boy and Little Bear had stood up to Roger St. Pierre, resisting his hollow threats and shallow promises, until the farmer-in-charge had been demoted, then eventually fired. That would be a model for him now.

Both Rocky Boy and Little Bear had been able to confront Roger St. Pierre at Fort Assinniboine because they were strong. Little Bear in particular had a dominant personality that would brook no opposition from his councillors. Now, Chief Smallboy found himself chairing meetings where he had no real say, where councillors had no respect for his opinions or for his leadership. "This new type of 'leader' has emerged now—elected Indian councillors who I have seen with my own eyes come to a meeting half drunk," he said. "This is a fact. Nobody can deny it."

They work side by side with the white government agents, and they go to extremes sometimes to obtain financial gain and recognition for themselves. What I say is something which I have observed myself, and this is why I will not accept the concept of leadership on the reserve any longer; because consciously I do not want to repeat what others have been doing with their people, as so-called "leaders."[30]

Bribery, he claimed, was common on the reserve. He had not been aware of this weakness in the democratic system until he became chief himself. "I was honest with my people," he said. "I did not stand alongside the white man, nor did I follow his dishonesty, and I did this for the benefit of the Indians... ."

I, too, at one time, made a living by using the Moo-ni-yaw's (white man's) tools, and by living like him. Although I was able to maintain a good livelihood for myself, I decided to give everything up. While I worked for myself, I did not depend on the chiefs or the councillors to do anything for me. I did my own work, and everything I achieved was accomplished through my own effort and hard work.[31]

Practically speaking, disrespect for the opinions of the seasoned chief and the unpredictability and irresponsibility of the councillors were not Smallboy's main concerns. What he wanted to address, arising from half a century of conflict with government bureaucrats, was the domination of reserve life by the Department of Indian Affairs. As Smallboy complained in his initial address to Queen Elizabeth II in 1971:

For years I was Chief of the Ermineskin Band at Hobbema, and all during that time I tried to help my people, but found there was little to do on the reserve. The Department of Indian Affairs ran the reserve; the Department devised the programs and the policies; the Department determined what our real needs, problems and aspirations were or should be. And still our problems were not solved and still the Department failed to respond in terms meaningful to our people or their needs.[32]

Smallboy argued that the Department of Indian Affairs seemed incapable of responding to the needs of First Nations people, despite its monopoly over their lives. The department not only ran the reserve, but devised its programs and policies often without consultation—without bothering to determine the "real" needs, problems, and aspirations of each individual. The fact that the department had no administrative or legislated capability to determine such questions for individual Indians was precisely the problem that Smallboy identified. The department had a monopoly on distributing malaise within the reserves through the ineptitude of a bureaucratic system that was not geared to solving problems in a creative or inspiring way—if at all.[33]

SEEKING MORE LAND

In the early 1960s, Smallboy held a series of meetings of supporters of the notion of acquiring more territory for his band. He was directed to seek formal advice from the government as to how to obtain more reserve land, preferably far away from cities and "civilization." The Ermineskin Band took up a collection to pay Smallboy's way to the Land Titles Office in Edmonton, where on behalf of the band he requested more land. "I explained to them that our reserve was getting overpopulated, and we had to have more reserve land," he said. "However, I was told that if I wanted more land I would have to buy it, and at the same time I would have to pay taxes on it."

> I saw and talked to others in the Provincial Government, who mentioned that nothing could be done for me. They said, "You will have to go to do your business with the Indian Affairs Branch." So I went to see the Superintendent or Regional Director [of Indian Affairs] and explained the whole situation to him. I told him that our reserve was getting overcrowded and that our proposal was to make room for the younger generation by relocating the older people who were unable to work for their living on the reserve. I also pointed out to him that I wasn't going to buy our land, nor was I going to pay any taxes. He said, "We do not own any land and there is no way that I can help you people."
>
> He explained that if we wanted to pursue this matter further, we would have to go to the Indian Affairs Department in Ottawa. So I asked our local Indian Agent and my councillors to assist me with travel expenses to Ottawa, and some of my colleagues made donations for my trip.[34]

On 9 May 1965, Smallboy left Hobbema for Ottawa, taking along Joe House of the Duffield Reserve as an interpreter. Although arrangements had been made for Senator Jim Gladstone to meet them at the train station in Ottawa, he did not show up, and they had to fend for themselves. They had set up a meeting for 10:00 AM the day after their arrival in Ottawa, but the Indian Affairs official had been told not to expect them, and the scheduled meeting was postponed to the following day. Again they arrived promptly, but were told abruptly to wait. They waited for an hour, while activity bustled around them.

"When the door was opened for us to go in," recalled Smallboy, "I met the two Indian Affairs officials from Edmonton whom I had spoken to already! One of them was the Regional Director, Ralph Ragan." The other was an official who had been in Alberta some time before—Robert F. Battle, by then director of the Indian Affairs branch. "Right then and there, I sensed the crookedness of the white man, because this is how he treats us people who are Indians. And as I spoke to the head man [Battle], he went on to say that he was sympathetic, but he was unable to give our people any land."

> He told me he could not rob the Provincial Government of any soil; he said if they wanted to give me land it would be entirely up to the Provincial

Government. From there on I did not know where to turn, and what steps I should take for legal advice to pursue this land question further.

It is difficult to beat the white man, the way he is, especially those like Mr. Battle, who has four heads. You have to be persistent and aggressive if you want to fight for your rights. Dishonesty and crooked business is powerful.

That time Mr. Ragan took me off to Mr. Battle's office in Ottawa, all the time they gave me to discuss my problem with them was twenty minutes. All this trouble of going to Ottawa was a waste of money! So I came home from Ottawa with nothing accomplished. But I learned through this experience the real crookedness of the white man.[35]

Smallboy's pursuit of freedom had led him to Ottawa and back without anything to show for it. This wild goose chase, apparently devised by an official at Indian Affairs, put Smallboy into a state verging on despair. He had no place to turn, nowhere to seek advice—and clearly nowhere to direct future requests and expectations. He had been thoroughly humiliated by officialdom. His request had, to him, been reasonable, but had been treated with total disrespect and complete disregard of the trouble he had taken to travel all that way at his constituents' expense to present his message. "My desires were beyond reach. No man can grasp anything that has been taken away from him beyond his desires and expectations," he said.

For many moons I thought of my sad experience of not accomplishing anything for the poor. It was like a parent going to town leaving his children behind and expecting to bring back to them something good. I took this sad experience with great emotion, and I was very hurt by the consequences.[36]

Yet Smallboy did not put all of the blame on the "white man." He recognized that Indian leaders of the past had been too weak, so that they were now dismissed by the authorities in Indian Affairs as irrelevant. This loss of dignity he put at the doorstep of the chiefs themselves:

This is why I say that we who are Indian leaders are the cause of all this, because we stand side by side with the white man, expecting him to admire and respect us. We are actually the ones, the Indian leaders, who are letting our people suffer, because we have a tendency to look for admiration. As Indian leaders, we must be willing to stand side by side with our own people at their own level, and to fight for them in order to win their respect and confidence. We must from day to day look at our poor Indians and observe just how the white man is treating them.[37]

Smallboy did not appear to comprehend the jurisdictional and constitutional realities facing the federal and provincial governments, which formed a subtext to their rejection of his request. Although the federal government was responsible under section 91 of the Constitution Act, 1867, for "Indians and lands reserved for the Indians," section 92 gave jurisdiction over Crown lands and mineral resources to the provinces. In particular, Ottawa and Edmonton had been quarrelling for over a quarter of a century before Smallboy's trip about whether the province was obliged to provide more land for reserves. Smallboy's position was that since the First Nations had not given up the mountains to Canada in the first place, Canada had no right to include the unceded land in the territory of Alberta when it first became a province in 1905. It comes back to the fact that most of the land included in Jasper and Banff national parks remains Indian land. In fact, all of the land east of the Continental Divide and west of the eastern range of the Rockies is Indian land, including the Kootenay Plains.

Smallboy's attempts to communicate directly with the head of the Bureau of Indian Affairs (as it was then configured) had come to naught: "Still our problems were not solved and still the Department failed to respond in terms meaningful to our people or their needs."[38] He listed some of the problems encountered by Indians on the reserves in the postwar years:

1) The reserves were overpopulated;
2) Employment opportunities were too limited;
3) The family unit was falling apart;
4) Alcoholism and general drunkenness were rampant;
5) Child neglect was altogether too common;
6) Too many Indians were in jail;
7) Too many Indian children were failing in school;
8) Disease was rampant on the reservation;
9) Individual Indians had lost their pride and dignity;
10) Indians collectively had been stripped of their religion;
11) The social order of the Indian had been disrupted;
12) The Indian's cultural identity had been destroyed;
13) Indians were left with little or no meaning to their lives;
14) Increasingly, Indians found their only escape in suicide.[39]

"Your government representatives are aware of the general status and condition of the descendants of the original people of this land," he told the Queen. "Collectively, the Indian people have been virtually destroyed as a cultural identity, with tragic results to the individual. But for all your awareness, it is we, the Indian people, who see every day what is happening to our brothers and sisters, to our children and grandchildren."[40] The federal government was aware of its failures, Smallboy claimed, but did nothing to ameliorate the situation. "As the years passed, we were directed from department to department to department," he said. Further discussion was fruitless, "since once again the Department knew what was best for us and refused to help in any way."

> We had tried to practice our religion and culture, but it was difficult to practice a good way of life on the reserve. We were also concerned with the future of our people and the importance of having the younger generation lead a good way of life; this is why we tried so hard and so long to acquire other land. But all those years of effort were for nothing.[41]

Hanne Marstrand Strong, who long claimed that Smallboy's medicine helped cure her daughter of cancer, later wrote in a news release on behalf of the Four Bands:

> Smallboy's decision to move his band to the mountains arose from his desire to teach his band the ways of his ancestors. He recognized that the influences and pressures of the modern industrial society were destroying his people's identity and threatening to break down their link to a great heritage. Smallboy became even more alarmed when many Indian people began to resort to alcohol in their frustration. The chief saw the necessity of leading his band to a return to the Indian traditional beliefs and value system.[42]

The key to the future, the Chief believed, was to acquire land far from modern influences and try to get back to "the Indian Way" that had been abandoned half a century earlier. After consulting with his most trusted friends and advisers, Lazarus Roan and Simon Omeasoo, he knew what he had to do:

> After a few moons, I decided to write a letter to Ottawa, and I explained to the Indian Affairs Department that I had reached my decision to leave Hobbema to inhabit the mountain region. I added that I would not bother them again, and if they wished to see me for something, they would have to come to me.[43]

CHAPTER 10

The Exodus

THE CAMP

As mentioned earlier, on the very day Pierre Elliott Trudeau first assumed the office of Prime Minister of Canada, the first teepees were erected at the Smallboy Camp on the Kootenay Plains in the foothills of the Rocky Mountains, well known among Indians as traditional sacred ground. The Plains were a fitting place for an attempt to return to a traditional Indian lifestyle. Recognizing that they were on "old Indian territory," Eugene Steinhauer, soon to become lieutenant-governor of Alberta, visited the site and concluded that the leaders had planned the move carefully.[1] Chief Smallboy, in consultation with his two councillors, Lazarus Roan and Simon Omeasoo, chose a site on an alpine meadow with a sunny southern exposure, protected on three sides by low poplar trees in the lee of high mountains near the confluence of the North Saskatchewan and Siffleur rivers. The Special Bighorn Reserve of the Wesley Band of Stoney Indians was not far away. A good dirt road led west from Rocky Mountain House to Nordegg, although from there to the Banff-Jasper Parkway, a hundred kilometres farther west, the road was seasonal and full of ruts.

The Department of Indian Affairs agreed to supply a trailer to the camp to serve as a schoolhouse—provided Smallboy moved the camp close enough to a negotiable road so that access to the trailer was assured. Accordingly, in the fall of 1968, Smallboy moved the mobile village, setting up his central teepee that doubled as a meeting lodge a few hundred metres off the barely passable gravel road that eventually was to become the David Thompson Highway. Steinhauer described it:

At this writing, Robert Smallboy and his group of 150 men, women and children are maintaining their stand to isolate themselves from the reserve system and away from the activities of the white man. It must be noted that those who joined Smallboy in the Kootenay Plains include some high school students and single men who have completed various training courses and are qualified to meet the standards of employment opportunities in the white society. Smallboy believes in education of the younger generation, but he has lost all faith and confidence in the Indian Affairs education system. The Indian Affairs Department has stated that a mobile training school will be set up for the group in the Kootenay Plains to meet the requests of the people.

The location of their camp contains a wide acreage of open range, partially covered with small trees and surrounded by mountains, with the North Saskatchewan River and creeks flowing through it. For transportation, they are sole owners of late model cars and pick-up trucks which are seldom in use, save for a trip to town to do their weekly shopping. There is, in addition, a number of horses owned by Smallboy that roam the Kootenay Plains which were trucked in from the Hobbema Reserve, and they are used by the people on field trips, i.e., hauling firewood and moving of camp from time to time.

In speaking to the members regarding employment, they anticipate winter employment will be slack, but foresee no difficulties regarding activities (social and economic) during the winter season. Meanwhile, the members are receiving welfare assistance from the Indian Affairs Branch, and from time to time they obtain a supply of wild meat and fish by hunting for their livelihood.

For social life, the members are complete abstainers of alcohol, and various cultural activities are put into practice by both old and young in order to break the monotony of the Kootenay Plains.

No one really knows the future of Robert Smallboy and his followers. But perhaps the master-minded Indian leader has certain predications which no one is aware of regarding the destiny of his people. This, of course, remains to be seen.[2]

Steinhauer's remarks, contained in a special Cree Studies edition of *The Western Canadian Journal of Anthropology*, go a long way to explain the difference between the reality of Chief Smallboy's permanent excursion into the woods and a *Walden*-like "back to nature" movement that sought to deny the validity of all technology. The Smallboy Band unabashedly used recent model cars and trucks for transportation. Bruce Cox of Carleton University noted in his preface to the Cree Studies issue that "the significance of Smallboy's acts is often lost on white interpreters":

In the popular press, the band's move from the reserve is seen as a romantic, back-to-the-bush movement. It is instructive to consider how truly radical Chief Smallboy's acts are. What he has done is to create a new relationship between his followers and the Indian Affairs Branch... . They have a new status and a new social identity. Though the camp has no resident Indian agent, school teacher or land manager, it continues to receive band payments and welfare allowances made to its members. Essentially, this amounts to the system of direct grants to bands which Indian nationalist leaders call for.[3]

Most early newspaper articles regarded the migration as an ill-conceived, flash-in-the-pan protest, and Smallboy as a "rebel" and a "renegade," despite his having been a successful farmer for fifty years and an elected chief of the Ermineskin Band for a decade. He was seventy years old—hardly a hothead! Visiting journalists were surprised to find him soft-spoken, gentle, and witty. Gradually, the image painted of him in the press began to change. Rather than berating the Chief and his new band, newsmen who took the trouble to go out to the Smallboy Camp began to express concern for the families that Smallboy had "shepherded" to the remote Kootenay Plains.

What none of them knew or understood was that Chief Smallboy had been here before—sixty years before, in Montana. For him, it was like coming home. At last he could see on the horizon some hope for "the Indian Way" that he had been extolling to his children for decades. His family could at last experience for themselves the idyllic kind of life that he remembered living as a child in the romantic Land of the Long Knives.

Journalists expressed concern for health care, to which Chief Smallboy replied with confidence, "We have our own medicine." They were concerned about religious worship, to which Smallboy replied, "We will teach them the right way of life ourselves." They were concerned most of all with the education of the children, to which Smallboy replied, "We will teach them the way of their ancestors." As Cox remarked:

Critics have often queried how effectively the message of university-educated spokesmen like [Howard] Adams and [Harold] Cardinal reaches the brother on the trap-line... . One cannot well maintain that Robert Smallboy has been much influenced by the seditious influence of the universities. Chief Smallboy is 72 and speaks no English, yet his analysis, and his actions, are as radical as those of younger, university-educated Indian leaders. Presumably the future belongs to both sorts of leaders; we need not attempt to choose between them.[4]

In fact, Smallboy was motivated more by memories of the freewheeling days of his youth than by any sophisticated political theory. To him, what he was doing was common sense, a simple means of protecting the Cree culture that he saw was under attack by the dominating culture, which itself was spinning out of control. He saw a need to cocoon, to withdraw to a quiet place to allow the wings of Cree culture to develop without interference from the bombardment of television. This had worked in the past, with the Sunchild and O'Chiese bands west of Rocky Mountain House. His uncle, Peter O'Chiese, had finally obtained a reserve of his own, following the Second World War, after surviving for more than half a century in the woods.

Although Stan Reid of the *Edmonton Journal* referred to Chief Smallboy's exodus from Hobbema as "one of the strangest stories of the year," his initial report on the event seemed to contain a measure of contempt, with its conclusion that Smallboy was "trying to set back the clock" and the dissidents "are a bunch of Indians who decided to go back to the way of their fathers—and who are not finding it easy."[5] However, there was more truth in this statement than Reid could ever have possibly imagined.

OFFICIAL RESPONSE

From the beginning, Arthur Dahms, the Indian agent for Rocky Mountain House, was optimistic. "I think they're going to make it," he said on 10 September 1968, after his first visit to the camp. He worked determinedly to set up a meeting between Chief Smallboy and senior officials at Indian Affairs. The Chief had said that if officialdom wanted to speak to him, they would have to come to him: he was certainly not going to waste his time to travel to Edmonton—or Ottawa—again to see *them*.

Sure enough, they did go to him. In October 1968, the *Edmonton Journal* announced, "BREAKAWAY INDIANS WIN OUT: OTTAWA OFFICIALS PAY VISIT."[6] The visitors included a somewhat subdued Ralph Ragan, Edmonton-area supervisor Thomas Turner (whose jurisdiction included the Hobbema reserves), and two other Indian Affairs officials from Edmonton. They stopped at Rocky Mountain House long enough to pick up Arthur Dahms. Crammed into a department car, the officials were required to drive a total of 500 kilometres—200 of which were unpaved, winding, forestry trunk road—in order to speak to the Chief.

They came with concessions. Smallboy had from the beginning insisted that the adult Indians in his group should claim and receive their usual treaty and Ermineskin Band fund money. Ragan assured him that the members of his camp could continue claiming federal payments for

GROUP OF TEPEES I.R. HOBBEMA

Starting from scratch. When the nomadic Cree of Montana were rounded up in 1896 and shipped to Hobbema to form the Montana Band, they lived in teepees until they could build more substantial houses. GLENBOW ARCHIVES, NA-650-1

A cast iron stewpot hangs by a chain from a tripod over an efficient fire: logs arrayed like the sun were gradually pushed inward as they burned. Blankets and Hudson's Bay blanket coats helped keep out the chill. GLENBOW ARCHIVES, NA-1905-24

Children would catch rides on a travois for both transportation and (as here) entertainment. GLENBOW ARCHIVES, NA-1164-1

The Chiefs of the Four Bands meet in Hobbema. They have been identified by Chief Charlie Rabbit as (left to right) Chief Francis Bull (Louis Bull Band), Chief John Bear (Montana Band), Chief Joe Samson (Samson Band), and Chief Panee Ermineskin (Ermineskin Band). GLENBOW ARCHIVES, NA-1223-20

A pow-wow at Hobbema. FROM BOB SMALLBOY'S PHOTO ALBUM

Bob Smallboy's teepee at Hobbema. FROM BOB SMALLBOY'S PHOTO ALBUM

At the Calgary Stampede in 1965, Chief Smallboy proudly carried the Union Jack. FROM BOB SMALLBOY'S PHOTO ALBUM

Grin and bear it. Ralph Ragan and Chief Bob Smallboy meet (all too briefly) in Ottawa after Smallboy took pains to travel there to request more land. After waiting one day plus an hour, Smallboy was given twenty minutes to make his pitch. For him, this was a decisive moment. His treatment in Ottawa led directly to his decision to move to the Kootenay Plains. FROM BOB SMALLBOY'S PHOTO ALBUM

Chief Smallboy at the time of his move to the Kootenay Plains in 1968. FROM BOB SMALLBOY'S PHOTO ALBUM

SKINNING MOOSE HIDE

The tanned hides of moose or elk would be scraped clean of hair to make leather. Skills such as those needed to make leather were revitalized at the Smallboy Camp. GLENBOW ARCHIVES, NA-2770-4

Chief Bob Smallboy's cabin at the Smallboy Camp near the Brazeau River—where he lived and died. GARY BOTTING

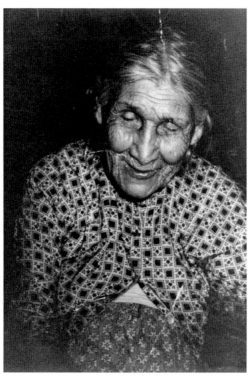

Smallboy's mother, Isabelle Coyote *Apitchitchiw*, at 112, just before her death in 1977. FROM BOB SMALLBOY'S PHOTO ALBUM

The Chancellor and Principal Companion
of the Order of Canada

Le Chancelier et Compagnon principal
de l'Ordre du Canada

to — à

Chief Robert Smallboy

Greeting:

Salut:

Whereas, with the approval of Her Majesty Queen Elizabeth the Second, Sovereign of the Order of Canada, We have been pleased to appoint you to be a Member of the Order of Canada

Attendu que, avec l'assentiment de Sa Majesté la Reine Elizabeth Deux, Souveraine de l'Ordre du Canada, il Nous a plu de vous nommer Membre de l'Ordre du Canada

We do by these Presents appoint you to be a Member of the said Order and authorize you to hold and enjoy the dignity of such appointment together with membership in the said Order and all privileges thereunto appertaining

Nous vous nommons par les présentes Membre dudit Ordre et Nous vous autorisons à bénéficier de ce jour de la dignité de telle nomination ainsi que du titre de membre dudit Ordre et de tous les privilèges y afférents

Given at Rideau Hall in the City of Ottawa under the Seal of the Order of Canada this thirty-first day of December 1979

Fait à Rideau Hall dans la ville d'Ottawa, sous le Sceau de l'Ordre du Canada, ce trente et un jour de décembre 1979.

By the Chancellor's Command

Par ordre du Chancelier.

Le Secrétaire général de l'Ordre du Canada

Secretary General of the Order of Canada

Chief Bob Smallboy's Certificate of Membership in the Order of Canada, 31 December 1979. (FROM BOB SMALLBOY'S ESTATE)

Eugene Steinhauer and Chief Bob Smallboy present Pope John Paul II with a document outlining their concerns with respect to Aboriginal Rights in Canada. VATICAN PHOTO

Chief Smallboy in London, England, in 1981, where he attempted to convince the House of Lords to intervene to protect the rights of First Nations in the patriation of the Constitution. FROM BOB SMALLBOY'S PHOTO ALBUM

Albert Lightning, Fred Bruno, and Chief Bob Smallboy in London, England, 1982. FROM BOB SMALLBOY'S PHOTO ALBUM

The ceremonial teepee of famous elder and medicine man, Albert Lightning (Buffalo Child), featuring the white buffalo, the spirit of which he claimed periodically appeared to him (Hobbema, 1983). GARY BOTTING

Chief Smallboy and translator Chief Gordon Lee outside Smallboy's cabin at the Smallboy Camp in August 1982. GARY BOTTING

Author Gary Botting reviews a genealogical chart with Chief Smallboy (1982).
GENE LEAVITT

Chief Smallboy enjoys a pensive moment in his small but neat cabin (July 1982).
GARY BOTTING

Although Smallboy steadfastly refused to speak English, he seemed to have no problem reading the newspaper.
GENE LEAVITT

Chief Bob Smallboy sports a new blanket, a gift from Chief Gordon Lee (JULY 1982).
GARY BOTTING

Old Sun Dance lodges on the Kootenay Plains. GARY BOTTING

which they had been eligible while living at Hobbema. Those followers of Smallboy who came from other bands would also continue to receive their band money. Dahms confirmed that none of Smallboy's band had applied for relief or provincial welfare payments; indeed, provincial officials were adamant that the Province of Alberta was not responsible for welfare payments, since the "maverick band" was comprised of treaty Indians who fell under federal jurisdiction.

Although the Department of Indian Affairs had negotiated an agreement whereby the province would give assistance to treaty Indians living off reserve, the province argued that the Smallboy Band had not established itself off the reserve, but rather was camping temporarily on provincial land. Ragan admitted that this was a blow. "We were disappointed that the province let us down," he told a twenty-five-member delegation from Hobbema, some of them anxious relatives who protested Smallboy's exodus. "There will be no force used to have children with the group attend school. We'll work out the problem with the Chief and his people." Ragan said Smallboy had requested that a school be established at the camp and "this request is being studied."[7] During his October visit to the Smallboy Camp, Ragan promised a mobile schoolhouse. However, by year's end, as drifting snow sealed off the Smallboy Band from the outside world, the school had not yet arrived. It did not arrive, in fact, until well into the new year.

In the meantime, Lazarus Roan's daughter, Violet Omeasoo, herself a mother of six, insisted that the children receive some semblance of formal education. She herself took on the task of teaching the children in the central teepee. "We brought the children away to grow this Indian way, to grow up with it, and I don't think they will miss anything," she told Paul Grescoe of *Weekend Magazine.* Translating for Chief Smallboy, she added, "We try to get back to the Indian Way. The younger boys learn to hunt. The younger girls, they have to make hides. There's always something to do."[8] All the adults pitched in with whatever skills they had. Dorothy Smallboy's contribution was making preserves, sewing, and knitting.

The first year was hell. Winter's cold assaulted Dorothy's twelve-by-fourteen tent as she knitted socks furiously to keep her family's feet warm. Her knowledge of food preservation and sewing became invaluable.

"The only things I took were my cook-stove, my mattress, and my sewing machine. We bought flour and rolled oats, but I made my own jam. We ate berries and wild meat." For warmth, Joe stacked hay bales against the sides of the tent for insulation and built wooden walls the following year to minimize the cold.

"Still, some of the ladies couldn't hack it … making fire all winter,"

Dorothy explained. "I was raised like an Indian so I was used to it. But my husband was a farmer. He had to learn how to hunt."[9]

Soon, the press came to accept the Smallboy Camp as a permanent fixture in the west country. Grescoe remarked:

> Chief Robert Smallboy and his 140 followers are making their last stand. It may be the last stand, too, for the culture of the Canadian Indian.
>
> They moved for many reasons, the chief says, but the most important motive was to escape the corruption of the white man's society that has afflicted the Crees since the 1700s, and to raise their children in the old and simple Indian style of life.
>
> They are teaching the children to hunt and trap and treat hides, to know the forest and the mountains and the animals, to respect their elders and to despise liquor and the licentiousness it can cause.
>
> If they succeed, they may have preserved a vestige of an Indian civilization from being buried by the overwhelming culture of the Canadian white man.[10]

There was always the temptation to go back to the comparative "civilization" of the reserve, but most of the Smallboy and Roan clan toughed it out. Dorothy Smallboy told Dianne Meili:

> I only remember one winter when we were hungry. It was after we'd moved from Kootenay. It snowed so hard we couldn't get out. We didn't have anything to eat. I guess my dad was telling everyone not to worry … that it was just a matter of time before Joe [Dorothy's husband] would run out of sugar and have to make a run for the store. He finally went. Some guys shovelled the snow in front of the truck, and they made it.[11]

Smallboy continued to maintain until he died that the Crees' treaty with Queen Victoria did not include the mountains and the Kootenay Plains, the land that had been left out of Treaty Six. Nor did any of the treaties include reference to the oil and other mineral wealth beneath the topsoil. Harold Cardinal made this point succinctly in *The Unjust Society*:

> As far as the Indian signatories were concerned, and certainly in line with Indian thinking today, the treaties were not intended to take away Indian mineral rights. The treaties, as our people understood them, meant the surrender of surface rights only so that the land could be shared with other peoples, without jeopardy to Indian claims to what lay under the surface.[12]

Hence the newfound wealth of oil that Alberta enjoyed was actually the property of the Indian. Not only that, the Queen's representatives had guaranteed a certain amount of land for each man, woman, and child, so that reserve lands would increase as the Native population grew. Therefore, the Indians should be getting more and more land each year. This new land could be drawn from the Indian land that the Crown in right of Alberta had claimed illegally—the land that had not fallen under Treaty Six or Treaty Seven—in short, the national parks and the Kootenay Plains.

Predictably enough, Indian Affairs department officials were adamant that Treaty Six offered no prospect of new land. But they said they intended to respect Chief Smallboy's decision to camp in the foothills and to help him as much as possible to ensure the survival of those at the camp.

Smallboy's argument that the Indians owned the mineral rights beneath the soil was to have a major effect on the Indian economy, if only because of findings by successive courts that the Indians did indeed own the mineral rights on their reserves. Oil had been discovered on several Alberta Indian reserves in the 1940s, but the exploratory wells had merely been capped for future reference. Not until the late 1960s, after Smallboy had moved to the Kootenay Plains, did these and other new, deeper wells come into production, producing revenue for the Four Bands in Hobbema in a big way.

During his nine-year tenure as chief of the Ermineskin Band, Smallboy had encouraged oil exploration on reserve land, and once the price of oil shot up in the early 1970s, the entire reserve was to benefit. The Four Bands became the richest in Canada. Thus Smallboy's first concern—poverty on the reserve—was quickly addressed, the Indians suddenly having wealth beyond their dreams.

After his move to the Kootenay Plains, Smallboy remained chief of the Ermineskin Band until a referendum of those band members who remained at Hobbema decided that he be removed from office. In order to do so, the band members at Hobbema had to first declare his band as separate from the main Ermineskin Band.

To many back at Hobbema, Smallboy's exodus was simply an embarrassment that, unlike the renegade chief himself, would not go away. A petition signed by 113 Ermineskin Band members requested the Band Council to unseat Chief Smallboy "because he has deserted us." Some called him "an old hippie." To their credit, Smallboy and his followers weathered these abrasions and insults, and the provincial government, on whose land they were allegedly squatting (although Smallboy adamantly denied this), retained its official "hands off" policy.

MOTIVATION

In December 1968, less than six months after having moved to the Kootenay Plains, Smallboy explained in a public address what had led him to move with his band from Hobbema and why he intended to stay in the foothills. His concern, he said, was for the future of his children and grandchildren and for a good, peaceful life for them in a place far from the influences of the modern world. He told of his abortive trip to Ottawa and said he had spent two years after that "trying to negotiate the land question and getting the people prepared to vacate their homes on the reserve." The advantages of life on the Kootenay Plains were numerous, he said: members of his band had time to think freely, to cope with the realities of life as they arose. The young people were living in peace and were learning to adapt to the good values of a life close to the land—"this land that we dwell on is clean."[13]

Despite minus-twenty-degree weather, there had been no health problems in the camp in the first six months; in fact, the only problem of any kind was the delay in receiving the promised schoolhouse from Indian Affairs. It finally arrived at the Smallboy Camp in two parts, in the form of two small construction trailers, one of them a teacherage complete with teacher. The students could not fit into the single-room trailer standing up, let alone sitting at desks.

The teacher was powerless to expand the facilities; in fact, a consignment of books issued by Indian Affairs in November 1968 had to be stored in the classroom, further reducing the floor space. Furthermore, the teacher was not made to feel at home at the camp and began to show signs of becoming "bushed" in the worst sense of the word. He was not popular with either the children or their parents, and after his contract expired in the summer of 1970, he disappeared—along with the teacherage.

Smallboy's request for a large tent to serve as a school went unanswered. Determined to teach the children themselves, Chief Smallboy requested assistance to send one of the band's teenagers to Calgary to study as a teacher's aide, but the department did not seem to take this request seriously.

Hardly anyone had expected the Smallboy Camp to last through the first winter, let alone the second. Yet the band prospered. Thanks to the business acumen of Chief Smallboy and Lazarus Roan, the band found adequate employment for everyone and actually made money.

THE BIGHORN DAM

At the time, the huge Bighorn Dam on the North Saskatchewan had passed the planning stage and was nearing construction, but the site of the future reservoir upstream on either side of the river—to be called

Abraham Lake, after the Stoney family that lived there—had to be cleared of trees, brush, and debris. The Stoney Indians on the nearby Bighorn Reserve would have nothing to do with the project, regarding it as an encroachment on their traditional hunting grounds.

The practical Lazarus Roan had no such compunction. All through 1969 and 1970, he led the band's clearing of the land for the reservoir, and from the standpoint of the beleaguered provincial government, the Smallboy Band's co-operation became economically expedient. It was cheaper to use labour already in place than to ship in work crews from points east who, in all likelihood, would not be happy with the attendant isolation.

Although the work was welcome, it soon became obvious that the "scab" activity of the Smallboy Band was generating friction with the Stoneys, who understandably felt that their land and principles had been compromised by the interlopers. After all, the Stoneys had to live forevermore with the devastating change in the landscape, and their hunting grounds had become seriously altered, if not eradicated, by the dam construction and flooding of the river basin. Furthermore, many Stoney graves had to be exhumed from a cemetery near the river bank. The remains—mostly of children—were rather summarily relocated to a new burial ground west of Abraham Lake on the North Saskatchewan River at Two O'Clock Creek. The Stoneys demanded that Smallboy move his camp off "their" land.[14] Recognizing the Stoneys' historic ties to the region, the Smallboy Band Council eventually complied. But in moving back onto Treaty Six land, the band lost ground in the bid to claim the Kootenay Plains and the Rocky Mountains as "Indian land" for all First Nations, as Smallboy clearly recognized.

Chief John Snow put the conflict between his band and the provincial government in the starkest terms:

> For the Stoney Tribe in particular, the greatest battle for land rights in recent years was also with the Province of Alberta. It was also unsuccessful, climaxing in one of the blackest days of our history and the virtual destruction of any possibility of a decent livelihood for those of my people living on the Special Bighorn Reserve on the Kootenay Plains.
>
> When I assumed the chieftainship in January 1969, I was only too well aware of the Bighorn-Kootenay Plains land claim. I had also heard of provincial government plans to build a dam somewhere on the North Saskatchewan River, but I thought it was another long-range scheme for the future development of provincial water resources and electric power. Being a rookie politician, I was not aware that plans for the construction of the dam were already well under way. Before I discovered how far this had gone, work crews had moved in with heavy equipment and begun massive

destruction of the beautiful North Saskatchewan Valley, near the Bighorn Reserve. Wesley Band members from the reserve came to Morley and told me of bulldozers knocking over Indian log cabins, destroying Indian graves, and ruining traplines as well as traditional hunting areas.

I went to the Bighorn-Kootenay Plains areas to look over the situation for myself. What I saw was unbelievable. Land that had belonged to the Stoneys—land that the Stoney Indians still claimed—was being bulldozed without consideration for, or consultation with, my people.[15]

The Stoney Tribal Council was unanimous in their opposition to the construction of the dam, given that their land claims had not yet been settled, and in the middle of March 1969, Chief Snow fired off a letter of protest to Premier Harry Strom:

Dear Premier Strom:

On behalf of the Stoney Indian Council at Morley I am writing to you concerning the Bighorn Dam project. It has been thought up, planned, and is now actually being built without at any time consulting the Indian people of the Bighorn Indian Reserve. It appears that the Government has once again ignored the Indian people on this very important matter that directly affects their way of life.

Snow requested a meeting between band representatives and appropriate provincial cabinet ministers before the end of March 1969. "Indian graves have already been destroyed by bulldozers clearing the land," he wrote. "All clearing must be stopped immediately so that these graves can be relocated, before the markings are destroyed and the locations lost forever."

Snow implied that his band had received a runaround not unlike that experienced by Smallboy, which had been partly responsible for Smallboy moving to the Kootenay Plains in the first place: "We do not want to talk to representatives who do not have authority to make decisions," Chief Snow wrote. "We have talked with one of your representatives in our council meeting on March 11th and all he could tell us was that he had no authority and would have to talk to other people about this." He suggested a meeting with Premier Strom in his office. "Please arrange this meeting at once and let us know when you will meet with us," he wrote in his letter to Strom. He identified ten problems that arose with the construction of the dam:

1) Indian Graves.
2) Indian homes to be flooded.
3) Indian land to be flooded.

4) Hunting area.
5) Grazing land for horses.
6) Traplines.
7) Sun Dance and Recreation Areas.
8) Historical and Cultural significance to the Indian people of the flooded area.
9) Disruption of Indian way of life through development of area.
10) Fear of living below the dam.[16]

As a result of his letter, Snow was invited to address the Alberta Legislature in the spring of 1969. There, he asked several blunt rhetorical questions:

> Why did the Provincial Government not inform the Indian people about the plans for this construction of the dam at Bighorn? Was this ignorance on the part of the Government? Was it disrespect on the part of the Government to the native people who have lived in the Bighorn area for centuries?[17]

Chief Smallboy himself claimed to know nothing of this conflict. Nor did Chief Snow realize that the province was actively soliciting the Smallboy Band as a workforce to clear the land, not only pitting one Indian band against another, but pitting two traditionally friendly tribes—the Assiniboine and the Cree—against one another.

For Lazarus Roan, who had negotiated the work contract for his people with the provincial government, clearing the land was simply gainful employment. But for the Stoneys, the effects of the dam construction were much more long-lasting:

> The destruction of the land was a terrible thing to watch. Haze filled the air as growing things were burned off to clear the ground. Homes were swept aside by heavy machinery, graves turned over or swallowed by the new lake.
>
> Even more far-reaching in its result was the almost complete disappearance of game from the area. The people living on the Kootenay Plains have always been among the most independent of the Stoneys.... But with hunting destroyed and little employment for unskilled labour in the area, 95 percent of the Bighorn residents live on welfare today.
>
> The damage—physical and psychological—that the building of the Bighorn Dam caused my people can never be calculated.[18]

The Smallboy Band did eventually respect the position of the Stoneys and in 1974 withdrew from both the land and the Abraham Lake project.

Chief John Snow had already expressed his view that the mountains belonged to the First Nations, but the two chiefs, Snow and Smallboy, did not seem to recognize that they were fighting precisely the same battle, even using the same ammunition: the argument that the mountains had never been ceded to the Queen and therefore remained "our sacred places."

In contrast to the Stoney experience documented by Snow, Smallboy claimed that his band was self-sufficient:

> This is how the Great Spirit wants us to live, and we are here to live with nature as her people. We have had no difficulties obtaining food. We hunt for meat and fish. The people eat whatever they wish to consume. If they want to eat fish, all they do is go down to the river and get it. And these are some of the reasons why they will not return to Hobbema. We shall never return to the reserve![19]

CHAPTER 11

The Kootenay Plains

GAPS IN THE TREATY

The David Thompson Highway that was eventually to run right through Smallboy's winter campsite is named after the greatest cartographer ever to map the North American continent. At the end of the eighteenth century, David Thompson spent a great deal of time calculating the height of mountains and tracing the routes of rivers to their sources. He created the first detailed maps of the Red Deer, North Saskatchewan, Brazeau, and Athabasca rivers, and he understood more than anyone the vastness of the land.[1] Seventy years later, much of the land he mapped in the North-West Territories would be appropriated by the Crown under Treaty Six. However, a significant strip of land mapped by Thompson east of the Continental Divide was not so appropriated. The Kootenay Plains were the southern part of this strip that was not already occupied by Jasper National Park and Banff National Park—all of which Smallboy claimed as "Indian land."

The Kootenay Plains and the Bighorn Wildland, as well as a substantial chunk of what is now the national parks, had not been included in Treaty Six or Treaty Seven when they were signed in 1876 and 1877. The land in question was included in Treaty Eight only as an afterthought, without consultation with the Cree, Stoney, and Peigan tribes who had hitherto occupied the Kootenay Plains and who traditionally regarded the Plains as sacred. This was the land that Chief Smallboy and his camp chose to occupy in 1968. He stated his position unequivocally: "In the Treaty our chiefs surrendered most of our lands. But the Rocky Mountains were never surrendered by treaty. The White Man now desires to take those lands which we did not surrender."[2]

Smallboy clearly believed there had not been a meeting of minds between the Indians and the Queen's representatives who signed the treaties: the negotiators had deliberately and specifically excluded the Rocky Mountains from the treaty because they were recognized as being Indian land.[3] And as for Treaty Eight, the northern tribes who were signatory to that treaty—the Slave, Chipewyan, Beaver, and Swampy Cree—had never occupied the Kootenay Plains, had never expressed an interest in it, and therefore had no right to bargain it away. In any case, the bulk of the land covered by Treaty Eight was geographically remote, cut off from the Kootenay Plains and the White Goat Wilderness area by Jasper National Park, which itself was Indian land since it had never been properly ceded to the Crown by its inhabitants.

It is clear that Lieutenant-Governor Alexander Morris and the Indian commissioners representing the Crown did not include most of the Rocky Mountains in Treaty Six, opting for a boundary following the eastern range of the Rockies rather than the more westerly Continental Divide. The best argument in favour of Smallboy's claim of the panhandle for the Indians was that, in 1876 and 1877, Morris and the commissioners undoubtedly had at hand Thompson's maps of the territory. They must have known that the boundary following the eastern range of mountains left a considerable tract of land outside the treaty. Therefore the omission of the land from Treaty Six in 1876 could not have been accidental. Nor was it a question of ignorance, which in any case would have been no excuse.

There is no question that the Kootenay Plains had been occupied by successive tribes of Indians long before the signing of any of the treaties—as attested to in the diary entries of several explorers, including David Thompson himself.[4] Fur trader Alexander Henry reported in November 1810:

It seems Thompson and his hunting party had a run-in with Peigans west of the Little Red Deer River and had had to stay some time in one of the Indian camps before crossing the Saskatchewan. So they missed the brigade, and then got chased by hostiles from the [Peigan] camp at the bend. They lost them on the Brazeau. Thompson stayed there while Cousin Will came back to the Saskatchewan where he met the brigade going up again.

I went to find Thompson, and persuaded him, since the Indians were so hostile here, to go on north and try crossing by the Athabasca pass, which is outside Peigan territory. I came back to arrange to have horses sent up to transfer the goods across country to where he waited, and by now he is on his way through that miserable muskeg country north of the Brazeau River.[5]

That "miserable muskeg country north of the Brazeau" was just a couple of miles down the road from the present location of the Smallboy Camp.

According to the fur trader William Henry, Thompson was uncharacteristically "spooked" by the Indians when he trespassed on the Kootenay Plains in 1810, territory on which he knew he was not welcome even by otherwise friendly tribes:

> Before sunrise the next morning we set off across country as fast as the horses could go though when we reached the Brazeau the fallen timbers slowed us greatly. The new snow would cover our tracks but I was greatly puzzled, for this wasn't like Mr. Thompson, running from the Indians. He had outfaced them many times; he understood their ways, had always got on with them and had good friends among their chiefs. Yet now he was determined to hide along this river.[6]

Thompson told Alexander Henry (cousin to William Henry and also a fur trader) that the Howse Pass route west of the Kootenay Plains was "impractical since the Peigans would always harass and prevent our passage."[7] He made it clear that this strip of land was occupied by various Indian tribes, who fought savagely to keep it in their control. Although up to that time he had enlisted the aid of the Peigans under Chief *Kootenay Apee*, his trespassing on the sacred Indian land of the Kootenay Plains had not been appreciated.

The Indians present at Fort Carlton and Fort Pitt would have been told that the land they were ceding did not include the mountains, but started at the eastern range of the Rockies. On that basis, they signed the treaty. Had Alexander Morris and the commissioners—or their advisers—included the land farther west, they may have had more difficulty obtaining the compliance of representatives of the First Nations who considered the mountains to be their sacred places.

NONCOMMUNICATION

Quite apart from the omission of this disputed strip of land from Treaty Six, Smallboy claimed that there was no "meeting of the minds" between the Indian chiefs and elders who had signed Treaty Six (including Ermineskin, Bobtail, Coyote, and eventually Big Bear) and the Queen's representatives. He and his descendants insisted that the First Nations who concluded treaties with Canada had a language that extended beyond words or names, including symbols, rituals, and metaphors that were universally understood among Indians without the need for written words, but which were all but ignored by the white negotiators. The

Queen's representatives simply were not educated in or aware of these nuances, and the interpreters—especially interpreters of the cloth—rarely bothered to enlighten the emissaries since, from their point of view, the rituals smacked of paganism and idolatry, to which they were compelled by religious beliefs and assumptions to close both their eyes and minds.

At the original treaty negotiations with Morris in 1876, the Métis interpreters were so concerned with translating every uttered word that they consistently failed to indicate the significance of component parts of physical symbols, rituals, and seemingly obscure metaphors that were equally a part of the communication of the chiefs. This symbolic language was understood by every Indian present, but not by Lieutenant-Governor Morris. Most significantly of all, where treaties were concerned, was the "dance of the pipestem," culminating in the smoking of the peace pipe—the best articulated speech of all. During the negotiations of Treaty Six, the gathered Indians performed an elaborate pipestem ritual at Fort Carlton on the first day of treaty talks (18 August 1876, four days after the commission had arrived), as described by the secretary to the Treaties Commission, A. G. Jackes, MD:

> In about half an hour they were ready to advance and meet the Governor; this they did in a large semi-circle; in their front were about twenty braves on horseback, galloping about in circles, shouting, singing and going through various picturesque performances. The semi-circle steadily advanced until within fifty yards of the Governor's tent, when a halt was made and further peculiar ceremonies commenced, the most remarkable of which was the "dance of the stem." This was commenced by the Chiefs, medicine men, councilors, singers and drum-beaters, coming a little to the front and seating themselves on blankets and robes spread before them. The bearer of the stem..., carrying in his hand a large and gorgeously adorned pipe stem, walked slowly along the semi-circle, and advancing to the front, raised the stem to the heavens, then slowly turned to the north, south, east and west, presenting the stem at each point; returning to the seated group he handed the stem to one of the young men, who commenced a low chant, at the same time performing a ceremonial dance accompanied by the drums and singing of the men and women in the background.
>
> This was all repeated by another of the young men, after which the horsemen again commenced galloping in circles, the whole body slowly advancing. As they approached his tent, the Governor, accompanied by the Hon. W. J. Christie and Hon. Jas. McKay, Commissioners, went forward to meet them and receive the stem carried by its bearer. It was presented first to the Governor, who in accordance with their customs, stroked it several times, then passed it to the Commissioners who repeated the ceremony.

The significance of this ceremony is that the Governor and Commissioners accepted the friendship of the tribe.[8]

Although fifty-two chiefs and councillors signed Treaty Six at Fort Carlton on 23 August, there is no evidence that the white observers had any comprehension whatsoever of the significance of the elaborate pipestem ceremony to the assembled Indians. To Dr. Jackes, the most significant part of it was not the ritual itself, but the "stroking" of the pipestem by the white officials, by which, from their narrow point of view, they indicated their acceptance of the obvious friendship of the tribe. But neither the governor nor the commissioners had actually smoked the pipe. Therefore, due recognition had not been given to the essence of the pipestem, from the Indian point of view: to "our belief systems, our religious and social values, our laws, our way of life."[9]

The consensus among the chiefs of the First Nations who had not yet signed Treaty Six seemed to be that they had to try harder to get the message across to the representatives of the Queen. Therefore, they quadrupled their efforts. On 7 September, at Fort Pitt, according to the lieutenant-governor, "The Indians approached with much pomp and ceremony, following the lead of Sweet Grass." Morris reported:

> The stem dance was performed as at Fort Carlton, but with much more ceremony, there being four pipes instead of one, and the number of riders, singers and dancers being more numerous. After the pipes were stroked by the Commissioners, they were presented to each of them to be smoked, and then laid upon the table to be covered with calico and cloth, and returned to their bearers.[10]

As far as the Indians were concerned, the commissioners, by actually smoking the pipes, had indicated their recognition of Indian values represented by the pipe and pipestem. In one gesture, they had agreed in deed, if not in word, to preserve the Indian belief systems, religious and social values, laws, and way of life, to share the land, and to guarantee sustenance for the Indian people.[11]

"The peace pipe that they all smoked, Indian and white, signified to the Indians what we did *not* give up in the treaties," said Marie Smallboy.[12] The interpreters at the Treaty Six negotiations did not explain this or put it into words. This is the part of the treaty that was not translated:

> The stem of the pipe that they all smoked is the road that we walk—the Indian way, our belief systems, our religious and social values, our laws, our way of life. We did not give them up.

The bowl of the pipe is usually made of rock or stone. It represents the land and everything on it. It was *there*. But just because it was *there* does not mean that it was ours to give away. The land does not belong to anyone. Just because it is not ours to give away does not mean that it is yours to take. We did not give it up.

The tobacco in the bowl represents the people. Smoking the tobacco is a prayer for sustenance for whatever is needed for continued life. That is what *Keskayo* was bargaining for at Blackfoot Crossing. For whatever was needed for continued life. We did not agree to give up our way of life. We did not agree to give up our land. We did not agree to sell our souls.

Every pipe speaks of what we did not give up. We know where we belong.[13]

Following the smoking of the four peace pipes at Fort Pitt on 7 September 1876, Morris, at the request of Sweet Grass, proceeded to set out all the terms of the treaty, as he understood them, a process that lasted for three hours. The collected Indians listened politely, but over the next two days, continued to raise questions. Only twenty-nine chiefs and councillors signed the treaty on 9 September. Conspicuously absent from the negotiations were Bobtail (named "Short Tail" by the lieutenant-governor) and Big Bear (named "Great Bear"), who came a day too late.

When he did arrive, it was clear that Big Bear was emissary not just for the Plains Cree, but also for the Stoneys, who traditionally accompanied the Cree in the hunt.[14] Morris put off his scheduled departure until the following day. Then he had another, longer meeting with Big Bear, who was advised by Sweet Grass to sign the treaty: "Say yes and take his hand," Sweet Grass urged him.[15] However, Big Bear stuck by his principles. He would first have to consult with the other Plains chiefs.

THE STONEY CLAIM

According to Chief John Snow, a Stoney, the many chiefs who signed the numbered treaties believed them to be primarily treaties of peace. In *These Mountains Are Our Sacred Places,* he claims they did not understand the notion of legal title, nor was this notion explained to them. "Given the difficulties in translation and the different cultural attitudes toward the use and ownership of land, our forefathers did not realize that they were ceding land to the whiteman for all time," he wrote.[16] This misunderstanding arose because the Canadian government obscured its intentions with outright lies. As Harold Cardinal remarked in 1969:

By and large, the articles of all written treaties between the Indians of Canada and the government of Canada must be considered misleading because they omitted substantial portions of what was promised verbally to the Indian. Additionally, they carry key phrases that are not precise, or they state that certain things were ceded that, in actual fact, were never considered or granted by the Indians who signed the treaties.[17]

In addressing Bobtail and the other Cree delegates present at Blackfoot Crossing in 1877 for the signing of Treaty Seven and an adhesion to Treaty Six, the lieutenant-governor was asked by Chief Bobtail and the other chiefs as to the real meaning of the proposal. According to one witness—the mother of Peter Wesley, who had lived on the Kootenay Plains for most of his life—the lieutenant-governor told them, simply:

> To make peace between us. We will have friendship when and where ever we meet. I am asking you to put your rifle down in exchange for a peace treaty. The money I am just about to give you is for this purpose. Not to kill each other. And furthermore I am not going to take over your land, but I am willing to pay you money if you put down your rifle and make peace with me. This is what I mean.[18]

Wesley's mother, who like Chief Smallboy's mother was in attendance at Blackfoot Crossing, insisted that this was the whole of the answer given by the lieutenant-governor. "Nothing besides peace-making was talked about," she avowed. Peter Wesley said that his mother "talked and understood Cree very well. That was why my mother understood all the conversations held between the Governor and the Chiefs."[19] Chief Snow added:

> If my forefathers had known what all this would mean to our people: the disappearance of the buffalo and diminishing of other game, the restrictive game laws, the plowing and fencing off of all the lands, more whiteman's diseases, attacks on our religion, culture, and way of life, the continual eroding of our other treaty rights; if they could have foreseen the creation of provincial parks, natural areas, wilderness areas, the building of dams and the flooding of our traditional hunting areas, they would never have signed Treaty Seven.[20]

And Bobtail might never have signed the adhesion to Treaty Six. Yet the consequences of not doing so would have been dire, as Big Bear eventually discovered when his entire band nearly starved to death in 1882.

The Earl of Dufferin, then the governor general of Canada, recognized the original right of Indians to the land in the absence of a treaty:

No government, whether provincial or central, has failed to acknowledge that the original title to the land existed in the Indian tribes and communities that hunted or wandered over them. Before we touch an acre we make a treaty with the chiefs representing the bands we are dealing with, and having agreed upon and paid the stipulated price, oftentimes arrived at after a great deal of haggling and difficulty, we enter into possession, but not until then do we consider that we are entitled to deal with an acre.[21]

Years later, in *These Mountains Are Our Sacred Places*, Chief Snow, as chief of the Wesley Band, presented a very strong argument demonstrating that the Kootenay Plains had traditionally been First Nations hunting grounds. He suggested that the inclusion of the panhandle of land in Treaty Eight was a deceit that should be undone. Snow also demonstrated that in 1909, the Department of Indian Affairs recommended that 23,680 acres of the Kootenay Plains be applied for on behalf of the Stoney Indians. The superintendent general of Indian Affairs put this proposal to the minister of the Interior, who had "signified his willingness to consent to the setting apart of such additional lands as may properly be reserved for these Indians."[22] Yet in 1939, the general superintendent of Agencies wrote to his colleague in the Reserves and Trusts Division:

I personally know that there would be absolutely no chance of getting a Reserve set aside for these Indians by the provincial Government, although very anxious to get them out of that district. The Indians refuse to move, and I would advise that the matter be left in abeyance as long as possible. The moment we start asking for a reserve for them, we will be starting something which we will never be able to finish. I have told the Provincial Government repeatedly that we could not move the Indians out of the district, as they have lived there so long.[23]

The Stoneys were granted a 5,000-acre reserve in 1947, despite the fact that the superintendent had stated that he "would not recommend an area as small as 5,000 acres because it would mean the starving out of these people in a very limited time."[24]

Peter Wesley, later known as "Moosekiller," was the first Stoney to lead an Indian band to the Kootenay Plains at the end of the nineteenth century.[25] When he left Morley, Wesley told the Indian agent:

My children are hungry; they cry in the night. My young men have empty stomachs and there is no meat in my camp. So I and mine go back to the Kootenay Plains. There we shall have meat and the children shall grow fat and happy. Grass grows there for our horses and no snow lies there in the winter.[26]

Wesley and his relatives and the Abraham family, after whom Abraham Lake is named, were the only First Nations people inhabiting the Kootenay Plains at the time Treaty Eight was signed, yet nobody in the families or connected with them was ever consulted.

By the time Chief Smallboy arrived on the Kootenay Plains in 1968, Stoney Indians had been living there continuously for more than seventy years, since before Bobtail Smallboy was born. This is why the Cree honoured the Stoney request to vacate the Kootenay Plains proper and move to the Brazeau River, one hundred kilometres to the north.

TRUDEAU'S "WHITE" PAPER

In Ottawa in 1969, Prime Minister Pierre Trudeau had no inkling of what was going on in the new Smallboy Camp, and the people in the Smallboy Camp had not the slightest interest or concern in what was going on in Ottawa. Yet the two geographically and culturally remote leaders—Trudeau and Smallboy—were on a collision course. Already the Liberal government had been toying with the idea of phasing out the reserve system, a move that would ostensibly allow the Indian to join the ranks of mainstream Canadian society as part of the "cultural mosaic" that was thought to define Canada, in contrast to the American "melting pot."

While Trudeau's intentions might have been honourable, he found as much opposition to the idea from among the Indian tribes as he did from among the general population. Over the next year, he attempted to defend the position of his ironically named "White Paper." But finally, with mounting pressure from Indian chiefs, such as Smallboy, he was forced to abandon his plan for assimilation of the Indian.[27]

Trudeau outlined the highlights of his proposed policy in a speech given in Vancouver on 8 August 1969:

> I think Canadians are not too proud about their past in the way in which they treated the Indian population of Canada and I don't think we have very great cause to be proud.
>
> We have set the Indians apart as a race. We've set them apart in our laws. We've set them apart in the ways the governments will deal with them. They're not citizens of the province as the rest of us are. They are wards of the federal government. They get their services from the federal government rather than from the provincial or municipal governments. They have

been set apart in law. They have been set apart in the relations with government and they've been set apart socially too.

So this year we came up with a proposal. It's a policy paper on the Indian problem. It proposes a set of solutions. It doesn't impose them on anybody. It proposes them—not only to the Indians but to all Canadians.

This is a difficult choice. It must be a very agonizing choice to the Indian peoples themselves because, on the one hand, they realize that if they come into the society as total citizens they will be equal under the law, but they risk losing certain of their basic rights and this is a very difficult choice for them to make... .

One of the things the Indian bands often refer to are their aboriginal rights, and in our policy, the way we propose it, we say we won't recognize aboriginal rights. We will recognize treaty rights. We will recognize forms of contract which have been made with the Indian people by the Crown and we will try to bring justice in that area and this will mean that perhaps the treaties shouldn't go on forever... . But I don't think that we should encourage the Indians to feel that their treaties should last forever within Canada so that they be able to receive their twine or their gun powder. They should become Canadians.

Aboriginal rights, this really means saying, "We were here before you. You came and you took the land from us and perhaps you cheated us by giving us some worthless things in return for vast expanses of land and we want to re-open this question. We want you to preserve our aboriginal rights and to restore them to us." And our answer—it may not be the right one and may not be one which is accepted but it will be up to all of you people to make your minds up and to choose for or against it and to discuss with the Indians—our answer is "no."[28]

Obviously, neither Trudeau nor the bureaucrats in Ottawa drawing up the White Paper had any inkling of the pain and suffering Smallboy's grandfathers in both Canada and the United States had endured for decades in attempting to secure relatively tiny reservations in Montana and Alberta; otherwise they would not have considered such a cavalier proposal.

Smallboy objected to Trudeau's grand plan. He recognized that it would grant Indians permission to sell off their reserve land over a long period of time. Smallboy believed that this would lead to exploitation. What he wanted was more reserve land, not less. When he had asked the provincial government and Indian Affairs about obtaining more land in the unarable foothills, the government had mockingly told Smallboy that the Indians in his band could trade the arable land of Hobbema for land in the foothills acre for acre—a disdainful suggestion that underrated

Smallboy's own successful farming knowledge. Now, the federal government was showing its true colours: it had intended to phase out the reserve system altogether.

Chief Smallboy pointed out the unfairness of the Trudeau plan from four different vantage points. First, he said, many Indians on the reserve had nothing, neither land nor money. Second, should the reserves be abolished, the Indian would be exploited by the white man and Indians would have to live according to the values of white society. If experience was any guide, he said, the Indian would not be given work in the larger Canadian society simply because he was Indian. Third, no matter how much the Indian may feel committed to hanging on to his land, every person eventually had his price: "A person who is desperate will do anything to survive; he will not consider it to be a difficult decision to sell his land."[29] Fourth, the Indian would be subject to the same laws as the white man when it came to the disposition of land, and the white man, who understands his own systems better than the Indian does, would be at a legal advantage. The "freedom" to move to the towns or cities is no freedom at all, Smallboy said.

> "Oh, I can go here, I can go there," they will say; but that is when they will have engineered their own downfall. Everything will be made difficult from that point on. There would be confusion and suffering—that's what would happen to the Indian first. There would be ways to force the Indian to look at his land and look on it as a burden; and finally he will be moved to sell all his land. And that is the goal of the white man—the goal he started towards a long time ago.[30]

Smallboy's own goals were far more important than sniping at his potential nemesis in Ottawa. Over the next decade and a half, all manner of Cree rituals were revitalized at the Smallboy Camp and on the nearby Kootenay Plains. Ritual sites abounded. Indians from all over North America visited Chief Smallboy and Lazarus Roan for guidance on how to perform the rituals they had already forgotten. A similar process had gone on at the Rocky Boy Reservation, as has been well documented by Verne Dusenberry.[31] Smallboy was now able to draw on the traditions preserved at Rocky Boy to provide a forum that would revitalize the pursuit of freedom for the First Nations and the resurrection of Native customs across the continent. From a First Nations standpoint, that was Smallboy's greatest and most enduring accomplishment.

CHAPTER 12

A Proposal to the Queen

THE SUBMISSION TO THE QUEEN

In February 1971, as part of a more generalized plan to secure permanency for the freedom they had obtained with the establishment of their camp, the Smallboy Band tried to obtain title to a large parcel of land in the forest reserve between the Cardinal and Brazeau rivers. But their situation remained tenuous, because as far as the provincial government was concerned, they remained squatters who were contravening provincial law. As long as they had been gainfully employed clearing the land west of the dam site, no questions had been asked. But now, the project was nearing completion and Chief Smallboy wanted assurance from the provincial government that they could receive a portion of Crown land for their own use. When all his efforts to obtain additional reserve land in the mountains had failed, Smallboy approach Queen Elizabeth II through the provincial government in an eloquent submission delivered on 18 February:

> May it please Your Majesty:
>
> We bring you greetings from the Indian people camped on the Kootenay Plains.... Through this submission we would make you aware of the status, condition and needs of my people.
>
> Camped on the Kootenay Plains, we are one hundred and eighteen men, women and children; we are nineteen families yet we are like one family.

It is the will of my people to present this proposal to the Governments of Alberta and Canada so that they may know the reasons for our actions.

We invite your various governments to develop new perspectives and to support our initiatives in dealing with what has come to be called "The Indian Problem."

We challenge you to depart from the "safe" paths of the parliamentary process, as is sometimes necessary to provide leadership in breaking new trails to better the human condition.

We ask that your governments recognize that we speak only for our group and that we do not wish to jeopardize or abrogate the rights and privileges of other Indian people.

We realize that some people in government do not agree with what we have done nor with what we propose to do. We realize the path our group has chosen may not be the best way for all other native people. But for our group it is the best way.[1]

The submission went on to outline the recent history of the Ermineskin Band leading up to the exodus and the band's plans for the future. "We must acquire land so that our way of life will be secure and stable, so that our people will not be forced into a series of endless moves," Smallboy wrote. "We have lived in tents all this time, but our people would like to build their own log houses and work hard to make of the land a good home for all. Our people are not lazy; nor do they fear sacrifice. We know we can do most things for ourselves, but we must have land."[2] He went on to list fourteen points "which must be covered if we are to acquire land on meaningful terms to our way of life":

1) We would like to own the land, but we realize that since we have made this request of the province this may not be possible, and we would therefore try to negotiate a long-term lease for use of the land.

2) It must be understood by both governments that we left the Hobbema Reserve for good and will never return there to live.

3) When we obtain our land we promise, as men of honour, never to ask for any more in the near future.

4) Though we have left the reservation we wish to retain our status as Treaty Indians so as to obtain the social, economic and educational assistance that is our right prepaid by our forefathers when they ceded the land under Treaty. Further, we do not wish to prejudice or jeopardize the rights and privileges of our people who wish to remain as inhabitants on Indian Reserve Lands.

5) Any rentals or taxes payable on the land requested are the responsibility of the Department of Indian Affairs.

6) Any claims or counter-claims between ourselves and the Hobbema Reserve will be dealt with as a local matter.

7) Education will be made available to our children, as is their right, but our councils will exercise greater control over our children's education than the Department of Indian Affairs has allowed us in the past.

8) We will assist in building our own school and our ceremonial lodges.

9) A power plant will be set up to furnish power, but only if power is a requirement for accredited educational facilities.

10) We will live together as a community, but a few of us will continue to raise livestock; so we will also need to grow hay and feed grain.

11) Our present community will establish itself first in our new area; any others who do not live with us now can join us at their own discretion and will be considered permanent residents only when they have proved themselves as stable assets in the community.

12) We will organize ourselves so that no problems will arise during our move once we have a commitment from the Government.

13) As Treaty Indians we feel we should be free to hunt game outside of Provincial Parks just for our consumption. We are also willing to cooperate with Provincial Game Authorities to protect the environment and game in our new area.

14) We do not believe in living on welfare; some of our members will work on occasional jobs wherever they can, and others will carry out some of our plans for development in guiding and outfitting, handicrafts and woodwork.[3]

He and his followers had been living, he said, as Indians had always lived—close to nature. "Our ancestors who lived this way were strong and healthy," he said, and so far returning to the traditional way of life was working out for the band.

A PETITION TO THE PROVINCE

Chief Smallboy complemented his submission to the Queen with a petition to the Alberta government, and he invited both the Government of Canada and the Government of the Province of Alberta to participate in "a process of cultural and spiritual revitalization by and among the original People of the Province of Alberta." He told Premier Harry Strom what Chief John Snow had already told him: that the Indian people collectively had been "virtually destroyed as a cultural identity, with tragic results for the individual."[4] But where Chief Snow had told Strom that the Alberta government was contributing to the problem by clearing and flooding Indian land without consultation, Chief Smallboy took a different tack.

His people living on the Kootenay Plains, he said, had been able to re-establish their ties to "the Mother Earth and the Supreme Being" by living their lives as the Great Spirit had intended man to live:

> It is the will of the Great Spirit that all men, all His children all over the universe, live as brothers and in harmony with their surroundings if they are to survive. The law of the Great Spirit is the same law that governs all His love, for any one man is no greater than his love for any other man, no matter what his ancestry or his place of origin.[5]

Commitment to Indian beliefs had caused his band to give up their homes and physical comforts in order to get back to Mother Earth and be one with the Creator, the Chief said. The preservation of this religion and way of life was deeply rooted in the land:

> On this land we will live as our Creator intended us to live; on this land we will raise our children in a proper manner; on this land we wish to return to our Creator, for our Creator has willed that we return to this land. It is the will of the Great Spirit that we preserve our identity as a people, to carry out our way of life and preserve our values and the heritage of our forefathers who were one with this land we love and were one with the Supreme Being. These basic rights of our people will be safeguarded only when we return to land we consider sacred.
>
> Here we can commune with the Supreme Being and teach our children the rich heritage which is rightfully theirs. Here on this land we will not tear the vegetation from the soil and pollute the earth. We respect the handiwork of the Supreme Being. Here we will not poison the lifegiving waters. We respect our font of life. Here we will not poison the air we and all living creatures breathe. We respect this source of life. Here we will not destroy your living creatures. We respect all life. Here we will not destroy our fellow man, degrade his race, destroy his heritage, defile his religion, deny his basic fundamental freedom. We respect these rights and always have respected these rights.
>
> Here we will be the guardians and protectors of this land returned to our trust. Here we can maintain our pride and dignity as a people whose origins are a part of this country. Here, we can set an example for our race—and for the rest of humanity.[6]

This was high-sounding rhetoric, and some of it was downright untrue, especially the bit about not destroying living creatures: the whole point in moving to the west country was to live off the land, including hunting and fishing. Part of the petition took unsubtle aim at what the dominant culture had done to the Indian: nobody could deny that white society had degraded the Indian, destroyed his heritage, defiled his religion, and denied his basic fundamental freedoms.

A PRAYER TO THE PREMIER

Chief Smallboy's main message was delivered on Friday, 26 February 1971, at the Third Annual Premier's Prayer Breakfast, which terminated a rather convoluted intergovernmental meeting attended by provincial, federal, and First Nations officials. Smallboy had been joined by Lazarus Roan, Eugene Steinhauer, Michael Steinhauer, and Harold Cardinal—all of whom supported the Chief in the establishment of the new Smallboy Band and equally supported the notion of establishing an additional reserve in the foothills. Eugene Steinhauer interpreted Chief Smallboy's verbal address, which he delivered impromptu as a supplement to the written submission to the Queen and petition to the province. "We have come all the way from the mountains to come here to make this proposal," he said, outlining what he wanted to discuss at the prayer breakfast: 1) the land question, 2) education for the children, 3) the maintenance of First Nations culture, including hunting and trapping, 4) the economy, 5) land use, and 6) transportation development, including construction of a road and a bridge.

The land question, he recognized, was one that would take time to resolve. But he made clear that education was as much a priority for him and his band as it was for the white man:

> The first thing I would like to talk about, which the white man takes as a priority in all cases, is education. We did not reject education. We still do not reject it. We would like to have our children taught right on their own home grounds where we live, and we want our kids to have the basic requirements in education—to learn how to read and how to count and how to write and talk English, so that they can get along in the world as it is. We also suggest that we have control of the curriculum that goes with the education of our children, and control of the administration itself and how the school should be run and managed. However, I would expect the white man to provide the facilities so that the school, or education, will be able to function efficiently. I say this because we have not the financial resources to take care of education requirements—we have not got the money that is necessary.[7]

Smallboy said his band wanted to maintain their culture and livelihood as Indian people "by hunting the animals that presently exist in the mountains," even though "we realize that trapping and selling of furs is rapidly deteriorating and there is not much economic benefit that can be obtained from that."[8] He asked that the land be protected, yet

> we would not like the white man to exploit the land itself, or to use it as a game area, or a park area, for the purpose of benefiting the affluent society. Rather, we would like to obtain this land area ourselves. We, as Indians, would like to have this land open to us at all times, permanently. The reason why I am saying this is because we have seen that the white man commercializes everything that he does as far as trying to protect nature is concerned, and this could happen over there too.[9]

He said that the band had found enough standing timber in the area to maintain an economic livelihood. "Some of the younger generation are talking about raising livestock, and the land over there is fit for growing hay and raising green-feed which would supply enough feed for the livestock."[10] He also stated his expectation that a road would be built, including a bridge if necessary, because "sometimes we run into difficulties as human beings. Sometimes it is necessary to get someone to a hospital almost immediately and this is why we would need a road."[11]

THE RESPONSE

Despite Smallboy's eloquence, the federal and provincial officials in attendance at the prayer meeting did not feel the same way. Unfortunately, the timing was all wrong. For one thing, the Stoneys led by Chief John Snow were clamouring to get exactly the same land for their own purposes and were complaining that construction of the Bighorn Dam had ruined the hunting habitat, rendering it all but unusable. If the Stoneys could not make a go of it, after living for most of the century on the Kootenay Plains, how could Chief Smallboy's band succeed? For another, Prime Minister Trudeau's White Paper on the reserve system had received major flak from several of the Indians present, including Smallboy, who suspected the government of giving Indians the right to sell their reserve lands so that the government could buy the reserves out from under them, thereby forcing the Indians to integrate with the larger Canadian society. This short-sighted view, Smallboy believed, would condemn Indians to ghettoized life in Canada's major cities. Furthermore, the Trudeau government was still smarting from the country's reaction to the imposition of the War Measures Act in October 1970 and wanted to avoid issues that might tarnish its reputation for arbitrariness even more.

Alberta's Premier Strom was in an even less enviable position, for the Big Blue Tory Machine, led by Peter Lougheed, which was eventually to rout Strom's Social Credit Party, was already moving into high gear for the provincial election. Provincial officials wanted to play it safe in an election year. Any agreement with Chief Smallboy could become a major campaign issue very quickly, especially if it was perceived that Strom had been playing off one side against the other in the war of words between the Stoneys and the Cree over living in and hunting on the sacrosanct Kootenay Plains. Smallboy used the same wording about the mountains being sacred places as did Chief John Snow six years later with the publication of his book *These Mountains Are Our Sacred Places.* "It is the will of the Great spirit that we preserve our identity as a people, to carry out our way of life and preserve our values and the heritage of our forefathers who were one with this land we love and were one with the Supreme Being," Smallboy said. "These basic rights of our people will be safeguarded only when we return to land we consider sacred."[12]

Several Indians came forward with testimonials in Chief Smallboy's favour, including Ralph Steinhauer, the cousin of Eugene Steinhauer, soon to become Alberta's first Aboriginal lieutenant-governor. At a time of personal crisis, Ralph had turned to Chief Smallboy and his band for social and spiritual guidance. "I take this request very seriously and I support it very seriously," he said of Smallboy's attempt to acquire the land upon which his camp now stood, "because if more people like myself can use the facility that they have—the guidance that they can give to our people—and return back to our communities and be able to help our own people, then they are doing a service not only to the native people, but to all others that have to live with native people." Steinhauer claimed to have gained from Chief Smallboy "an identity which I will never lose, and which I am not afraid to profess at any time or place—of being an Indian first. I am proud of this, and what has given me this pride is the effort of these people. It is through them that I have regained this."[13]

Harold Cardinal explained that the Smallboy request had nothing to do with the actual treaty claims that had not been settled; rather, it was a matter of acquiring sacred ground "where they can practice and develop their religion."[14] Eugene Steinhauer, who had translated Smallboy's speech and submission, agreed with Cardinal that the land that Chief Smallboy had requested was indeed considered sacred.

The question of land use on the Kootenay Plains was already on the agenda for the All Chiefs Conference later in the year, and it was the subject of a position paper drafted by the Treaty and Aboriginal Rights Program, of which Chief John Snow was then director of research. The organization protested proposed provincial legislation that would have

banned hunting on Crown lands without any consideration for First
Nations traditional hunting rights:

> The government is well aware of the fact that the Indians consider certain
> areas of crown land to have religious significance. These areas are holy
> grounds where we Indians can go to communicate with the Great Spirit.
> We hold special pow-wows, dances, and most of all, Sun Dance ceremonies
> in these areas. The government knows about these facts.[15]

Lazarus Roan, always the practical one of the triumvirate at the Smallboy
Camp, avowed that the camp would not become a refuge for undesirable
social types who could have a harmful influence on the children, but would
rather serve people like Mike Steinhauer, who recognized that they had
problems of a social or spiritual nature that they wanted to overcome. The
sacred grounds were perfect for this type of therapy, he said.[16]

Nonetheless, neither the provincial nor federal government officials
seemed impressed with Chief Smallboy's proposal. This wasn't surprising,
in that most of the people representing the governments were bureaucrats
without decision-making power. Those who had such power did not want
to assume responsibility for paying for the roads or educating the children. The Smallboy Camp had already moved half a dozen times since the
summer of 1968. What guarantee would there be that the Smallboy Band
would not move again in the future?

"You have my word," Chief Smallboy responded simply. "I shall die
there."[17]

Other officials questioned the consistency of Smallboy's desire to build
a road, keep livestock, and develop a sawmill when the reason for leaving
their present location close to the North Saskatchewan was ostensibly to
escape the encroachment of civilization in the first place. Lazarus Roan
responded that the livestock and sawmill would be one way of their
becoming self-sufficient in a manner consistent with the Cree tradition
of living off the land; both would be used for internal consumption, not
for profit.

Frustrated by what he regarded as government stonewalling, once
again, Chief Smallboy himself had the final word. "If the land is not
granted to my people, I shall be moving my camp to that area anyway," he
said.[18] And that's exactly what he did.

That statement, vintage Smallboy in its honesty and bluntness, probably put the nail in the coffin of provincial co-operation from the Strom
government. Symptomatic of political reaction against Chief Smallboy's
position was a law passed in the provincial legislature in May 1971 prohibiting public camping on Crown land for more than thirty days. An

amendment to the legislation that would have excluded Indian and Métis bands from the thirty-day limit was defeated, giving the province the legal right to remove Chief Smallboy and his band by force.

But Smallboy refused to budge. "If they come for me and tell me to leave," he said, "I will do as my grandfather would have done. They can put a rope around my neck but I will not move from this land!"[19] Then he added in a more subdued tone:

> We have a natural love for this piece of land. When the buffalo still existed, our forefathers always chose this land. The Indians could make a living from this land. When Queen Victoria came asking for land for her people, the Indians, having a kind heart, gave it. Now we are asking for the same thing. If there was any kindness, we would be given the land we are asking for.[20]

This was parallel to the perception of Chief John Snow, who wrote:

> My people were hospitable and generous and shared what we had with the newcomers. We were quite prepared to share the land as well. Despite the fact that many of them arrived preaching the Christian virtues of brotherhood and understanding and Christian emphasis on spiritual things over material things, their actions proved that what they wanted was to own and control the land and to control the minds and actions of my people as well. At least this is the way we Indians have experienced the history of the last centuries.[21]

MOUNTING OPPOSITION

Be that as it may, public opinion had shifted against Chief Smallboy. Lougheed's Progressive Conservative government took office in Edmonton in September 1971, amid mounting pressure to deal with the "squatters" on the Kootenay Plains once and for all. "SMALLBOY NOW A TORIES' HEADACHE," the *Red Deer Advocate* proclaimed in a front-page headline, and on 5 November 1971, the paper published an editorial upbraiding the Conservatives for taking a soft line with Smallboy during their first two months in office:

> What a precedent to set! Can any person or group of persons—of whatever color—squat on Crown land and thereby establish proprietary rights to it? We can think of a lot of sites in the West Country we'd dearly love to possess, land now held in the name of her Majesty for the unhindered enjoyment of all Canadians.... .

If it's said Chief Smallboy's Group comprise a special case, what about all the other people of native blood in this province? Can any of them expand their land holdings simply by moving onto Crown land?

… This is no romantic adventure. It's a case of people taking the law into their own hands and expecting the rest of society to support them while they are doing it… .

If Smallboy and his band really want new land for settlement, then have them do it like any other Canadian: homestead lands are still available (and government aid in financing them).

But give them land merely because they happen to have taken a fancy to it? Bad for them and impossible for society.[22]

Chief Smallboy countered such attacks, which missed the point entirely as far as he was concerned, with increased criticism of the white society that had led him to move his band to the Kootenay Plains in the first place. "We have no desire for anything in Hobbema that we would go back for," he said.

Besides, the white man is not providing the kind of life for our people that we have here. There are many curious white men coming to our camp to see how we live. They feel that everyone should live like the white man in order to get by in this world. But this is not so! We are different, because this is how the Great Spirit wants us to live, and we are here to live with nature as people.[23]

As he had written in his submission to the Queen, journalists in particular "have told lies about us, laughed at us, and even tried to make trouble for us. But we are still here and are now certain that we have done what is right":

We had moved so that changes could be brought about for a better way of life for our families, and to a large degree these changes have come about: the social problems of the reserve have not found their way to our community; our family and community ties are strong; our children and grandchildren are happy; we have recaptured our pride and know what it means to be an Indian; our young men are confident and will learn how to gain respect in the future.

Here we have found peace and quiet within ourselves. Here we feel once again the spiritual essence as well as the material composition of all things. Here we are at once men and children of the Great Spirit, we are at once proud and humble. Here we are at peace and here we are happy. Here is life and the meaning of life.[24]

Life, Smallboy said, is more temporal than the land. He had the future of his children and grandchildren to think about, and the children and grandchildren of those who had opted to travel with him to the Kootenay Plains. The whole point of requesting land in the foothills in the first place was not so the band could benefit economically—if that were the case, he could have continued operating his profitable farm in Hobbema. His goal was to maintain the Indian culture in as pure a manner as possible.

Chief Smallboy claimed once again that the First Nations had never ceded the mountains and the Kootenay Plains to Queen Victoria, so that they were not part of the treaty and remained Indian land. As for the land that had been ceded by treaty, the treaties were only concerned with the topsoil, not with the minerals beneath the ground. The mineral wealth of Alberta belonged to the Indian. The treaties had also been broken in the sense that the Queen's representatives and their successors had not shown the slightest inclination to protect Indian culture and interests. Therefore, the Chief argued, there had been a breach of contract. Finally, the foothills that fell under the treaty remained Indian land because they were not arable. The Queen had only negotiated for arable land for the settlers—not land they could not use. This was a different argument from the one he had used to claim that the Rocky Mountains and the Kootenay Plains were Indian land that had never been ceded in the first place. Now he was attacking the integrity of the whole of Treaty Six, as well.

"It is you who make the laws," Chief Smallboy told government representatives when they tried to persuade him to move off the Crown land,

> and you have made a law that states when you buy something, you must pay, and if you do not pay, then what you bought can be taken from you. All I am doing is taking back some of my land—land which is not being used by anyone—because you have not yet paid in full for what you took.
>
> I am using your law.[25]

Two years earlier, Harold Cardinal had written in *The Unjust Society*: "The white man took what we gave him, and more, but we never received payment. It was planned that way. The truth of the matter is that Canadian Indians simply got swindled. Our forefathers got taken by slick-talking, fork-tongued cheats."[26]

From 1971 until Chief Smallboy's death in 1984, neither government did anything to budge Smallboy or the Smallboy Band from the land he had chosen. He became a passive, immovable object rather than an irresistible force. Even the full weight of government legislation could not prevail against him. Gradually, Native opinion swung behind him, and by 1978, he had become an important influence in Native politics, particularly as one who stood on principle, who doggedly pursued freedom for his people, and who patiently waited for the time when the rights of the First Nations to their sacred land—the Kootenay Plains and the mountains—would be recognized. Native leaders came to Smallboy's camp from far-flung reserves to consult with him, and they pledged support for his cause.[27]

CHAPTER 13

Native Rights and the Constitution

INDIAN LAND

Chief Smallboy's dogged pursuit of freedom for his people entailed defending Native and Aboriginal rights, and he did this by travelling widely, arguing in London and Rome that these rights should be enshrined in the Constitution, which Canada was seeking to patriate from Britain. Closer to home, the pursuit of freedom included protecting hunting and fishing rights, as well as the Smallboy Camp and the fragile and impressionable minds of the young.

After the initial rhetoric had died down and the Social Credit government was soundly defeated by Peter Lougheed's Progressive Conservatives in 1971, the general population of Alberta seemed to remain blithely unaware of what was going on out in the foothills. Albertans revelled in the greatest economic boom of the province's history. Still, Smallboy remained distrustful of a system that had let him down so often. During the 1970s, the focus of the camp remained educating the children with respect to hunting and trapping and treating and tanning hides, teaching traditional cooking, Indian medicine, sewing, beadwork, and the basics of animal husbandry—and storytelling. The children were also taught to honour and respect the elders and to perform the ritual functions of the Indian way.

On a more practical level, the younger members of the band became adept hunters, usually consulting with Chief Smallboy or Lazarus Roan before going off to hunt for bighorn sheep, deer, elk, moose, or black bear, all of which commonly ranged the mountains to the west. Joe Smallboy had enough horses to take hunters on extended trail rides into the mountains, and several members of the band were qualified guides. Others chose to fish. Jackfish and other species of pike were the most common, but other fish abounded in the streams, from dolly varden and brown trout to bass and perch. Smaller animals, of course, were fair game: rabbits, sharptail grouse, spruce grouse, ducks, and geese were common fare. But more often than not, someone would bring steaks or roasts or pork chops or chickens from town, along with a supply of eggs to supplement those laid by the few free-ranging chickens at the camp.

Constitutional rights, including Aboriginal and treaty rights under sections 25 and 35 of the Constitution Act, 1982, including the right to hunt and the right to self-governance (especially in areas not legally ceded by treaty), remains a major issue in Canada. The Smallboy Band has actively sought to obtain standing in litigation against strip-mining operations that threaten to destroy the integrity of the land surrounding their camp, but to little avail, since the Alberta Court of Queen's Bench regards members of the Smallboy Band—at its current location—as being squatters who have no rights. No judicial decision has been made with respect to Smallboy's more important claim that the Kootenay Plains, the Bighorn Wildland, the White Goat Wilderness, and most of Jasper and Banff national parks are Indian land by virtue of the fact that they were never given up to the Canadian government by the Indians who inhabited them and claimed them as sacred lands throughout the nineteenth century—a claim that endures to this day.

FRIENDS OF SMALLBOY

Lazarus Roan, a self-styled philosopher and medicine man of some repute, was better equipped than most to formalize some of the political thoughts expressed by Smallboy in his speeches, and although Smallboy was the primary spokesman for the group, Roan's imprimatur could be seen on many of the position papers emanating from the camp. He usually attended speeches given by Smallboy and was quick with the answers whenever Smallboy appeared lost for words.

Before he died in 1977, Roan taught Indian medicine to those who were eager to learn, including his son Wayne, who became a pre-eminent medicine man in Hobbema when he moved back there in the late 1970s. Similarly, when Simon Omeasoo died, his granddaughter Janet moved to Hobbema and eventually to Calgary to complete her Bachelor of Education degree; she still teaches on the reserve.

Isabelle, who had stood by her son through good times and bad, also died in 1977 at 112 years old. Smallboy alone was left to lead his much-diminished band.[1] At its low ebb in the mid-1970s, the Smallboy Camp dwindled to twenty permanent members.

From Smallboy's standpoint, the most difficult decision he had to make in all the years that he was at the camp near the Brazeau River concerned Leonard Peltier, an American Indian Movement leader accused of murdering two FBI agents, who arrived at the camp in the spring of 1976 and took up residence, briefly, in the teacherage and then with one of the women in the camp. According to Smallboy, the police had been on the lookout for him and asked Smallboy if he had seen him. When Smallboy was noncommittal, the police said they would be back in two days. Smallboy conveyed this message to Peltier, giving him two days' notice to vacate the camp. When he did not do so, Smallboy simply directed the police to the teacherage, where Peltier was arrested. Peltier left a borrowed gun propped up against the teacherage wall, as if he had been expecting to be arrested. Dorothy Smallboy recalled:

> I remember some guys knocking on our door and asking if they could camp across the road. We didn't think anything of it. We lent them a stove. The next thing I knew there were helicopters and police all over the place. I finally went down to the school to see what was going on. I walked in, and there was a constable there. He said the guys were Americans wanted by the police for murder.[2]

The extradition hearing that followed constitutes one of the darkest episodes of Canadian-American diplomatic skullduggery, with the FBI leading suborned evidence to secure Peltier's extradition. Thirty years later, Leonard Peltier remains in custody at Fort Leavenworth, serving two life sentences. Yet had the judge and minister of Justice known that the FBI had deliberately misled them, there is little doubt that Peltier would have avoided extradition on the basis that his alleged crime—not to mention the motivation behind the extradition—was entirely political.

Shortly after this nadir in the life of the camp, Smallboy met Hanne Marstrand, the wife of the influential chairman of Petro Canada, Maurice Strong, a Canadian entrepreneur and adviser to Prime Minister Pierre Trudeau and Governor General Ed Schreyer. Marstrand and Strong became staunch supporters of Smallboy as a visionary who had set up an alternative camp for the lost and destitute. In the following years, they lobbied tirelessly to advance the Chief's agenda, although sometimes without a clear understanding of what that was.

Knowing how he had suffered during the first decade of his inhabiting the Kootenay Plains and points north to claim it for all Indians, Strong nominated the Chief for membership in the Order of Canada, the highest official distinction a Canadian can achieve. He and Marstrand followed up the nomination with accolades from Smallboy's peers and contemporaries, who praised him as a visionary, a warrior, a man of principle, and a bold Indian chief and elder, who had stared adversity in the face, who had rejected the corrupt world, who had presented an alternative universe to those who hovered on the brink of despair—and who had made it all work.

Marstrand credited Smallboy's medicine ceremonies with curing her youngest daughter, Suzanne, of cancer.[3] She set up the International Smallboy-Camp Support Fund and, in 1979, initiated a site investigation study with a view to requesting the federal government to cede a remote part of Jasper National Park, the South Esk, to the Smallboy Band in perpetuity.[4] The study went hand-in-glove with Strong's nomination of Chief Smallboy for the Order of Canada. The land in question fell neatly into the "Treaty Eight panhandle" that remains unresolved as far as Indian treaty rights are concerned.

Thus, by the end of the decade, officialdom was once again trying to track down Chief Smallboy in the backwoods, this time to present him with the country's most prestigious civilian medal. The "immovable object" of the early 1970s had, at the ripe age of eighty-one, become a force to be reckoned with. On 16 April 1980, Chief "Robert" Smallboy ("Bob" simply wasn't proper) was presented with the Order of Canada medal and certificate by Governor General Schreyer—in Ottawa—two decades after his first abortive trip there to ask for more land for his people. This time, Ottawa paid his fare, and the whole town, it seemed, was there to greet him.

Despite the attempt by Marstrand to obtain a small piece of Jasper National Park for the Smallboy Band, Chief Smallboy had staked out as Indian land a much larger chunk of real estate excluded from Treaty Six. So had the Stoney Indians, who traditionally had lived with the Cree for centuries.

The Alberta government did not particularly object to Smallboy living on the land in the Brazeau Valley and in fact made concessions to make sure roads were kept open and health care was provided to those who needed it. The federal government continued to co-operate with the provincial government in providing educational facilities. Indeed, how could any of them object to what Smallboy was doing, now that his efforts had been rewarded with the presentation of the Medal of the Order of Canada? So the Smallboy Band was left to its own devices. This was exactly what the Chief wanted.

AMENDING THE CONSTITUTION

Despite being left on its own, the Smallboy Band was not completely out in the cold where Canadian politics was concerned. Years earlier, Chief

Smallboy had made clear his opposition to Trudeau's White Paper, to the extent that it suggested the abolition of the reserve system. However, he was all in favour of Indian self-governance. He was also very much in favour of enshrining Native rights in the Canadian Constitution.

Having had dealings with Ottawa and finding that not even the Department of Indian Affairs was concerned in any meaningful way about the plight of the Indian, Smallboy was leery about what might happen if the Constitution—the British North America Act, a statute of the United Kingdom—should ever be brought to Canada. How would the Canadian government handle the Constitution once it was here? Was the rest of the Canadian government as incompetent as the bureaucrats he had encountered in Ottawa two decades before?

The Constitution certainly needed an overhaul, as far as Smallboy was concerned, because it did not properly protect Native rights. But how could this be achieved? Smallboy had been told, and believed, that this kind of constitutional change could only be effected by going to Great Britain to attempt to get Westminster to change it.

From the beginning, Canadian Indians were opposed to attempts to "patriate" the Canadian Constitution in the form of the BNA Act, since Native rights were not specifically identified within it. Prime Minister Trudeau, for his part, was concerned that civil liberties and legal rights be enshrined in the Constitution as the Canadian Charter of Rights and Freedoms, which would apply to all governments in Canada and their employees and agencies, whether provincial or federal. Previously, the Canadian Bill of Rights, a federal statute, had applied only to the actions of the federal government, although copycat legislation had been adopted by several of the provinces. Therefore Trudeau requested the British Parliament to pass a new law, the Canada Act, which would transfer the BNA Act and a new Canadian Constitution Act to Canada to form the new Constitution.

Strangely, Smallboy had always felt more allegiance to Great Britain than to Canada.[5] As far as he was concerned, the treaties of the nineteenth century had been made with Queen Victoria, the Queen of the United Kingdom. They had not been made with Canada, whose ignorant bureaucrats had brushed him off in Ottawa and whose Indian agents, from Tom Quinn to Ralph Ragan, had, in his opinion, been abusing and insulting his people since Confederation. Smallboy led a delegation to Europe in November 1981 to hear the decision of the Court of Queen's Bench in an application by the Indian Association of Alberta for judicial review of a decision of the United Kingdom Secretary of State for Foreign and Commonwealth Affairs, made a year earlier, that treaty obligations entered into with the First Nations of Canada were not owed by the

Queen in right of her government in the United Kingdom. The court refused leave, saying that treaty obligations had been transferred from the United Kingdom to Canada and were outside the jurisdiction of a municipal court.[6]

By the time this judgment came down, Smallboy and his delegation had already approached the Bishop of London with their concern about inclusion of Aboriginal rights in the Constitution. On 10 November 1981, the Lord Bishop brought the issue of inclusion of Aboriginal rights to the attention of the House of Lords, as reported in the British *Hansard*:

> *The Lord Bishop of London*: My Lords ... I wish to speak about one aspect of the proposed patriation of the British North America Act 1867; namely the effect that it would have upon the aboriginal peoples of Canada.... We feel that we have a moral obligation to draw attention to the concerns of the indigenous peoples of Canada, whose representatives have consistently relied upon reasoned argument in presenting their claims... .[7]

He said that the "solemn treaties with the British Sovereign" gave the indigenous people "certain rights, including that of self-government."[8] However,

> [t]he representatives of the aboriginal peoples draw attention to the almost total absence of recognition and protection of the rights of aboriginal nations in the proposed constitution. The indigenous people of Canada are asking that their aboriginal, treaty and self-government rights might be entrenched in the proposed Canada Act; that they be accorded full status as delegates at constitutional talks; and that amendments of those sections of the constitution dealing with their rights be made only with their agreement.[9]

The federal government of Canada had declared that "the position of the native peoples will be a matter for discussion once the new constitution is in force," he continued. However, the indigenous peoples expressed fear that without constitutional guarantees in place, "the limited protection they enjoy at present will quickly disappear when proposals to implement general intention are put forward."[10] The Lord Bishop added:

> Apart from their concern for the preservation of their way of life and culture, which they have sought to maintain in the face of very considerable difficulties, for the Indians a treaty is a most solemn matter. It is sacred. It is made by a person to a person, and it carries with it personal obligations; or, in the words, incorporated into the treaties themselves, it is to last "as long as the sun rises, the grasses grow and the rivers flow." I would suggest,

that generally speaking, the world today has something to learn from the obligation which an Indian sees he is bound to by treaty.[11]

Whatever the legal position may be, said the Lord Bishop, "I believe that we must demonstrate by fuller consideration and by a fuller answer that we have the interests of the Indians, the Metis and the Inuits at heart, and it is for this reason that I raise the matter again. I ask your Lordships to accept that we have a moral obligation to do so."[12]

Smallboy had flown to London in time for his eighty-third birthday, but despite his age, he did not pull any punches about his mission. "For thirteen years now," he said, "I have lived in the mountains. I have been requesting from the Government some land where I can live in peace. So far, I have not noticed that they are willing to give me any of my land. I do not disturb anyone, nor do I cause any wrongdoing. But they would rather chase me away."[13] In speech after speech, he pointed out the parallels between England of the nineteenth century and the Indian reserves of today. At the beginning of December 1981, he delivered this short but punchy speech, which gave the British a new perspective on their role in concluding treaties with the Indians:

It is with much gratitude to the Creator that I stand here on this land, where our Treaties originated a long time ago.

The Queen thought well for her people. She saw her land was becoming overpopulated, and she knew more land would be required. So she appointed several of her people to come to us and to make Treaty for our land. The Queen was wise towards her people, and they arrived there asking us for our land.

Then, as today, the Indian had much respect for Mankind. Honest friendship was his way of life and belief. And he knew all things of his land. He was resourceful, and he lived a good life on his land. But he did not consider being stingy. He used a kind-hearted approach to the Queen's people, and it did not take long to answer them.

Our grandfathers knew there was much land, so they shared, rather than keeping survival from their fellow man. Our grandfathers believed in the laws of our Creator. It did not matter that there was a lot to give. Our land was plentiful.

The Indian did not know the white man's ways. The Indian believed the white man would keep his promises forever, and he did not expect the white man ever to turn his back against the Indian.

So the Queen's people came home satisfied, knowing the Queen's wishes were fulfilled.

But now, today, we come to the British for help with what is now a big problem before us. We can see it will cause us many problems. As well, we can see it will bring much hardship for our children in the future. Our Treaties with the Queen are being broken!

Yet I see that the sun still walks across the sky, and in the mountains where I live, I still see the rivers continue to flow. Only those promises they made to us are gone. We look back at what was promised and it looks now that they did not keep their promises for more than a day![14]

TURNING TO RELIGION

Somewhat disheartened by the Court of Queen's Bench decision, yet elevated in spirit at having witnessed the case for the First Nations being advanced in the House of Lords, Chief Smallboy and other Native leaders, including his good friend Albert Lightning of the Samson Band, who had always stood by him through triumphs and defeats, plotted strategy for their trip to continental Europe the following month. This time, the two octogenarians decided, they would shame the Canadian government into enshrining Native rights into the Constitution by appealing to as many religious leaders as possible, including the spiritual leaders of the Islamic, Buddhist, Jewish, Protestant, and Roman Catholic faiths. Smallboy delivered this address to the Islamic community in January 1982:

Long ago—over one hundred years have passed—my great-grandfather, *Keskayo* (Bobtail), signed a treaty with Queen Victoria's representatives. In the Treaty, our chiefs surrendered most of our lands, but only the topsoil which they had asked for. And the Rocky Mountains were never surrendered by treaty. In return for the surrender, the Queen's men promised certain things. It was agreed by our chiefs and the Queen's men that those agreements would last for as long as the sun would shine. Our chiefs were promised assistance towards survival for the Indian people. It was upon these assurances that our chiefs agreed to sign the treaty, and to surrender some of our lands.

But now it has been made known to us that the Government wishes to put an end to all these things which they had promised to our grandfathers. The white man now desires to take those lands which we did not surrender. My mind is heavy with concern that our young ones growing up will be without land in the future. I wonder why this should be?

The white man already owns more than what he needs for his people. He has derived much wealth and prosperity from those lands which they have taken from us. But still, he wishes to take from us those lands which our grandfathers had withheld for our future generations. We are already a poor people, but he wants to put the Indian people into greater poverty.

It is our belief that we were placed here on our lands by our Creator. It is the same belief of our grandfathers. It is also our belief that our land is sacred and we should show it respect. When the treaties were signed the sacred pipe was used in reverence to our Mother Earth.

On these lands we have remaining, we are able to follow our spiritual beliefs and hold observances of respect towards our Mother Earth.... .

Our wish is to remain as Indian People, to be free to follow the manner of our worship of our Creator. I ask for your prayers. I ask you as spiritual leaders of your people to pray for the Indian people of Canada. And I too will ask our Creator to give blessing to you and your children.[15]

The following month, Chief Smallboy travelled to Rome with Eugene Steinhauer, Chief Lawrence Wildcat, Chief Gordon Lee, and Hanne Marstrand Strong (who sponsored the trip) for a historic meeting with Pope John Paul II. Immediately afterwards, Smallboy held a press conference during which an Italian journalist asked him, "As a spiritual leader of your people, what advice would you have to offer to the European countries?" The Chief's answer was full of ironic overtones:

As I have travelled throughout your country, I have seen many things that are of good appearance. The houses in which your people live, the cars that they drive, and the clothes that they wear—all of these are attractive. It looks as though most of your people are living well.

But then I also see soldiers with guns standing everywhere. It looks from that as if you were anticipating some problems! What I have seen is that there is much affluence on one side, but it also seems there are some things that are not right within your country.

In every country I have seen, it is the same. Money has become the God of the white man. They have more respect for money than they have for God. A man owns a house but he is not satisfied: he looks at his neighbour's house and he desires to have that, too. He has his land, but still he wants to own the land of his neighbour.

And in this way, it begins to happen that the people learn to think with this mentality. They have a country, but since they cannot be satisfied, they look towards the country of their neighbours. And so it is, because of the European's need to accumulate possessions, he chooses to have war with his fellow man.

Today, this day we are seeing now, is a day that I shall not forget for as long as I am alive. For me it is a day of great significance. For it is on this day that I met with the Pope. He is a man who is working for something that is good. He studies the laws of God and he possesses much wisdom, which is good.

And now, you ask that I should give words of advice to your people. I can only say that you listen carefully to the words of the Pope, and try to understand his teachings. Those are the only words I can give you. I say this, since you have asked me to do so. And I wish to thank Kisemanito [i.e., the Great Spirit] for giving me the blessing to have met with one of His greatest servants.[16]

THE CONSTITUTION ACT, 1982

The timing for bringing pressure to bear to change the proposed Constitution to include Aboriginal rights was perfect: Trudeau wanted the Constitution under Canadian control as soon as possible, and certainly before the next election. He also knew that Chief Smallboy was a man of his word—one who meant what he said: had he not spent the past ten years demonstrating that fact? Trudeau simply could not wait another ten years, or even a single year, to have the Constitution brought home to Canada. He had already lost one election and could not afford to delay patriation of the Constitution beyond another. And so he gave the First Nations just about everything they wanted, with promises of more to come, including mandated conferences built right into the Constitution, which First Nations leaders would attend. At last, meaningful talks. Not like the excusatory drivel encountered by Chief Smallboy when he visited Ragan and Battle in Ottawa fifteen years before.

Having heard Chief Smallboy and the rest of the delegation, some members of the British parliamentary system, from the Lord Bishop of London down, were insistent that protection for Aboriginal rights be addressed in England and that Canadian draftsmen work overtime to effect a compromise. Finally they came up with a grandfather clause with respect to Aboriginal rights that would prove to make all the difference in the way Indians were treated and perceived in Canada. Section 25 of the Canadian Charter of Rights and Freedoms now reads:

25. The guarantee in this Charter of certain rights and freedoms shall not be construed so as to abrogate or derogate from any aboriginal, treaty or other right or freedom that pertain to the aboriginal people of Canada including

a) any rights or freedoms that have been recognized by the Royal proclamation of October 7, 1763; and

b) any rights or freedoms that now exist by way of land claims agreements *or may be so acquired.*

This last phrase, added in 1983, was the best hope that Smallboy and all Treaty Six and Treaty Seven Indians had to acquire the "panhandle" of land that he believed was stolen from them in 1899 when it was incorporated into Treaty Eight, including the Kootenay Plains, which Smallboy had first claimed as Indian land in 1968.

Part II of the Constitution Act, 1982, dealt exclusively with the "Rights of the Aboriginal Peoples of Canada":

35. (1) The existing aboriginal and treaty rights of the aboriginal peoples of Canada are hereby recognized and affirmed.

    (2) In this Act, "aboriginal peoples of Canada" includes the Indian, Inuit and Métis peoples of Canada.

    (3) For greater certainty, in subsection (1) "treaty rights" includes rights that now exist by way of land claims agreements or may be so acquired.

The all-important clause was the reference to "land claims agreements." Like section 25(b), this clause was added in 1983 with the passage of the Constitutional Amendment Proclamation. So was section 35(4):

    (4) Notwithstanding any other provision of this Act, the aboriginal and treaty rights referred to in subsection (1) are guaranteed equally to male and female persons.

And finally, underlining the importance of these provisions as parts of the Constitution of Canada, section 35.1 added:

35.1 The government of Canada and the provincial governments are committed to the principle that, before any amendment is made to Class 24 of section 91 of the "*Constitution Act, 1867*", to section 25 of this Act or to this Part,

   (a) a constitutional conference that includes in its agenda an item relating to the proposed amendment, composed of the Prime Minister of Canada and the first ministers of the provinces, will be convened by the Prime Minister of Canada; and

   (b) the Prime Minister of Canada will invite representatives of the aboriginal peoples of Canada to participate in the discussions on that item.

The first such constitutional conference was held in March 1983 pursuant to section 37 of the Constitution Act, 1982, which mandated including in the agenda "an item respecting constitutional matters that directly affect the aboriginal peoples of Canada, including the identification and definition of the rights of those peoples to be included in the Constitution of Canada." The prime minister was directed to "invite representatives of those peoples to participate in the discussions on that item." Subsequent constitutional conferences were to be held at two-year intervals, and each "shall have included in its agenda constitutional matters that directly affect the aboriginal peoples of Canada." Section 37 further directed the prime minister to invite "representatives of those peoples to participate." Thus Smallboy's secondary concern—that Indians be made to feel welcome in Ottawa and not be brushed off as he had been when he took the trouble to go there—had been addressed once and for all by the supreme law of the land. Never again would the Indian voice be lost in the administrative wilderness of red tape and bureaucratic bungling.

Thanks in part to the efforts of Chief Smallboy and his entourage, Aboriginal rights were indeed enshrined in the Canadian Constitution in much the way Smallboy had envisioned. Once again, his persistence on behalf of his people and their revitalized way of life had paid off, to the extent that the Trudeau government in 1984 seriously researched methods of implementing First Nations self-governance, an issue that First Nations leaders have since debated and advanced in the courts and in negotiations with the Canadian and provincial governments with increased success.

THE PAPAL VISIT

Following Smallboy's visit to the Vatican, the Chief asked me, as his spokesman, to extend an invitation to Pope John Paul II to visit the Smallboy Camp, and considerable correspondence followed between governmental offices in Canada and organizers of the 1984 papal visit. On 5 November 1983, I wrote to Pope John Paul II, reminding him of Smallboy's visit to him in Rome, saying the Chief "has been instrumental in rejuvenating hope and pride among his own people to the extent that he has led them back from the brink of despair to relative spiritual prosperity."

Chief Smallboy lives a humble and secluded—at times lonely—life, which hides his own greatness. He is regarded by his people as an oracle; but he has no pretensions. He is simply a wise and loving man. Like you, a leader, like you, one of the "great servants" of God. I do not know what power you have over your itinerary while you are in Canada, but would it be possible for you to have a brief audience with Canada's pre-eminent hereditary Indian chief?

Forgive me for being so forward. Smallboy has worked miracles to restore the faith, hope and confidence of his people and to bridge a gap between native and white Canadians. I believe that by one simple gesture, you can help him complete that bridge.

I sent copies of the letter to Prime Minister Trudeau at 24 Sussex Drive and to Governor General Ed Schreyer at Rideau Hall, with covering letters. The first reply, dated 15 November 1983, came from Rideau Hall:

Dear Mr. Botting:
I am replying to your letter of November 5, 1983, addressed to the Governor General. His Excellency was deeply moved when I showed him your letter. The itinerary of the Pope's Visit to Canada in 1984 is being arranged by the president of the Canadian Conference of Catholic Bishops, the Right Reverend John Sherlock, to whom I am copying your letter as well as my reply to you… .

The answer from the Canadian Conference of Catholic Bishops, dated 18 November 1983, looked hopeful:

Dear Mr. Botting:
In order that your most eloquent plea might be brought to the attention of those responsible for the Papal Visit, I have taken the liberty of forwarding a copy of this correspondence to the Archdiocese of Edmonton which will be welcoming the Holy Father. I will ask them to get in touch with you if there is any possibility of them responding in a positive way to your plea on behalf of Chief Smallboy. I do hope that some way can be found to arrange the meeting which you are so graciously seeking to arrange.

Then came the letter from the president of the Alberta Papal Visit Committee, dated 19 January 1984:

Dear Mr. Botting:
The many letters that you have written on behalf of Chief Robert Smallboy have all finally landed on my desk. The eloquence with which you state your case is most impressive and if there was any way that I could possibly accommodate your request I would do so. I have, however, a multitude of requests and a very great shortage of time in which His Holiness will be available to us… . As you can probably realize, there have been very many valid and heartrending requests for special interviews with the Holy Father, however he is just unable to deviate from the very tight schedule that has been imposed upon him and it is with great regret that I must tell you that I cannot respond favourably to your eloquent plea.

Ultimately, however, fate took a hand in deciding whether the Pope and Smallboy would meet again in person at the Smallboy Camp, for by the time the Pope visited Canada, Chief Bob Smallboy was dead.

CHAPTER 14

Being Kind to the Soul

SERMONS IN THE MOUNTAINS

Through the 1970s and into the 1980s, Chief Smallboy sought to show others the path he had followed in his pursuit of freedom. He kept busy teaching the traditional way of life and warning of its alternative: a white, materialistic society where money was the root of all evil. Indian people who manipulated one another for the sake of money were no better than the white men who had led Indian culture to the brink of extinction in the first place, he maintained. "Now is a good time to talk about these things," he would say to the children gathered for classes at the beginning of each school year. "In the future, upcoming generations will want to hear about what we are doing now, and why. I will tell you how these things have come to pass, so that you may tell your children and your grandchildren." And then another important lesson in oral history would begin.[1]

Rather than the program of education encountered in most school curricula, Smallboy advocated "turning to the ways we have left behind: the sweetgrass, with which we have been blessed; the pipe, the pipestem, and tobacco—all the things we are now gradually allowing to slip into mere remembrance.... We were blessed with many things that were good, but we have turned our backs on these." He said that even though many of his people now lived as the white man does, "we should apply these [traditional] gifts to our lives and in our prayers."[2] Before such solemn discussions, he would light the sweet grass and pray, to show the younger ones how it was done and to get them to revere such symbols of the presence of the Great Spirit.

Sometimes these lectures would start out as homily:

> That which the Creator made in the beginning, the purpose for its existence cannot be lost. We see every day the Sun and that for which it was created in the beginning—to sustain life on this earth. Today, the Sun still functions according to its purpose, no more and no less than it ever did. That is the function assigned to the Sun by our Creator.
>
> For everything we see in the universe, there is a purpose. That is how the Creator made all things. Many things—the wind, the rain, the snow—the weather—all these still function in the way each has functioned since the beginning of Creation.[3]

Sometimes, they became stern sermons:

> But these things we no longer give any consideration to, as we are a people lost. In following the white man's tracks, we have lost many things along the way. We have lost our identity.... We have lost our direction by following the white man.[4]

Then he would bring his audience home again:

> The white man has brought us much grief. And from that, we are reminded of those things with which we have been blessed. To utilize those things to give purpose to our existence, we now resort to those things that we have left behind. The sweetgrass, with which we have been blessed; the pipe, the pipestem, and tobacco.[5]

STORY TIME

Smallboy was not always the stern schoolmaster. He had a lighter, more endearing side and a sense of humour punctuated by a magnificent smile when he saw the funny side of things. And he had a way with kids. He would bounce his tiny great-granddaughter on his knee until she giggled in delight and, at breakfast, spoon soggy cornflakes and milk into her mouth with amazing dexterity, all the time chatting away in Cree, telling this story or that about the exploits of the Grandfathers—mostly for the benefit of the four bigger grandkids sitting in a row on the sofa, their proud father, Joe, sprawled at the kitchen table and Dorothy, the hovering mother.

His only complaint, he said, when he at last handed the baby back to his granddaughter, was bad circulation in his legs caused by diabetes, a condition he had been afflicted with for several years. He massaged his legs gingerly where the baby had been sitting. "It seems," he said to his assembled grandsons on the sofa, "that good health lasts but one day. Be kind to your body. That way, you can be kind to your soul."[6] He talked a bit about diet and exercise—he still went for walks every day when the weather was fine, and he insisted on chopping his own wood and cooking for himself. And he told endless anecdotes about life as it used to be, as well as life at the camp as it was then, stories suitable for young as well as seasoned ears.

"There once was a dog lived around here," Chief Smallboy recounted, "whose hind legs were twice as long as his front ones. He kept tripping over himself when he ran. His father must have been a Chihuahua, his mother a German shepherd—" His eyes twinkled mischievously. "It wouldn't have worked the other way around. This dog was built in almost the same manner as my truck—high in the back end, short in the front."

"Chief's Truck Dog!" says one of the girls in sudden recognition.

"That's what *you* called him. I called him something else—"

"What happened to him?"

The Chief shrugs, then grins. "I'll bet Paul knows! Or Lorne—"

Sheepish grins from the squirming boys on the sofa.

"Sure you do—you remember the big roundup. No, not the cattle—the *other* roundup a few years back? Remember all the dogs we had back then? Every time we had visitors from Hobbema, they would bring their dogs. Not just their pets, mind, but their culls—stray dogs they didn't want to keep or had grown tired of. They'd let them go for a run out here—then drive away before the dogs figured out that they had been abandoned.

"That's how the dog population got out of control out here. Pretty soon there were more dogs than people. Eventually there were so many that they formed rival packs—and started acting human. One pack would pull down a deer, the others would chase 'em off and eat it. Then the smaller ones started going after the chickens."

"Mom's chickens," said one of Dorothy's daughters.

"So I declared a general roundup of all the dogs."

"Oh, *that* roundup!" said one of the boys. "When you ordered all the dogs to be shot!"

"Well, that's not quite like it was," replied the Chief, glancing sideways at his visitors. "You see, you have to listen carefully when an adult speaks."

"That's because they don't always mean what they say," one of the girls explained to her sister.

The Chief's frown commanded instant silence. "Sometimes they *do* mean what they say. Yes, I ordered the roundup—"

"You said, 'Shoot any stray dogs you can't catch,'" said one of the boys.

The Chief grinned at his grandson, who guiltily stared at the floor. *Busted.*

"Three rounds," he said. "Someone shot three rounds with his 0.22 at Chief's Truck Dog—and didn't hit a thing but the outhouse." He paused for effect. "The outhouse back of my place." Then he added in a more subdued tone, "I know, because I was in it!"

Squawks of laughter from the girls.

"Hey, I wasn't aimin' to hit him. The dog, I mean, I was just tryin' to scare him was all. But when *Mosôm* come out of that outhouse yellin' like crazy with his long johns around his ankles? That's when we *both* got *real* scared!" He chuckled. "You were some pissed!"

The shooting had prompted the Chief to rescind the last half of his order. The dogs, he declared, would be rounded up humanely and tied in the back of his truck. Except for Chief's Truck Dog, who having dodged three bullets had earned a reprieve. And then the Chief had explained his plan.

News of the Chief's solution to the dog problem went through the camp like grassfire. The whole camp got in on the act and soon only the closest pets, including Chief's Truck Dog, whom Smallboy had adopted, were left to roam the camp.

When the truck was full, the Chief drove all the dogs to Hobbema and in the central parking lot—the town being tiny—cut them all loose to find their own way home. The owners who had abandoned them not only got their dogs back—they got the message. Never again were dogs a problem at the camp.[7]

GOOD MEDICINE

Although Smallboy encouraged the young people in the camp to enjoy life to its fullest, young people were also expected to respect the elders and to respect the traditional procedures they taught, whether those lessons be in social mores or medicine. Knowledge was a gift that would only be given to those who had proven themselves worthy to receive it, and arcane knowledge in particular could only be transmitted through solemn ritual:

> When someone desires to acquire certain knowledge then there is a specific way of doing this. With men, tobacco or the sacred pipe was and is still used as a way for asking for certain information ... In the old days, and even now, the seeker of knowledge should be regarded as being of self-worth by the one who possesses the desired knowledge. It should not be given to someone totally unknown of character by the one who possesses knowledge: that should not happen. Knowledge was valued, and considered

sacred, something that should not be abused. People passed such knowledge only to those persons considered worthy and considered not likely to show disrespect.[8]

Among the things that had been lost, but which had been rediscovered and revitalized at the camp, said Chief Smallboy, was appreciation for the fine art of Indian medicine. Indian medicine, properly administered, brought remedies to sickness without side effects, he claimed, whereas "white" medicines often led to drug dependency and addiction:

> The elders would describe the medicine of the Indian—the medicine roots, certain flowers and herbs that they would use for sickness. Each medicine was good for a specific illness. The medicine men and women used these medicines to bring cures for many of their sick. These medicines were not feared by anyone, as people knew what they were. Medicines brought remedies to sickness, and they did not create other forms of health problems, or bad side-effects. Those medicines brought about the desired results. And to this day, those medicines are as fruitful and beneficial as they were when our Creator placed them on this earth: they are still like new.[9]

He described several different medicines and their uses and several rituals that were used to help cure chronic afflictions, always with an appeal to the Great Spirit for assistance:

> The elders possessed much knowledge of the laws of the Creator as to how one should live on this earth with his fellow man. They taught a way of life that allowed them to avoid offending others. They called it *manah-tisiwin*. They also knew how to derive life and health from certain trees, plants and roots. Some were blessed with this knowledge, and some were taught by other elders.
>
> All medicinal plants were approached with much respect. A person could not just pull a certain medicine plant out of the ground and expect to benefit from the life-giving power placed there by the Creator. There were certain rituals performed, imploring the Creator for his blessing. Great care was taken to ensure that the manner of taking medicines was followed properly and in a manner showing respect for the Creator.
>
> Our Mother Earth was blessed with life-giving powers by our Creator. We can see all around us that life exists on Earth. And Man is part of this creation. We are all children of Mother Earth. And man, if he is to survive, must show respect towards his Mother.
>
> We must teach the young ones all of these things. We must give instruction to the young ones who do not have knowledge of these matters.[10]

Women taught their daughters about their bodily functions, including the power of menstruation; there were taboos against menstruating women being involved in certain rituals, including the Sun Dance. "When a young girl reaches the age of womanhood, she is at that point of her life blessed by our Mother Earth with the gift to give life," said Chief Smallboy.

Her first period is celebrated in a spiritual manner. Certain rituals are conducted to honour the attainment of womanhood. The first period is looked upon as the most secret occurrence—the gift of life to humanity by our Mother Earth. From that point on, she is capable of bringing life into this world. She has become Woman.

It is one of the most important times of any woman's life. So again there is a manner of preparation involved by which the young woman must be prepared for womanhood. Usually it is performed in this way: she must not come in direct contact with certain members of her family such as brothers; she should stay in one room (and long ago they would be confined to a teepee specifically erected for that purpose); and at least four older ladies must stay with her throughout the four days of isolation.

The old ladies would tend to her needs, but their role is much more than merely to look after her. They must be fully knowledgeable about life. During this time, they give her instruction on all matters of life—including such things as marriage and the purpose of marriage.

These procedures must have worked, since separations were seldom seen in Indian society back then. The methods for raising children were explained to her. Family relationships. The importance of all these things were explained to her. Man-woman relationships were described to her during those special days. Everything that a woman needs to know, these were the things the young woman was told.

Today, as it was then, these matters should be talked about and the old procedures revived for the benefit of young women entering adulthood. It is a very important time in a woman's life.

So it is that these things enable a young woman to understand the demands of her lifegiving fertility, and she enters her life of potential childbearing without shame. The Old Women play an important role in explaining what those things are that occur during this time.[11]

Chief Smallboy was very much a proponent of preventive medicine—of keeping healthy and fit for as long as one is able to do so. He called this "Being kind to the soul":

A healthy state of the body and a pleasant state of mind contribute to a relationship of closeness with the soul. This was the advice of the elders, and it is true. Life unfolds according to the advice of the elders. It really is not for long that one enjoys good health. Old age arrives too soon, and one's movement soon becomes slow and weak. That is why our elders gave this advice.[12]

Later, he remarked, "The elders encouraged the young people to take good care of their appearance and physical health. If they looked after themselves in this way and had respect for themselves, they would live in harmony with their soul." He added that, in Hobbema, "the Indian doesn't understand the meaning of this simple principle, or its purpose. Today we have forgotten the principle of being kind to the soul."[13]

MODERNITY AND MATERIALISM

Whenever Chief Smallboy gave advice, there was always a subtle subtext: Beware of the modern world that was only the turn of an on/off knob away. These warnings he himself had received as a child, and in the process he had acquired a healthy suspicion of modernity. "When I was your age," he would say, "I would listen carefully to the elders as they discussed how life would be in the future."

> They foretold the manner of life the young ones would follow—how the young ones would follow the ways of the white man and how they would abandon those things the Indian had been blessed with and how he would stand in the midst of the white man, and would be content to live in this manner.[14]

Alberta was going through unprecedented prosperity as he intoned these warning words. It soon became clear that his primary target in the early 1980s had changed from poverty, his main concern in the 1960s, to the glut of money that was pouring into the Ermineskin Reserve from unexpected oil revenues. The Four Bands suffered from an embarrassment of riches. The individual bands at Hobbema began to invest in a great number of institutions on and off the reserve, including oil refineries, trust companies, film companies, and farm land surrounding the reserve. Smallboy's initial dream—of reversing the spiralling poverty that he saw as being so central to the difficulties encountered at Ermineskin while he was chief—came to be realized without much help from him, and in a manner that even he could not have anticipated.

Now, everyone on the reserve, man, woman, and child, took home about five hundred dollars in oil royalty money each month. They bought ridiculous things: massive television sets, fast cars and trucks, video games, and all the liquor and drugs they could consume. The partying was nonstop.

Much of what Smallboy taught at the camp had to do with materialism and the pursuit of riches. He recognized that the world back at Hobbema was spiralling out of control and that many of the children and teenagers who were listening to his words were already toying with the idea of abandoning the ideals of an Indian way of life for the temptations and comforts of "civilization."

Materialism, Smallboy said, was the greatest danger of a modern "white" education. Ultimately, money remained the root of all evil:

> To the Indian child, all the white man's things appear attractive and impressive, especially these days. The young people have an easy life. The kind of life they choose is not difficult.... All the inventions of the white man make life easy. There is no hard work involved....
>
> How can an Indian follow the white man's paths, even when he knows that his children are being ruined, even though his children are unable anymore to talk the language of the Indian? ... The white man's education has created this confusion.[15]

Attitudes ingrained in school were further shaped at home, especially in an environment where everything revolved around doing things for money. "People steal, even kill, for money. They cheat over money. It is money that comes to control the lives of people. But the young ones do not understand: they will not take advice. They do not understand that in the Indian Way, money does not exist, nor any of the evils it generates."[16]

Eerily echoing Chief Smallboy's words was a statement by Chief Eddie Littlechild, who had remained in Hobbema during the years Smallboy had been away at the camp. He had since taken over Smallboy's former mantle as chief of the Ermineskin Band. After the oil money started coming in to Hobbema, "there was so much money that people thought it was growing on trees," he said. "The money played a big part in the abuse of alcohol and drugs. The people weren't interested in going to work. The younger people don't know what it is to work for their money. We didn't realize the problems that the money could create."[17]

During the early 1980s, one of the unanticipated side effects of this newfound wealth was a suicide epidemic that did not end for seven years. Hobbema had one of the highest suicide rates not just in Canada, but in North America. Of the Four Bands, *Globe and Mail* reporter Geoffrey York remarked: "These reserves are far from ordinary. There are none of the overcrowded, rundown shacks that pass for housing on most Prairie reserves. Most of Hobbema's band members live in split-level or ranch-style homes, worth at least $100,000 each."[18] He estimated that by 1983, at the peak of the oil boom, annual royalties hit $185 million a year for the

Four Bands—$2.1 billion over fifteen years—much of it filtering through to families. "In the history of Canada, very few communities have ever been transformed from poverty to wealth so suddenly. As the oil money poured into Hobbema, the social upheaval was traumatic."[19]

The use of alcohol and drugs such as cocaine increased, as did domestic violence, separation, and divorce. But most of all, the suicide rate sky-rocketed. "From 1985 to 1987, there was a violent death almost every week at Hobbema, and the suicide rate for its young men was eighty-three times the national average. There were as many as three hundred suicide attempts by Hobbema Indians every year."[20] In addition, dozens of Hobbema residents died in car accidents, often attributed to alcohol abuse. A dozen died this way in 1987 alone.[21]

What was causing this malaise? Like Smallboy, York blamed the money. And once again, as in the 1960s with the issue of poverty, this new crisis landed at the doorstep of Indian Affairs. "In the last ten years, the federal government has just pulled out," lamented Chief Simon Threefingers of the Louis Bull Band. "They say, you have money, that's it, period. They're glad we have money because they can have nothing to do with us."[22]

Professor Leroy Little Bear at the University of Lethbridge noted that the Indians at Hobbema "were not ready, mentally, for that flow of money," since they had been "at the bottom of the social scale" and suddenly received "an endless flow of money without the requisite train-ing."[23] As York remarked:

> The story of Hobbema is proof that money by itself cannot repair the damage that has been done to native culture for more than a century. When the flow of money is too great and too sudden, it becomes yet another threat to traditional cultural values. The shift from poverty to wealth was as wrenching as the shift onto the reserves in the nineteenth century.
>
> The fate of any community is a product of a complex web of factors. At Hobbema, the influx of money was certainly one factor. The lack of proper management and control of the money was another. And the history of the community—a history of dire poverty and harsh treatment at residential schools—had an equally important influence. The invasion of oil money was the culmination of a century of turmoil, just one more way in which the har-mony of an Indian community was destroyed by powerful outside forces.[24]

The problem the influx of money was causing on the reserve had been identified as early as 1984 by Joe Dion in a report commissioned by the Department of Indian Affairs. Blaming the influx of oil revenues for social disruption, alcoholism, drug addiction, and the escalation of suicide and other violent deaths, Dion described the penalties for not preparing the Hobbema Indians for their change of fortunes as "heavy and tragic."[25] He said these effects "have extended out to weaken the social fabric of entire communities"—the exact opposite effect of what could and should have happened with responsible counselling from Indian Affairs. He recommended that the department appoint a trustee to administer the money, with a long-range plan for authority over the money to revert to the bands.[26]

Later, York's analysis was startling:

> In the 1980s, most of the suicides and other health problems at Hobbema were linked directly or indirectly to alcohol, solvent abuse, cocaine, or other drugs.... .
>
> Public health officials reported twenty-one deaths from alcohol or drug abuse in one eighteen-month period at Hobbema. In fact, 40 percent of all deaths at Hobbema in the late 1970s and early 1980s were caused by accidents, poisoning, and violence, mostly related to alcohol or drugs. About 70 percent of adult admissions to hospital were a result of alcohol abuse, and an estimated 25 to 30 percent of the parents at Hobbema were failing to provide proper care of their children, largely because of alcohol abuse.[27]

All of this, Smallboy had anticipated and, in the early 1980s, had monitored from afar. He did not allow drugs or alcohol or television sets at the camp. Much time was spent counselling people visiting from Hobbema who were contemplating suicide. Those who had been facing despair at Hobbema found solace in the peaceful surroundings at the camp, away from the hectic speed that life at Hobbema had brought even to the most innocent of residents. Peace itself was good medicine.

SURVIVAL

"The hard times are coming," Smallboy warned me during an interview conducted in August 1982. "These have been foretold by our Elders. Our Elders have foretold that the white man will experience poverty and confusion. It will soon be his turn to experience hardship."[28] Indians like himself who had learned to survive under harsh conditions would be at an advantage, because "the Indian's main concern is survival, and as long as he has enough to surive, he is satisfied. All he asks is the will and health and satisfaction to do things for himself. He is not afraid of hardship as long as his survival is assured."[29] By contrast,

> [t]he white man does not teach his children how to survive under trying conditions. His way of life has become too easy. How then can he survive?

He does not teach his children survival under difficult conditions. He doesn't know anything about suffering. He doesn't know how to survive with nature. It is said that food and all those things which make life easy will eventually no longer exist as they are today. When the explosion occurs, how will any of these networks survive? When the cities explode, where will people get food to eat?

The machines that produce food will be destroyed. This is what our Elders have foretold. Money will be worthless; it will be of no benefit to anyone. That is the thing that the Elders were talking about when they said that this world would be contaminated by pollution. Starvation and hunger will be common human suffering.

The Indian knows the meaning of suffering, but the white man knows nothing of these things. He does not know hardship, nor is he able to teach his children the way of survival, the sense of survival. His children do not know how to cope with hardship, hunger or starvation. It is so, since they have lived an easy life. His survival is at his fingertips—as he pushes buttons for heat and light. When these things are no more, how is he to survive? Under trying circumstances, he will experience only hardship.

The white man does not give counsel to his children on these matters.[30]

Smallboy recognized that his comments were a generalization extending to people who had come to depend upon modern urban comforts. He was quick to add that one French man at the camp took his children into the bush, where they learned to sleep outdoors. On the other hand,

[t]here are many Indians who do not have belief in these things…. . But when the time comes and there is fighting in our country, there will be nothing left. We will all be poor. We will experience hunger. We shall die from starvation. On that, I have said enough.[31]

BAD MEDICINE

Smallboy spurned modern medicine. "The Elders foretold that we would abandon our own medicine and that we would learn or become dependent upon the white man's medicine rather than our own," he said, "and we are doing exactly what they foretold":[32]

When we have a pain, we take a pill and the pain goes away and we are deceived into thinking that we are well again. But once the pill's effect wears off, the pain returns and we must swallow more pills. The white man's medicine only dulls the pain, but it does not bring remedy.[33]

He believed that modern pharmaceuticals were addictive and soul-destroying.

Smallboy's unabashed prejudice against modern medicine seems to have stemmed in part from a story told to him by *Waskahte*, describing the Plague of Sores in 1870. "There is one more thing regarding the epidemic," he said during an interview in London on 2 December 1981:

> There was one person who went from camp to camp, a person named Pere Lacombe, Catholic Priest. He spoke Cree and also the language of the Blackfoot. He went around checking on the people. He was not afflicted with the disease. He had no sickness.
>
> It happened that he asked one of the Indians to travel to another camp to find out if the people were also sick at that camp. But the Indian was reluctant to go for fear of contracting the disease.
>
> The priest then told the Indian, "I will give you some tablets so that the disease cannot be passed on to you." And with that, he gave him the tablets, and the Indian left for the other camp.
>
> The Indian arrived at the other camp and saw that the people there were afflicted and dying in great numbers. He then returned, and nothing happened to him. The disease had not been passed on to him.
>
> The priest had medicine to help the sick recover. But he didn't use it for that. Instead, he used it for his own good. And he was a man of prayer, my grandmother told me—supposedly a man of prayer![34]

For Smallboy, this was one more example of the white man manipulating his knowledge for his own good, at the expense of the Indian. He lamented the fact that the Indian now uses "white" medicine for virtually any illness, rather than turning to Indian medicine men for assistance or advice. The average Indian had become a pill-popper, using the slightest excuse to try another drug. "The more we take the more we need," he said. "That is not how it was with the Indian's medicine."[35]

Surgery was every bit as repugnant to Smallboy as pharmaceutical drugs, and Indian reliance on it another example of "how we have lost our way":

> To bring remedy to our sickness, the white man uses the knife to cut away that which causes the sickness. He cuts us open, like an animal being dressed. But once a person is operated on, his movement of life is weakened. The elders had foretold that we would abandon our own medicine and that we would learn or become dependent upon the white man's medicine rather than our own. And we are doing exactly what they foretold.[36]

FROSTBITE

In March 1983, this oft-expressed position against surgery left Chief Smallboy facing a terrible ethical dilemma. In January, Smallboy had visited the Navajo and Hopi reservations in Colorado and New Mexico. He was honoured in Colorado at an ecumenical development in a valley southwest of Denver, and he was even invited to attend a special session of the United Nations in New York dealing with Aboriginal rights. But eventually such demands took their toll. Perhaps his supporters expected too much of their seemingly indefatigable, but eighty-four-year-old chief.

On the way back from Colorado, the Chief and his three travelling companions stopped in Banff for the night and checked into a motel. The younger men left the Chief at the motel to get some rest, not realizing that, by that time, he was more hungry than tired. He decided to look for a restaurant by himself.

A cold front had rolled in. Chief Smallboy, having just come from the south, was not dressed for cold weather. Leaving the restaurant, he became disoriented and couldn't find his way back to the motel—not surprisingly, since in Banff many of them look alike. Temperatures were falling by the minute, and both his legs were numb from the cold, his circulation compromised by chronic diabetes. By the time he found his way back to the motel, they were both frozen.

The Native healer who later treated Smallboy gave more attention to the leg that hurt the most. The one that was frozen the worst received only a cursory glance. On his insistence, Smallboy was taken directly back to the camp, via the Banff-Jasper Parkway and the David Thompson Highway. To his horror, he was unable to walk.

The leg that had been left untreated quickly deteriorated, becoming gangrenous; yet he insisted that only Native medicine be used to treat him. He did not want surgery. Only when it was pointed out to him that there was ample evidence that Indians had practised amputation long before white contact did he consent to be taken to Wetaskiwin General Hospital—but only for a consultation. Of course, since gangrene had set in, they recommended immediate amputation. However, he demurred. All they could do was give him a whopping dose of antibiotics and hope for the best.

Confined to a bed at his brother Johnny's place just off Highway 2A in Hobbema, he greeted friends and relatives sombrely, convinced that this would be his deathbed. Dozens of family members, mostly women, stood vigil. As day after day went by, more and more people urged him to have his offensive leg removed. The dilemma he faced was holding to his principles of avoiding surgery and dying or having his gangrenous leg amputated and living for a few more months.

Following in the tradition of the Grandfathers—of Big Bear and Little Bear, and Bobtail and Coyote, and Rocky Boy—he stuck to his principles until the choice was made for him. He passed from delirium into a coma. At that point, the Four Bands Council stepped in, and an ambulance was summoned. He was taken to the emergency ward at Wetaskiwin General Hospital, where a rescue amputation was performed.

After the surgery, Smallboy became very despondent, believing that a significant part of his soul had already departed, hacked off by a white man's scalpel. His depression was exacerbated by the fact that nobody on the medical or nursing staff at the hospital spoke Cree, despite the fact that five thousand Cree Indians lived on four reserves within twenty kilometres of the hospital and 40 per cent of the users of the hospital were Cree.

HOSPITAL

Smallboy found himself confined to a hospital bed in a small room with impersonal service that, he claimed, verged on the contemptuous. Much of his food—such as cheese sandwiches—he could not eat. But if the food was terrible, the service was worse. His only solace, apart from frequent visits from his son, Joe, was the almost constant attendance during this time of his granddaughter Jessie, then twenty. She talked to him, consoled him, encouraged him, fed him. She was like a personal nurse to him. Yet there was only so much she could do in a hospital governed by strict rules, one that apparently had no time and little patience for elderly Indians.

Smallboy's greatest concern, however, was something that Jessie could not help him with: the hospital's strict no smoking policy extended to the burning of sweet grass. Both she and the Chief were forbidden from lighting his sweet-grass braid so that the Chief could cleanse himself spiritually in accordance with the most basic sacred ritual that the Cree possess.

When I visited him on 23 March 1983, Chief Smallboy bitterly lamented the fact that his leg had been removed against his will. But he was equally upset that he was not allowed to light a sweet-grass braid to smudge and purify himself. Every time he lit his braid, he told me, the smoke detector would go off, and there would be hell to pay. The last time, the nurse had confiscated his matches.

More than once during a visit, I discreetly lit a sweet-grass braid. The Chief held the bedsheet over his head like an oxygen tent as he performed his ablutions, bathing himself in the smoke. We felt like two kids smoking our first clandestine cigarette, terrified lest the smoke alarm should sound.

At the Chief's request, on 24 March 1983 I wrote a letter of complaint to the hospital administrator, Peter Langelle, copying it to the Four Bands Council that was meeting the next day in Red Deer. It stated in part:

Chief Smallboy is probably the most significant spiritual and cultural leader of the North American Indian alive today; he is regarded as a culture hero and important elder statesman by native peoples across the continent and by many others besides. In token recognition of his influence and prestige as a chief, he was awarded the Order of Canada in 1980 by the Governor General, and a year ago he was honoured in London and Rome as being the spiritual leader of the Native delegation. He is a man of much wisdom and insight, a spiritual man who has rubbed shoulders with other great men who in turn have recognized his greatness—men of the stature of Pope John Paul II and Mohammed Ali.

Today, this great chief lies in a hospital bed in Wetaskiwin General Hospital without access to any of the comforts of his daily routines: the sweetgrass braid lies beside him unburned; and his spirits are low. If he lights the sweetgrass, the smoke alarm in his room will summon the nurse, who up to now has not been particularly understanding of the Chief's needs. But to a Cree who has become used to practicing the Old Ways—and Smallboy made his reputation precisely because he insisted on following the Old Ways—to start the day without the sweetgrass ritual is like being deprived of water to wash with. As water purifies the body, so the sweetgrass purifies the spirit and helps put one in touch with the Great Spirit. Such rituals are as important as eating; almost as important as breathing.

I simply suggested what Chief Smallboy himself had requested: to be able to light his braid of sweet grass in a corner of the sunroom early each morning before the other patients arose. "I guarantee that his spirits would rise enormously," I wrote. "I think you would find that this simple step would help the Chief more than sedatives ever could."

Another request concerned his diet. Rather than cheese sandwiches, which were his daily fare,

> if he is allowed to eat nutritious Native foods such as whitefish or trout or chicken he would be a lot more comfortable and his condition might improve faster. He has a healthy appetite when presented with traditional foods; but eating habits die hard.... It grieves us to see his spirits so low, and we shall do everything in our power to help him along the road to recovery.

I discussed Smallboy's concerns about his medical treatment, including the surgery, with his surgeon, Dr. Terrence Drolet. On 26 March 1983, Dr. Drolet informed Joe that, in his opinion, the Chief would have to stay in the hospital for at least another month. When he heard this, the Chief immediately demanded to be returned to the camp far from doctors and nurses, so that he could die in peace.

We all knew that this would be the best medicine for the Chief, getting him back to the camp north of the Kootenay Plains, where he belonged. And so, with our encouragement and Joe's assistance, he took French leave.

As it turned out, he was to live on for more than a year.

FINAL DAYS

Although Smallboy could no longer walk, he had many loving hands to take care of him. Joe, then sixty-three, had provided him with ten grandchildren—and he and Dorothy had adopted two more! Clara and Elizabeth also had large families. Everyone pitched in to help.

There was no doubt that the Chief felt a great deal of pain during the last year of his life, but he bore it stoically. Occasionally, Jessie or his other grandchildren would take him for walks in a wheelchair so that he could see the distant mountains and valley that had become so much a part of his life, his heritage.

In the spring of 1984, his other leg began to deteriorate, and again Smallboy suffered from the side effects of gangrene infection: nightmares, cold sweats, headaches, and waking dreams and hallucinations. But this time he refused to give in to the scalpel. Knowing his end was imminent, he called his family about him, and they sat vigil once again for many days. This time, he was determined not to call the doctor.

On Friday, 6 July 1984, he told his grandsons where to hunt for elk. He said he had seen in a dream where the elk would be, and they must go and hunt tomorrow. They did as they were told and sure enough returned on Saturday afternoon with two large elk. "Enough for a feast," the Chief murmured when told of their good fortune.

On Sunday, 8 July, just before dawn, Smallboy asked to be carried outside on a litter. He then asked his daughter for a glass of water, and she brought it to him where he lay next to the worn dirt path beside his cabin. He gestured for his son, Joe, to light the sweet-grass braid so that he could bathe himself in its healing aroma. Joe lit the braid and with solemn urgency helped direct the sweet smoke over his father's face. Smallboy nodded thanks, and Joe smudged himself, then handed the smoldering braid to his son, who took it away.

Chief Smallboy allowed his hand to drop to the soil. He patted it. Tried to smile.

"Good land," he murmured, hardly audible. "Good land."

As the sun began to glimmer through the trees on the horizon, Chief Bob Smallboy breathed a final sigh that seemed almost of relief.

THE FUNERAL

The formal announcement of Smallboy's death, issued to the press by Four Bands administrator Gordon Lee, was in the form of an obituary and eulogy written by Hanne Marstrand Strong, who was present at the funeral:

> Chief Robert Smallboy of the Cree nation died early Sunday morning, July 8, 1984. With his passing Indian people of this country have lost one of their greatest spokesmen of modern times.
>
> In 1968, ... Smallboy courageously led a group of 140 followers into the foothills of Alberta.... Once Smallboy settled in the serene mountain area, he began the task of teaching the Indian Way. Much emphasis was placed on instilling respect for all mankind and an appreciation for nature.
>
> It was not long after his move there that visitors came from all parts of the world, seeking counsel and knowledge which was readily given by community members.
>
> Since then Chief Smallboy has revived a new sense of dignity and a strong sense of Indian awareness, not only to his small band, but he has provided an example that is sought and respected by Indian communities throughout North America. Chief Smallboy's influences and philosophy have gone beyond the realm of the Indian community; his courage to live by his convictions has earned him international recognition.... .
>
> Chief Smallboy was of the same mold as Chief Joseph and Chief Sitting Bull. He will leave behind a legacy that will be written on stone. It is a legacy of wisdom, courage and humility.[37]

Although eloquent, the eulogy was not accurate. The fact is, Chief Bobtail Smallboy's own personal heroes were not Chief Joseph, the law-abiding Nez Percé chief who by brilliant strategy outwitted three U.S. Cavalry divisions in his 2,866-kilometre trek to elusive freedom, or Sitting Bull, the great Sioux chief who sought refuge in Canada after his decisive defeat of General Custer. Rather, Smallboy's heroes were his personal *mosôms*: his great-uncle Big Bear, who resisted signing Treaty Six, seeing that it was a one-sided trap that would lead to the demise of the Indian; his great-grandfather Bobtail, who had named him after himself and who had held out for a year until 1877 before signing his adhesion to Treaty Six only when assured that the land was being "loaned" to the Queen by the Indians; and his paternal grandfather, Rocky Boy, who wept and starved for his people, perhaps more than any other chief but Big Bear, on the long road to obtaining a reservation in his name—a year after his death.

Smallboy's funeral was attended by many First Nations people from as far away as Ontario and New Mexico. "News of his death travelled like brushfire," remarked Violet Omeasoo. The two hundred mourners lined up in a long procession that filed by the Chief's open casket, paying their last respects. The casket, draped in a Union Jack—the only flag Smallboy truly respected and paid allegiance to—was carried to the grave site in a solemn procession led by Joe. Prayers, eulogies, and songs were offered in Cree, and his war bonnet, the one he had worn in Europe for his visit with Pope John Paul ii, was placed on top of the flag.

As if on cue, the camp dogs began a mournful keening, a combination of whines and moans and howls and barks and yowls and yips and yarps that drew an echoey response from the mountains miles away. Off in the distance, timber wolves began to howl in eerie chorus as Chief Bobtail Smallboy's casket was lowered into the ground.

Epilogue

No leader has emerged to replace Chief Bobtail Smallboy in the pursuit of freedom or in the quest for recognition that the Treaty Eight panhandle is rightfully First Nations land. Although Joe Smallboy tried to fill his father's boots for a while as leader of the Smallboy Band, he was more cowboy than Indian chief. While Joe loved telling stories, his wife, Dorothy, was the practical one and became the social organizer for the camp. They travelled everywhere together, often to meetings in Hobbema, when the interests of camp residents were involved. Their sons developed a keen interest in hunting and guiding, while the girls learned handicrafts from their mother—developing a facility at cooking bannock or fry-bread, putting up preserves of saskatoons or chokecherries, and sewing fancy beadwork on leather pouches or bracelets.[1] Their talents had not changed much from those described of women and children at Little Bear's camp in Montana more than a century ago.

The Roans in particular did not like the way Joe ran things, saying he was more concerned with his horses than his community. Following the death of Joe and Dorothy Smallboy in a car accident in 1995, the camp divided into two factions: the Smallboys and the Roans. When Wayne Roan, who had lived in Hobbema ever since his father had died in 1977, was elected chief by the Roan majority, the Smallboys were understandably incensed. Just as the younger Roans did not accept Joe Smallboy as chief, so the younger Smallboys had not accepted Wayne Roan. Roan was beaten up in 1997 after he moved back to the camp from Hobbema, in what police characterized as a domestic dispute, and was hospitalized with a broken jaw. He has lived in Hobbema ever since.[2]

As long as the land along the Brazeau remained vacant and unused, the Smallboy Band had a legitimate claim to using the land as they might have used it before Treaty Six came into force. But as forestry, mining, and oil companies encroached year by year, the argument that the camp had a right to independent existence under Treaty Six began to wane. The interests of the province and mining consortiums like the Cheviot coal mine have come to take precedence over squatters' rights—both judicially and politically.

Disputes between the Smallboys and the Roans as to how to approach these competing interests have contributed to the long-standing animosity that has divided the camp. Litigation against Cardinal River Coals Ltd. brought by Wayne Roan and others in an attempt to stop the giant Cheviot mine from strip mining the land adjacent to the Smallboy Camp was dismissed in 1997 because the Indians at the Smallboy Camp were deemed to be "squatters" who had no legitimate claim to the land.[3] However, the issue of whether the Smallboy community is squatting on Crown land pales in comparison to the Crown's own dubious status with regard to Jasper National Park, where it has been "squatting" for nearly a century.

Cardinal River Coals turned its attention elsewhere for the sake of political expediency. However, in the wake of the Federal Court of Canada decision, the Alberta and federal governments decided to isolate the Smallboy Band, most graphically by withholding $250,000 in annual education funding.[4] This led to the boarding up of the schoolhouse in 2003 after thirty-four years of operation—this at a time when the band needed government support as never before. Camp children are now forced to travel at least an hour's drive away to schools at the Bighorn Reserve, Hinton, and Rocky Mountain House.

With their boarded-up school and messy plywood-and-tarpaper shacks competing for attention with satellite dishes, the inhabitants of the Smallboy Camp appear to have lost sight of the twin visions of Chief Bob Smallboy and Lazarus Roan—the hope of establishing a healthy, traditional lifestyle and of claiming the mountains as Indian land. A Sun Dance held in the summer of 2004 organized by Wayne Roan—the first in seven years—may be the start of a healing process. But the Smallboy Camp has a long, long way to go to attain its founder's dream. As Joe's son Lorne explained, "My grandfather had the knowledge. That's why we were all together and had a happy time."[5] Lorne is currently trying to revitalize his father's backcountry guiding enterprise, training pack horses. Although Aboriginal tourism is currently all the rage in Indian communities across the country, tourists intent on experiencing the Indian Way expect more than mere squalor.

What is needed is another visionary who can put the Smallboy Band, and the First Nations generally, back on track in the quest for recognition of the fact that the Rocky Mountains, including the Kootenay Plains and much of Banff and Jasper National Parks, remain Indian land. Always as a part of Chief Smallboy's focus was the knowledge that his people had been blatantly deprived of their most sacred places by the Canadian government .

The putative acquisition by Canada in 1899 of what appears on a map of the treaties to be the panhandle of Treaty Eight was not a simple matter of miscommunication between the Indian and the white man, as could be argued with respect to most of the numbered treaties. Rather, the acquisition of the mountains north of the Red Deer River was deliberate sleight of hand. David Thompson and Alexander Henry had made clear in their diaries and journals that the Kootenay Plains and the mountain passes had been vigorously defended by Indians in the past. Accordingly, government negotiators left this sacred strip of mountainous land between the Continental Divide and the eastern range of the Rocky Mountains to the Indians. That is the only reasonable explanation for this strip of land being so pointedly left out of Treaty Six.

Twenty-three years later, when Indians were "settled" on reserves—on pain of imprisonment if they were found off their reserve without a pass or permit—the government included the "panhandle" of Treaty Eight in the land negotiated away by the more northerly tribes. There is no indication that these tribes, including the Chippewyan, Slave, and Beaver, and the northerly bands of the Woodland Cree, had any knowledge, interest, or attachment to the strip of land to the west and south of the land outlined in Treaty Six.

These lands, as Stoney Chief John Snow pointed out so poignantly thirty years ago in *These Mountains are our Sacred Places*, were not up for negotiation. As he wrote in 1977: "Much of this book deals with ... our still-unsuccessful efforts to claim our ancestral lands in the Kootenay Plains which had been promised at treaty."[6] He was articulating what Smallboy had already been saying for a decade with respect to the Cree claim to the same land.

The federal government has never properly addressed the fact that the Kootenay Plains, the Bighorn Wildland, the half of Banff National Park north of the headwaters of the Red Deer River, and a broad, profitable strip of Jasper National Park, including the Columbia Ice Field, were never the subject of treaty negotiations at all. The Stoney Indians who occupied the Kootenay Plains in 1899, when Treaty Eight was concluded, were not so much as consulted about ceding the land; neither were the Cree nor any other nations included in Treaty Six.[7]

Government negotiators of Treaty Eight did not give the issue of who occupied the Kootenay Plains and the surrounding mountains any consideration whatsoever. They knew that the First Nations included in Treaty Eight clearly did *not* occupy them and had no knowledge of them, let alone "interest" in them. This was not their traditional territory. To them, and to any objective observer, the "panhandle" between British Columbia and what was then the western part of the North-West Territories was an overlooked strip of land to which the government of the day took a fancy. The process of acquiring this land by reference to geographical descriptors on a map in an office in Ottawa had no legitimacy whatsoever.

The government negotiators arbitrarily incorporated the strip between the Continental Divide and the eastern range of the Rockies into a treaty concerned with different land, different people, and different issues altogether, specifically "with the Indians occupying the territory south and west of Great Slave lake" in the far-off North-West Territories.[8] It was a bookkeeping decision to cover all the residual bits of land left over from the negotiation of Treaties Six and Seven, without any consideration as to why this particular strip had been left out in the first place.

The Treaty Eight boundaries are framed in innocuous terms calculated not to draw attention to the average Indian band in the vicinity of Great Slave Lake or Lake Athabasca—who had absolutely no comprehension as to what the government was attempting to do or the vastness of the boundaries and what was contained within them. The white negotiators baffled these remote bands with detail, including, for example, making provision to honour their "rights" to comparatively insignificant islands in Great Slave Lake. But there was no mention of the mountains, the glaciers, the Kootenay Plains—all someone *else's* sacred places:

Commencing at the source of the main branch of the Red Deer River in Alberta, thence due west to the central range of the Rocky Mountains, thence northwesterly along the said range to the point where it intersects the 60th parallel of north latitude, then east along said parallel to the point where it intersects Hay River, thence northeasterly down said river to the south shore of Great Slave Lake, then along the said shore northeasterly (and including such rights to the islands in said lakes as the Indians mentioned in the treaty may possess), and thence easterly and northeasterly along the south shores of Christie's Bay and McLeod's Bay to old Fort Reliance near the mouth of Lockhart's River, thence southeasterly in a straight line to and including Black Lake, thence southwesterly up the stream from Cree Lake, thence including said lake southwesterly along the height-of-land between the Athabasca and Churchill Rivers to where it intersects *the northern boundary of Treaty Six, and along the said boundary easterly, northerly and southwesterly, to the place of commencement.*[9]

Try translating *that* into Chippewyan, Slave, or Cree! Interestingly, the treaty got the directions wrong even in English. They should have been "westerly" and "southeasterly" to the place of origin.

It is unlikely that any of the chiefs present at the signing of Treaty Eight in 1899 had ever visited what is now Jasper National Park, the Kootenay Plains, the Columbia Icefield, or the Angel Glacier at Mount Edith Cavell. Nor did the Indians to the north and east have any knowledge or comprehension of the implications of giving up the panhandle of land that had been excluded from Treaty Six.

To the extent that the First Nations of Treaty Six had been told that their sacred land was *not* being ceded to the Crown—that the boundary of the land that they were supposedly ceding was the *eastern* range of the Rockies, not the Continental Divide—the subsequent inclusions of those sacred places in someone else's treaty altogether amounted to an officially authorized act of fraud perpetrated on the Indian people, a crowning act of dishonesty that capped a century of acquisition-by-deception on the part of the Canadian Crown.

Smallboy believed that, since they were not given up in Treaties Six or Seven, the mountains remain Indian land, as both he and Chief John Snow pointed out four decades ago. Snow cited Governor-General Lord Dufferin's assurance: "No government, whether provincial or central, has failed to acknowledge that the original title to the land existed in the Indian tribes and communities that hunted or wandered on them."[10]

Both the Stoneys and the Cree took steps to occupy the Kootenay Plains. Smallboy did not occupy Banff or Jasper National Park in 1968, but he did not need to do so to make his point that the mountains west of the western boundary of Treaty Six had not been properly ceded to the Crown. Chief John Snow declared possession of the mountains in the very title *These Mountains are our Sacred Places*, while Smallboy in particular showed Indians the way to make what could become the most significant land claim by First Nations in Canadian history.

Obviously, the federal government is not about to abandon the profitable Banff and Jasper national parks or their millions of visitors each year without a legal fight. But the government can rest assured that the First Nations who are directly affected by the 1899 deception will eventually mount a claim for the land, a legal challenge that will no doubt wend its way through tribunals and lower courts before being taken to the Supreme Court of Canada for resolution. The First Nations will no doubt seek compensation for past and present usage of the park and be eligible to claim a substantial portion of the profits from taxes, leases, and rental revenues for the use of their property. Assuming the litigation is a success, Parks Canada will owe the First Nations a century of back rent.

It is likely that the First Nations will draw attention to their claim not only by occupying the land in the same manner that Smallboy occupied the Kootenay Plains, but also by educating visitors as to who actually owns most of Banff and Jasper national parks. Only then will it become clear to the average Canadian the enormity of the fraud. Indeed, what was taken from the Indians more than a century ago in a ruthless and legally baseless land grab is simply enormous.

No doubt it will be argued that the land that Canada sought to take by a stroke of a pen in Treaty Eight, without any consultation whatsoever, is now too valuable for Indians to own or manage. It was undoubtedly the opinion of the Indian negotiators of Treaty Six that the sacred mountains were too valuable to them to hand over to the government to manage—the mountains simply weren't negotiable. That is why the boundaries of the land the Cree agreed to cede extended only to the eastern range of the Rocky Mountains, and not beyond.

Once it becomes clear that Canadians are anxious to "keep" the land so ignominiously acquired by their government, the First Nations of Treaties Six, Seven, and Eight adjacent to Banff and Jasper national parks will be in a strong negotiating position to acquire a commensurately larger geographical zone within Alberta to replace their land within the park—not a token parcel of land, or yet another reserve, but a large enough portion of the foothills to compensate for the undoubted jewel of which they were defrauded in 1899.

The First Nations should be allowed to retain the Kootenay Plains, but replacement land for their portion of Jasper National Park should include portions of the adjacent forest reserves to the north, south, and east of the Kootenay Plains large enough in the aggregate to allow them to set up a self-governing zone parallel to that negotiated with the Nisga'a in British Columbia in 1999. Only then will Chief Bob Smallboy's dream be realized: the dream of his people living the Indian way in the mountains, in freedom, for as long as the sun rises, the grasses grow, and the rivers flow.

Appendix

1800   David Thompson first visits Kootenay Plains, Rocky Mountain House
Kootenay Plains occupied and jealously guarded by Peigan Indians
Birth of *Mukatai* (Black Powder), Chippewa father of Big Bear and Pleasant One

1801   David Thompson marries Charlotte Small, a Cree-Métis, at Île à la Crosse

1805   Birth of *Ocepihk* (Root), Cree mother of Big Bear and Pleasant One

1807   David Thompson returns to Kootenay Plains, recognizing it as Peigan land

1809   The Peigans, Bloods, and Blackfoot attack David Thompson and the Salish

1810   Alexander Henry reports "many warriors" defending Kootenay Plains

1825   Birth of Big Bear, Smallboy's great-uncle, his paternal grandmother's brother

1829   Birth of *Keskayo* (Bobtail), father of Coyote and namesake of Bobtail Smallboy

1837   Birth of *Nahkawewin* (Chippewa Speaker), mother of Rocky Boy

1840   Birth of *Mescakanis* (Coyote), Smallboy's maternal grandfather

1850   Birth of *Kakokikanis* (Hanger-On), Smallboy's maternal grandmother

1851   Birth of *Imasees* (Little Bad Man), later to become Little Bear

1852   Birth of *Asinikosisan* (Rocky Boy), Smallboy's paternal grandfather

1864   Coyote weds *Kakokikanis*, Smallboy's maternal grandmother

1865   Big Bear becomes headman of small band of Cree/Assiniboine near Fort Pitt
Birth of Smallboy's mother, Isabelle Coyote (Piché)

1867   Canadian Confederation; many Cree in Montana given this birth date
Birth of *Pekiskwewin* (Voice), Rocky Boy's second wife

1869   Smallpox epidemic spreads from Peigans to Bloods and Blackfoot to Cree

1870   Assiniboine-Cree alliance unsuccessfully attacks Bloods at Belly River
Rocky Boy weds *Miÿweÿihtakwan* (Pleasant One), Smallboy's grandmother

1871   Plains First Nations peace treaty concluded at Turtle Mountain, North Dakota
Birth in Saskatchewan of *Apitchitchiw* ("Shorty" Young Boy), Smallboy's father

1872   Birth of *Waskahte* (Walking-in-a-Circle), Coyote's second wife

1876   Plains Cree (except Big Bear, Bobtail) sign Treaty Six at Carlton House, Fort Pitt

1877   Bobtail and Coyote sign adhesions to Treaty Six at Blackfoot Crossing, Tail Creek

1882   Big Bear's band walks for 21 days without food; many starve to death
(December 8) Big Bear signs adhesion to Treaty Six at Fort Walsh

1883   Measles epidemic kills Pleasant One, leaves Isabelle Coyote blind

1885   Riel Rebellion culminates (for the Cree) in Frog Lake Massacre
Little Bear leads refugees into Montana, including Smallboy's parents

1886   Isabelle gives birth to a son in Havre; calls him *Apisisiw* (Little Boy)
Little Poplar and Yellowface, two brothers, reunited at Table Mountain

1888   Isabelle has a daughter, born in Browning; calls her *Apisisisiw* (Little Girl)

1894   Little Bear defiantly holds a banned Sun Dance at Montana's state capitol

1895   Congress approves appropriation to move Canadian Cree from Montana

1896 Chippewa/Cree rounded up and herded in cattle cars to Canadian border
       Once in Canada, Little Bear, though promised amnesty, arrested for murder
       Apitchitchiw and Isabelle Coyote are formally married in Hobbema
1897 Birth of Maggie Smallboy in Calgary
1898 Birth of *Keskayo Apitchitchiw*—Bobtail ("Bob") Smallboy—near Fort McLeod
1899 Treaty Eight purports to include mountains specifically excluded from Treaty Six
1900 Birth and baptism of Johnny Smallboy at Hobbema, Alberta
       Naming of Bobtail Smallboy; death of Bobtail (Alexis Piché)
1902 Rocky Boy asks President Roosevelt for land for his band of Chippewa/Cree
       Smallboy nearly drowns in Little Big Horn River, on Crow Reservation
1903 Rocky Boy first compiles list of members of his band
1904 Canadian Cree rounded up and relocated in western Montana
1908 Artist Charles Russell and others advocate a reservation for Rocky Boy and his band
       Yellowface, the Medicine Man, rides north to Cardston, the "Land of Answers"
1910 Land set aside for Rocky Boy "thrown open" for white settlement
1913 Little Bear confronts secretary of the Interior, protesting maltreatment of the Cree
       Linderman, Bole demand Fort Assinniboine be given to the Chippewa/Cree
1914 Roger St. Pierre hired to supervise distribution of rations to Chippewa/Cree
       Outbreak of First World War leads to clampdown on travelling Indians
1915 Chippewa/Cree gather around Fort Assinniboine; Smallboys in Hobbema
1916 (18 April) Rocky Boy dies; Smallboy family attends funeral in Montana
1917 Rocky Boy Reservation established; St. Pierre helps compile first "roll"
       Little Bear becomes first chief of Rocky Boy Reservation
1918 (3 June) Bob Smallboy marries Louisa Headman at Hobbema
1919 Spanish influenza epidemic takes *Kakokikanis*, at Rocky Boy Reservation
1920 Birth of Joe Smallboy
1924 Death of Coyote, by then a widely respected medicine man in Montana
1925 Sun Dance at Rocky Boy draws Smallboys and hundreds of others
1929 Great Depression allows Smallboy to flourish as a farmer
1935 Death of *Apitchitchiw*
1939 Outbreak of Second World War; again Smallboy's farm flourishes
1951 Sun Dance allowed to be held in Canada for first time in half a century
1952 Joe Smallboy and Dorothy Roan wed in arranged marriage
1957 Bob Smallboy first asked to run for chief of Ermineskin Reserve
1959 Bob Smallboy elected chief of Ermineskin Reserve
       Louisa Smallboy dies of pneumonia
1965 Chief Smallboy goes to Ottawa to negotiate more land, but is rebuffed
1968 Pierre Elliott Trudeau becomes prime minister of Canada
       Chief Smallboy and Lazarus Roan lead "Smallboy Band" to Kootenay Plains
1969 Trudeau and Minister of Indian Affairs Jean Chrétien issue "White Paper"
1971 Chief Smallboy makes submission to Queen regarding his mission
       Smallboy's healing camp endorsed by Mike Steinhauer, Harold Cardinal
1976 Leonard Peltier, wanted for murder of FBI agents, arrested at Smallboy Camp
1977 Isabelle Coyote (Piché) dies; Lazarus Roan dies; Smallboy Camp dwindles to 26
       permanent members
1979 Chief Smallboy nominated for Order of Canada
1980 Chief Smallboy travels to Ottawa to receive Order of Canada
1981 Smallboy asks British Parliament to enshrine Aboriginal rights in Canada Act
1982 Smallboy visits Pope John Paul II to seek support for Aboriginal rights
       Constitution Act, 1982, enshrines Aboriginal rights in Canadian Constitution
1983 Returning from U.S., Smallboy suffers severe frostbite in Banff, Alberta
1984 (8 July) Smallboy dies peacefully at Smallboy Camp

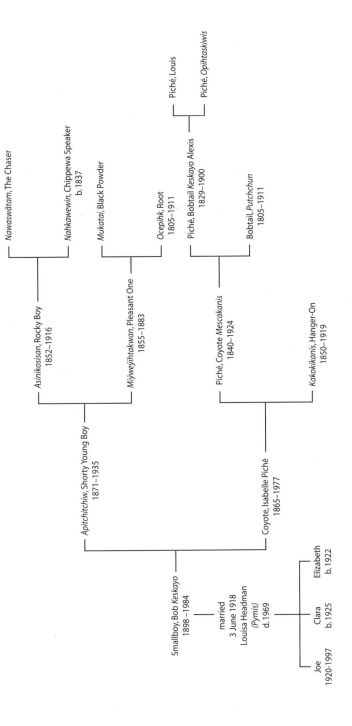

Notes

PREFACE

1. The play *Way To Go, Witigo!* was first produced by People & Puppets Incorporated in Edmonton in July 1972. Both the play and the story were published in *Issue Magazine* (1972), a joint publication of the University of Alberta and the University of Calgary.
2. That St. Pierre had an axe to grind against Cree members of the reservation, in particular the first chief of the Rocky Boy Reservation, Little Bear, and his friends, can readily be seen by his loose, often insulting translations of Cree nicknames into English, including the name he gave Little Bear's pockmarked wife ("Bad Face"), and those he gave to the impoverished Coyote's first wife ("Hanger Owner") and their blind daughter Isabelle ("Smooth Eyes").
3. Testimony of Marie Smallboy, Standing Committee on Aboriginal Affairs, Northern Development and Natural Resources (*Hansard,* 17 February 2003).
4. *Kruger et al. v. The Queen,* [1978] 1 S.C.R. 1 at 109.
5. Marie Smallboy, personal correspondence with author, 29 December 2004; Jessie Smallboy, conversation with author, 15 February 2005. Marie, the daughter of James Smallboy, is the granddaughter of Bob's younger brother, Johnny.

CHAPTER I: VOICE IN THE WILDERNESS

1. Pierre Elliott Trudeau, "Remarks on Aboriginal and Treaty Rights," in *Native Rights in Canada* (2nd ed.), eds. Peter A. Cumming and Neil H. Mickenberg (Toronto: General Publishing, 1972), 331. Trudeau called his White Paper "a policy paper on the Indian problem," to which Harold Cardinal responded, "An Indian, who probably wasn't joking at all, once said, 'The biggest of all Indian problems is the white man.'" Harold Cardinal, *The Unjust Society* (Vancouver: Douglas & McIntyre, [1969] 1999), 63. More seriously, Cardinal remarked: "If I were to accept the bothersome term *Indian problem,* I would have to accept it in light of the fact that our most basic problem is gaining respect, respect on an individual basis that would make possible acceptance for us as an ethnic group. Before this is possible, the dignity, confidence and pride of the Indian people must be restored" (22).
2. Chief Bob Smallboy, "Advice for Europe," trans. Eugene Steinhauer, in "The Indian Way: The Memoirs of Chief Bob Smallboy," ed. Gary Botting (unpublished manuscript, 1984), 42–43, and Appendix F.
3. Nancy LeClaire and George Cardinal, *Alberta Elders' Cree Dictionary* (Edmonton: The University of Alberta Press, 1998), s.v. "small"; Arok Wolvengrey, *Nehiyawewin: Itwewina* (*Cree: Words*) (Regina: Canadian Plains Research Centre, 2001), Vol. 1, s.v. "apihci-" and "apisci-", and Vol. 2, s.v. "small".
4. Married names Elizabeth Monture and Clara Rattlesnake.
5. Marie Smallboy, interview with author, Hobbema, 13 January 2005. She in turn cited as a source for this metaphor her great-uncle Peter O'Chiese, a first cousin of Bob Smallboy, who in January 2005 celebrated his 110th birthday.
6. Chief Bob Smallboy, "The Oral Tradition," recorded 11 January 1982, trans. Gordon Lee, in "The Indian Way: The Memoirs of Chief Bob Smallboy," ed. Gary Botting, (unpublished manuscript, 1984), 61–64.
7. Chief Bob Smallboy, "Decision to Leave Hobbema," trans. and ed. Eugene Steinhauer, *The Western Canadian Journal of Anthropology,* 1, no. 1 (1969): 113. The *Journal* is published by the Department of Anthropology at the University of Alberta, Edmonton.
8. To be even more precise, the Cree word for "Cree" is *nehiyaw* when used as an adjective and *nehiyawewin* when used as a noun. See LeClaire and Cardinal, *Alberta Elders' Cree Dictionary,* s.v. "Cree"; and Wolvengrey, *Cree: Words,* Vol. 2, s.v. "Cree."

9. Joan Oxendale, "Reflections on the Structure of Cree," *The Western Canadian Journal of Anthropology*, I, no. I (1969): 120.

10. Chief John Snow, *These Mountains are our Sacred Places* (Toronto: Samuel Stevens, 1977), 6.

11. Stan Reid, *Edmonton Journal*, 11 August 1968.

12. *Edmonton Journal*, 20 October 1968.

13. *Weekend Magazine*, 21 September 1968.

14. *Edmonton Journal*, 11 August 1968.

15. *Weekend Magazine*, 21 September 1968.

16. *Edmonton Journal*, 11 September 1968.

17. Jeff Holubitsky, "A spiritual foothold in the wilderness," *Edmonton Journal*, 18 July 2004.

CHAPTER 2: BIG BEAR AND LITTLE BEAR

1. Alexander Morris, *The Treaties of Canada with the Indians* (Toronto: Belfords, Clarke, 1880), 240.

2. Ibid.

3. Ibid., 192.

4. Ibid., 193.

5. Ibid., 242.

6. Hugh A. Dempsey, *Big Bear: The End of Freedom* (Vancouver: Douglas & McIntyre, 1984), 74–75. See also Rudy Wiebe, "Mistahimaskwa," in *Dictionary of Canadian Biography*, Vol. XI, 1881 to 1890, ed. Francess G. Halpenny (Toronto: University of Toronto Press, 1982), 597–600. Bill Waiser and Blair Stonechild suggested in *Loyal till Death: Indians and the North-West Rebellion* (Calgary: Fifth House, 1997) that Big Bear was using the metaphor merely to plead "that Indians not lose their freedom like tethered animals." However, Dempsey's interpretation of a horse being subjected to its master's control is a much more compelling image.

7. David Mandelbaum, *The Plains Cree: An Ethnographic, Historical, and Comparative Study* (Regina: Canadian Plains Research Centre, 1979), 171–72.

8. Recorded in the minutes of "Third Annual Premier's Prayer Breakfast," 26 February 1971.

9. *Edmonton Journal*, 20 October 1968.

10. Dempsey, *Big Bear*; Rudy Wiebe, *The Temptations of Big Bear* (Toronto: McClelland & Stewart, 1973).

11. Dempsey, *Big Bear*, 11.

12. Ibid., 25.

13. Exhibit 50.2-3739 A-M.

14. Mandelbaum, *The Plains Cree*, 171–72.

15. Wiebe, "Mistahimaskwa," 600.

16. Morris, *Treaties of Canada* (1880), 192.

17. Stonechild and Waiser, *Loyal till Death*, emphasize the role of Big Bear as conciliator in the conflict, as does Dempsey (*Big Bear*). Big Bear's sentence was actually for three years, but he was released in 1887.

18. "Peigan" is the preferred spelling, according to *Merriam-Webster's Collegiate Dictionary*, 11th ed. Hugh A. Dempsey consistently spelled it this way in his earlier books, but in *Firewater* (Calgary, Fifth House, 2002) adopted the spelling "Piegan," following other authorities such as Mandelbaum. The Peigans are one of three tribes of the Blackfoot Confederacy, the other two being the Bloods and Siksika ("True Blackfoot"). American usage refers to the people of the Blackfoot Confederacy collectively as "Blackfeet." See Mandelbaum, *The Plains Cree*, 9, 239. Retold here based on an account by Joe Smallboy in 1986, recounting a story told to him by his grandmother Isabelle Coyote.

19. Dempsey, *Firewater*, 67; see also Hugh A Dempsey, *Crowfoot: Chief of the Blackfeet* (Edmonton: Hurtig, 1976), 73–74.

20. See Dempsey, *Big Bear*, 40.

21. Ibid., 65.

22. Stonechild and Waiser, *Loyal till Death*, describe "the diminutive, wiry Big Bear, whose face had been disfigured by smallpox" (25). In the Rocky Boy census of 1917, not only did Roger St. Pierre name Little Bear's wife "Bad Face" in reference to similar disfigurement, he cruelly nicknamed Smallboy's mother, Isabelle Coyote, "Smooth Eyes," in reference to her blindness dating back to the 1883 measles epidemic. See "A Tribal Background Analysis of the Chippewa Cree 'Tribe' Born Before 1889," taken from the *Tentative Roll of the Rocky Boy Indians*, 3, in John C. Ewers, *Ethnological Report on the Chippewa Cree Tribe of the Rocky Boy Reservation, Montana* (New York: Clearwater, 1973), n. 3, 139.

23. Dempsey, *Big Bear*, 16–18.

24. Ibid., 18.

25. Ibid., 42.
26. Dempsey, *Firewater*, 67–69, citing the *Lethbridge News*, 30 April 1890. For parallel accounts, see Dempsey, *Big Bear*, 42; and Dempsey, *Crowfoot*, 60–61, 73–74.
27. Smallboy, "The Oral Tradition," 61–64 (see chap. 1, n. 6).
28. Geoffrey York, *The Dispossessed* (Toronto: McArthur, 1999), 91.
29. *Imasees* (Little Bad Man) did not become Little Bear until after he reached the United States in 1885.
30. York, *The Dispossessed*, 91–92.
31. Wolvengrey, *Cree: Words*, 511 (see chap. 1, n. 3).
32. Ibid. See Dempsey, *Big Bear*, 176–77.
33. Dempsey, *Big Bear*, 177.
34. See Stonechild and Waiser, *Loyal till Death*, 185–88.
35. Ibid., 188.
36. Ibid., 188–89.
37. Ewers, *Ethnological Report*, 70; William B. Fraser, *Big Bear, Indian Patriot* (Calgary: Historical Society of Alberta, 1966), 4–5.
38. Mandelbaum, *The Plains Cree*, 278–79.
39. Dempsey, *Big Bear*, 180.
40. Ibid.
41. Ibid.
42. Ibid., 177.
43. Ibid.
44. Ibid., 179–81.
45. 19 August 1885.
46. C. E. Denny, *The Law Marches West* (Toronto: J. M. Dent and Sons, 1939), 202–3.
47. Ibid., 196.
48. Wiebe, "Mistahimaskwa," 600. Although several authorities, including Dempsey (*Big Bear*) and Stonechild and Waiser (*Loyal till Death*) refer several times to Big Bear being "old" as in "the old chief," he was only sixty at the time of the Frog Lake Massacre and only sixty-three when he died. Being disfigured from smallpox, he may have looked older than his years.
49. See Wiebe, *Temptations of Big Bear, passim*; Dempsey, *Big Bear*, 133, 142, and 161; and Stonechild and Waiser, *Loyal till Death*, 114, 125, and 185. From this point on, *Imasees* will be referred to as "Little Bear."
50. William B. Cameron, *Blood Red the Sun* (Calgary: n.p., 1926), 217, cited in Ewers, *Ethnological Report*, 93. Little Bear is not to be confused with his namesake, the Little Bear who was hanged alongside Wandering Spirit and six others at Battleford on 27 November 1885. Accused and convicted of having murdered George Dill, Little Bear protested his innocence to the end.
51. Edward Ahenakew, *Voices of the Plains Cree* (Toronto: McClelland & Stewart, 1973), 108.
52. Stonechild and Waiser, *Loyal till Death*, 119.
53. Dempsey, *Big Bear*, 179.
54. Ibid., 169.
55. Hans J. Peterson, "Imasees and His Band: Canadian Refugees After the North-West Rebellion," *The Canadian Journal of Anthropology* 7, (1978): 21–37.
56. Stonechild and Waiser, *Loyal till Death*, suggest that the number of people fleeing with Little Bear did not exceed 100 people (227). Dempsey, in *Big Bear*, states, "*Imasees'* following of 137 people swung south past Birch Lake and headed for the Thickwood Hills" (179). This number corresponds to the number of refugees in Little Bear's band who were eventually rounded up in Montana the following December. However, Dempsey states that at the Thickwood Hills, about 30 men, women, and children of the original group travelled upstream to Battleford with Miserable Man, where they surrendered (179).
57. Stonechild and Waiser, 194.
58. Dempsey (1984), 179.
59. While Dempsey pegs the number of adherents to Little Bear's group at 137, this number is likely drawn from the count of men, women, and children in the group who surfaced in Montana months later. There is evidence that many more than this started off on the trek. About 40 people abandoned it after the gruelling first stage of the march to Turtle Lake, and more gave up once they got to the Thickwood Hills. Once they helped others reach the rendezvous point at Thickwood Hills, Four Sky Thunder and Miserable Man headed back upriver to Battleford with their extended families, where they surrendered to the authorities. Miserable Man was among those later convicted of murder in connection with the Frog Lake Massacre. He was hanged alongside Wandering Spirit and six others at Battleford the following November. Dempsey, *Big Bear*, 179, 224–26.

60. Mandelbaum, *The Plains Cree*, 172.

61. Interview with Bob Smallboy at the Smallboy Camp, August 1982.

62. "*Imasees* and his band continued south, avoiding patrols and foraging for food along the way. Three weeks later, they reached the South Saskatchewan River, a short distance down from The Forks. By this time they were starving." Dempsey, *Big Bear*, 179–80.

63. Ibid. Stonechild and Waiser, in *Loyal till Death*, adopt the account of W. H. McKay in "Lucky Man's Flight," *Canadian Cattlemen* (December 1948): "Their flight went undetected, apart from the momentary alarm raised by the accidental shooting of a man who refused to give up his boat so that the refugees could cross the South Saskatchewan River" (194–95).

64. Verne Dusenberry, "Rocky Boy Indians: Montana's Displaced Persons," *Montana Magazine of History* (Winter 1954): 181.

65. It took Little Bear and his band three weeks to get to the Forks (Dempsey, *Big Bear*, 179–80). If they maintained the same pace, the band would have taken another week to get from the Forks to Montana.

66. All of these individuals are listed in the 1917 Rocky Boy roll as having come into Montana in 1885. Some may have come independently later on in the year, following Little Bear's lead. See Stonechild and Waiser, *Loyal till Death*, 227–28.

67. Ibid.

68. *Fort Benton River Press*, 30 December 1885.

69. Thomas R. Wessel, "A History of the Rocky Boy's Indian Reservation" (unpublished; undated), Stonechild College Library, Havre, MT, call no. AI 970.49 W86.

70. Dusenberry, "Rocky Boy Indians," 2; "Tribal Background – 1917 Rocky Boy Indian Census," in Ewers, *Ethnological Report*, 139.

71. Dusenberry, "Rocky Boy Indians," 3. Colonel E. S. Otis of the 10th Infantry wrote in February 1888, "These Indians are workers, are eager to have land assigned them for cultivation and have some knowledge of soil tillage." *Senate Reports*, 4, no. 821, 54th Congress, 1st Session.

CHAPTER 3: THE GRANDFATHERS

1. Verne Dusenberry, *The Montana Cree* (Norman: University of Oklahoma Press, [1962] 1998), 161–63.

2. Bobtail is referred to as Short Tail in Ahenakew, *Voices of Plains Cree*, 37 (see chap. 2, n. 51). See also Morris, *Treaties of Canada* (1880), 193, 241 (see chap. 2, n. 1).

3. Ahenakew, *Voices of Plains Cree*. As Chief Thunderchild told Edward Ahenakew: "There was a general shout when three riders appeared. Two of them were scouts, the third was a Black-foot woman, very pretty. The scouts had killed her husband, and they gave her to Short Tail [i.e., Bobtail], the brother of Ermine Skin" (37).

4. Although several skirmishes between Cree and Bloods and Siksika tribes were reported subsequent to the Turtle Mountain Pact of 1871, including those led by Crowfoot against Big Bear (one of which claimed Crowfoot's son in 1873), it is significant that none of the skirmishes was directly instigated between the Cree and Peigan, who remained faithful to the pact. See Dempsey, *Big Bear*, 44 (see chap. 2, n. 6).

5. Testimony of Marie Smallboy, Standing Committee on Aboriginal Affairs, Northern Development and Natural Resources (*Hansard*, 17 February 2003).

6. Linderman identified "Stone-Child, whom belittling white men dubbed 'Rocky Boy,'" as one of the men who entered Canada with Little Bear in 1885, "bringing his own contingent of Chippewa braves." Frank B. Linderman, "The Rocky Boy Renegades," in *Indians at Work* (Washington, DC: Office of Indian Affairs, 1937, 1 January).

7. Testimony of Marie Smallboy, Standing Committee on Aboriginal Affairs, 17 February 2003.

8. Morris, *Treaties of Canada* (1880), 352 (see chap. 2, n. 1).

9. Ibid., emphasis added.

10. Ibid., 352–53.

11. Ibid., 354.

12. Marie Smallboy, interview with author, Hobbema, 13 January 2005.

13. Ibid.

14. York, *The Dispossessed*, 92 (see chap. 2, n. 28).

15. Marie Smallboy, interview, Hobbema, 13 January 2005.

16. Joe Smallboy, interview with author, Bentley, Alberta, 11 July 1986.

17. As told by Joe Smallboy, Bentley, Alberta, 1986.

18. Ibid.

19. Marie Smallboy claimed that Isabelle's father, Coyote, became one of the casualties of the Riel Rebellion in 1885 (personal correspondence, 28 December 2004). However, Bob Smallboy claimed that he saw Coyote in the first decade of the twentieth century when, as a boy, he attended a Sun Dance ceremony in the United States, to which "some even came from Maskwachees to participate, although it was far away. *My grandfather, my mother's father,* I saw down there, and my grandmother, and my mother's youngest brother." Chief Bob Smallboy, "Early Memories," trans. Gordon Lee, in "The Indian Way: Memoirs of Chief Bob Smallboy," ed. Gary Botting (unpublished manuscript, 1984), 51 (emphasis added). Then he added, more ambiguously, "My mother's father and mother and brothers and sisters all lived at Maskwachees. It was there that they had taken treaty, but that was a long time ago." See Morris, *The Treaties of Canada* (1880), 361–62.

20. Wolvengrey, *Cree: Words*, Vol. 2, s.v. "Riel Resistance" and Vol. 1, s.v. *"mâyahkamikan-"* (see chap. 1, n. 8).

21. The role of Isabelle as family historian was described by Smallboy several times between 1982 and 1984 and confirmed by Marie Smallboy in an interview with the author at Hobbema, 13 January 2005.

22. Francois Coyote eventually married an Isabelle Piché (one of half a dozen Isabelle Pichés on the Hobbema rolls) at Our Lady of the Seven Sorrows Church. Harvey Buffalo, an archivist for the Samson Band, told the author in an interview that his mother was also named Isabelle Piché (Hobbema, 11 January 2005).

23. *Tentative Roll of the Rocky Boy Indians*, 30 May 1917. A literal translation of his first wife's name is "Hanger-On" or "One Who Hangs On." The English version evolved to "Hanger-On-er" and eventually (possibly by clerical error) "Hanger Owner." See "A Tribal Background Analysis of the Members of the Chippewa Cree 'Tribe' Born Before 1889," in Ewers, *Ethnological Report* (see chap. 2, n. 22), produced from microfiche contained in the published collection *The Expert Testimony before the Indian Claims Commission*, 138, 140.

24. The descriptive name *Kakokikanis*, which rhymed with *Mescacakanis*, was probably given to her by Coyote and recorded by Rocky Boy.

25. Dianne Meili, *Those Who Know: Profiles of Alberta's Native Elders* (Edmonton: NeWest Press, 1991), 80–81.

26. Eleanor Brass, *Medicine Boy and Other Cree Tales* (Calgary: Glenbow Museum, 1982), n. p.

27. Dusenberry, *The Montana Cree*, 161.

28. Linderman, "Rocky Boy Renegades."

29. Conversation with Jessie Smallboy, Big Horn Reserve, 13 July 2005.

30. Morris, *Treaties of Canada* (1880), 192.

31. Dusenberry, *The Montana Cree*, 26–27, 30–31.

32. Morris, *Treaties of Canada* (1880), 223.

33. Ibid.

34. Ibid., 224.

35. Ibid.

36. Some sources say that Rocky Boy was born in Wisconsin, but this seems unlikely. The chief of police of Anaconda, Montana, reported in a letter on 10 February 1902 that Rocky Boy's "ancestors ... left Chippewa Falls, Wis., and came to Montana." Ewers, *Ethnological Report*, 138, 144–46. Little Bear's claim that his mother was Chippewa rather than Cree (along with his prosecution in Canada for murder after the United States returned him to Canada in good faith that an amnesty had been granted to all people in his situation) later helped him in his bid to remain in the U.S. and to become the first chief of the Rocky Boy Reservation. Little Bear told Frank Linderman that he had been born in Wisconsin, although in fact he was born in Little Hills, Saskatchewan (Ewers, *Ethnological Report*, 138, 145). However, Little Bear may simply have been stating what Rocky Boy had said: that his ancestors had come from Wisconsin. Ewers explained: "In the light of the known history of the movements of the Chippewa in migrations westward across Red River, it would seem most probable that it was the *fathers* of Rocky Boy and some of his followers who were born east of Red River, and that they themselves were born west of that river and were participants in a further westward migration" (146, italics in original).

37. Rocky Boy's brother Full-of-Dew was among those who sought refuge on the Flathead Reservation west of the Rocky Mountains in 1887. According to Frank Bird Linderman, Full-of-Dew did not rejoin his brother in Montana, opting instead to seek a separate peace west of the Rockies. Frank B. Linderman, *Montana Adventure: Recollections of Frank B. Linderman* (Lincoln, NB: Merriam, 1968), 134–35, 151.

38. Marie Smallboy, the granddaughter of Johnny Smallboy, agreed that Pleasant One was likely the mother of *Apitchitchiw*, whom she identified as "Joe Smallboy" or "Young Boy as he appears in the American Rolls." Correspondence with author, 29 December 2004.

39. Ewers, *Ethnological Report*, 71.

40. Ibid., 147, 155–56.

41. Ibid., 146–47.

42. Frank Bird Linderman, who knew both men well, found Rocky Boy to be a very gentle man, less aggressive than Little Bear, who was two years his senior (Linderman, *Montana Adventure*, 161).

43. In November 1908, Rocky Boy conspicuously left Little Bear's name off a list of one hundred band members drawn up for submission to U.S. Indian Inspector Frank C. Churchill. In his transmission of the list to Washington, Churchill observed "the common understanding that chief Little Bear and some fifty persons are a part of this group of roving Indians that for many years have been camping near the larger towns in the state" (Churchill to Secretary of the Interior, 10 November 1909, The National Archives). Three days after this transmission, Rocky Boy got wind of it and dictated a garbled letter of protest to Churchill in which he said, "I cannot do to take Little Bear's Band at all" (Ewers, *Ethnological Report*, 127). A fortnight before his death on 18 April 1916, Rocky Boy complained about Métis friends of Little Bear: "Then Little Bear trys to get them in here although he has no right to do this. I am the one that have to let them on if my tribe of Indians want them" (letter from Rocky Boy to Frank Bird Linderman, dated at Box Elder, MT, 1 April 1916).

44. Dempsey, *Big Bear*, illustrations.

45. They are also preserved in archival records in the Museum of the Plains Indian at Browning, MT; in the U.S. federal archives in Seattle, WA, and Denver, CO; at the Glenbow Institute in Calgary; and at the Alberta Provincial Archives in Edmonton. Reconstructing events and relationships from more than a century ago is complicated by the duplication or mistranslation of names. Connecting the dots and fitting the historical "facts" to the oral tradition remains a challenge, since accounts of the same incidents often vary. The process is more of an art than a science, since it involves a certain degree of speculation as to which versions of events are most consistent and most plausible.

46. Among these accounts is Linderman, *Montana Adventure*, 143, 152–53, 160–61, 207–8; see also the Linderman Papers, Archives of the Museum of the Plains Indian, Browning, MT.

47. Ewers, *Ethnological Report*, 143.

48. Dusenberry, "Rocky Boy Indians," 10, n. 22 (see chap. 2, n. 64).

49. The photograph could be miscaptioned, or there could have been a mistranslation: "mother" (*okawimaw*) for "grandmother" (*okomimaw*).

CHAPTER 4: MONTANA

1. *Senate Reports*, 4, no. 821, 54th Congress, 1st Session, 29 April 1896.

2. *Fort Benton River Press*, 24 August 1887.

3. Raymond Gray, "History of the Cree Indians" (unpublished manuscript, Montana State University Library, Bozeman, MT, 1942).

4. *Great Falls Tribune*, 9 November 1887.

5. *Senate Reports*, 4, no. 821, 54th Congress, 1st Session.

6. *Official Correspondence Relating to Admission of Montana As a State into the Union Including Proclamations and Official Addresses of Joseph K. Toole* (1892), State Archives of Montana, Helena.

7. Dusenberry, "Rocky Boy Indians" (see chap. 2, n. 64).

8. *Senate Reports*, 4, no. 821.

9. Ibid.

10. *Great Falls Tribune*, 6 June 1894.

11. *Havre Plaindealer*, 7 June 1894.

12. *Senate Reports*, 4, no. 821.

13. 10 January 1896.

14. Thomas R. Wessel, "A History of the Rocky Boy's Indian Reservation" (unpublished, undated), Stonechild College Library, Havre, MT, Library of Congress AI 970.49, W 86, pp. 17–18.

15. Linderman, "The Rocky Boy Renegades," 24 (see chap. 3, n. 6). See also Linderman, *Montana Adventure*, 99–100 (see chap. 3, n. 36).

16. 4 July 1896.

17. A. M. Hamilton, Secretary of the Saskatchewan Historical Society, in a letter to Anne McDonnell dated 12 January 1892 (now held by the Historical Society of Montana).

18. Marie Smallboy, interview with author, Hobbema, 13 January 2005. Dempsey, *Big Bear*, 112ff (see chap. 2, n. 6).

19. Later, Smallboy claimed to have had only one full sister, Margaret. However, Smallboy claimed that his mother gave birth to twelve children; it would be curious if all but one were boys. Marie Smallboy, who had seen the photograph before, identified Isabelle (interview, Hobbema, 13 January 2005).
20. Smallboy, "Early Memories," 45 (see chap. 3, n. 19).
21. Dempsey, *Big Bear*, 199.
22. Public Archives of Canada, R.G. 10, File 121698-19, A. N. McNeill, Assistant Secretary, Department of Indian Affairs, to E. J. Bangs, Farmer in charge, Stoney Reserve, 4 August 1897.
23. A permanent truce between the Cree and the Peigans was finalized at Turtle Mountain Reservation in 1871, the year after the Battle of Belly River.
24. Marie Smallboy, personal correspondence, 19 December 2004, and interview, 13 January 2005.
25. Ibid.
26. Smallboy, "Early Memories," 46.
27. Ibid., 47.
28. Ibid., 46.
29. Ewers, *Ethnological Report*, 113–18, 146 (see chap. 2, n. 22).
30. *Anaconda Standard*, 11 February 1902, p. 4, col. 2.
31. Cited in Ewers, *Ethnological Report*, 117.
32. Ibid.
33. Ibid., 116.
34. Ibid., 118–19.
35. Ibid., 119.
36. Ibid.
37. Ibid., 120.
38. Ibid., 120–21.
39. Ibid., 122.
40. Ibid.
41. August 1901.
42. Cited in Ewers, *Ethnological Report*, 122–25. See Summary Statement in 191, "Special Case Chippewa-Cree," Sec. Interior, 1913, Indian Office Records, The National Archives.

CHAPTER 5: THE NOMADIC LIFE

1. Smallboy, "Early Memories," 49 (see chap. 3, n. 19).
2. Ibid., 48–50.
3. Chief Bob Smallboy, "White Man's Education," trans. Gordon Lee, in "The Indian Way: Memoirs of Chief Bob Smallboy," ed. Gary Botting (unpublished manuscript, 1984), 76.
4. Samuel Bellow, Flathead Reservation Agent, to Commissioner of Indian Affairs, Flathead Agency, Jocko, MT, 29 February 1908.
5. Frank C. Churchill to Secretary of the Interior, Browning, MT, 14 October 1908, Indian Office Records, The National Archives.
6. U.S. Indian Inspector Frank G. Churchill to Secretary of the Interior, 3 November 1908, NARG 75.
7. Smallboy, "Early Memories," 48.
8. 28 January 1908. See Dusenberry, "Rocky Boy Indians," 1–15 (see chap. 2, n. 64).
9. *Great Falls Tribune*, 8 January 1909, cited ibid., 10.
10. Ibid.
11. See especially *Great Falls Tribune*, 8 January 1909.
12. *Helena Daily Independent*, 10 January 1909.
13. Cited in Dusenberry, "Rocky Boy Indians," 10.
14. Ibid., 11.
15. Smallboy, "Early Memories," 50.
16. T. W. Wheat to Commissioner of Indian Affairs, Brewing, MT, 20 April 1909; copy on file at office of the subagent, Rocky Boy Agency, cited in Dusenberry, "Rocky Boy Indians," 10–11.
17. Dusenberry, "Rocky Boy Indians," 12.
18. *Great Falls Tribune*, 6 November 1909.
19. Superintendent William N. Logan (Fort Belknap Agency) to Commissioner of Indian Affairs, 16 November 1909; "Memorandum," no signature, 12 February 1910, NARG 75.
20. *Cut Bank Pioneer Press*, 19 November 1909; Commissioner of Indian Affairs to Commissioner Fred Dennett, General Land Office, 12 January 1910, NARG 75.

21. *Havre Plaindealer*, 22 January 1910.
22. Dusenberry, "Rocky Boy Indians," 13 ff.
23. Churchill to Secretary of the Interior, 10 November 1909, The National Archives.
24. Dusenberry, "Rocky Boy Indians," 9.
25. Chief Bob Smallboy, "Being Kind to the Soul," trans. Gordon Lee, in "The Indian Way: Memoirs of Chief Bob Smallboy," ed. Gary Botting (unpublished manuscript, 1984), 94.
26. Ibid.
27. Ibid., 96; Chief Bob Smallboy, "The Role of the Elders," trans. Gordon Lee, in "The Indian Way: Memoirs of Chief Bob Smallboy," ed. Gary Botting (unpublished manuscript, 1984), 68–69.
28. 26 June 1896.
29. Dusenberry, *The Montana Cree*, 60–61 (see chap. 3, n. 1).
30. Ibid., 52.
31. 11 January 1913.
32. 19 January 1913.
33. 15 March 1913.
34. See chapter 6: Yellowface.
35. Chief Bob Smallboy, "Buffalo Hunting," trans. Gordon Lee, in "The Indian Way: The Memoirs of Chief Bob Smallboy," ed. Gary Botting (unpublished manuscript, 1984), 93.
36. Smallboy, "Early Memories," 52.
37. 8 August 1913.
38. *Great Falls Tribune*, 15 December 1913.
39. *Havre Plaindealer*, 27 December 1913.
40. Wessel, "Rocky Boy's Indian Reservation," 64 (see chap. 4, n. 14).
41. Paris Gibson and Charles Russell to Arthur E. McFatridge, 12 January 1814, NARG 75; Superintendent H. H. Miller (Fort Belknap Agency) to W. D. Cochran, Government Farmer, 29 January 1914; Miller to Cato Sells, 14 February 1914, Fort Belknap Records, Series 2, Federal Records Center (FRC), Denver, CO.
42. William W. Bole (ed., *Great Falls Tribune*) to Cato Sells, 23 May 1914, NARG 75.
43. 3 July 1914.
44. Assistant Commissioner of Indian Affairs Edgar B. Merritt to Commissioner Clay Tallman, General Land Office, 29 May 1915, NARG 75; Merritt to Superintendent Jewell D. Martin (Fort Belknap Agency), 19 April 1915, Series 1, FRC, Denver, CO.
45. Wessel, "Rocky Boy's Indian Reservation," 55–57.
46. Ibid., 59.
47. Jewell D. Martin to Commissioner of Indian Affairs, 21 September 1915 and 26 November 1915, Series 2, FRC, Denver, CO.
48. Wessel, "Rocky Boy's Indian Reservation," 131.

CHAPTER 6: YELLOWFACE

1. Chief Bob Smallboy, "Prophecies," trans. Gordon Lee, in "The Indian Way: The Memoirs of Chief Bob Smallboy," ed. Gary Botting (unpublished manuscript, 1984), 106–7. The phonetic rendering of Smallboy's pronunciation of Yellowface was *Kohsow-Ahtihkweyiw*.
2. Legend has it that Little Poplar was beheaded by Ward, a bounty hunter who supposedly sent his head to the Canadian authorities in the hope of collecting a reward. "Some say his skull was sent to a museum in Washington." Dempsey, *Big Bear*, 200 (see chap. 2, n. 6).
3. In the course of conversation about my then-landlord, the Cree elder and medicine man Albert Lightning, with Dr. Brigham Young Card at Red Deer College in 1983, I mentioned Bob Smallboy's repeated references to Yellowface as a powerful medicine man and prophet. The next day, Dr. Card provided me with a copy of his father's account of meeting Yellowface in the Cardston area in 1908, when the elder Card was a young Mormon missionary. It became apparent to me, as it was already apparent to Dr. Card, that his father, Joseph Y. Card, and Smallboy had unknowingly crossed paths in 1908, when Joseph was twenty-three and Bob Smallboy was ten. After Bob Smallboy's death, I used J. Y. Card's narrative as a basis on which to conduct further inquiries about Yellowface. The various stories of Yellowface in this chapter are drawn primarily from narratives first told to the author in 1985 and 1986 by Joe Smallboy, relying on his grandmother's account of what she had been told by the sister-in-law of Yellowface. Some liberties were taken with the dialogue, which was first written in 1986–87 as part of an earlier unpublished manuscript "Smallboy: Child of Freedom" (27–44).

4. See the parallel account of this "miracle" provided from a Mormon perspective in the narrative of Joseph Y. Card, provided later in the chapter. There are echoes of this "miracle" in other accounts by people close to Smallboy. For example, on 10 February 1982, Albert Lightning (1898–1991), also known as Buffalo Child, a respected elder of the Samson Band, gave this metaphorical account of the first conference on the Constitution:

> I was invited home by two men for supper. During this supper I was poisoned. I was wrapped as a corpse and left in the basement. A sympathetic White called the house, as he felt concern. Three policemen came. The men I had gone with were asked where I was. They said I had gone back to a meeting.
>
> One policeman stayed on. He found the "corpse" in the basement. The two other policemen got the men. They prepared the "corpse" to be taken to the Reserve.
>
> On the fourth day, the hammers were pounding on the box together. I came to life and started pounding too, and shouting. They opened the box. They were scared.
>
> "Don't run away," I said.
>
> They brought the three men I had had supper with, handcuffed. "According to the law, they are to be hanged or sentenced. They have killed you. What do you want me to do?" the official asked me.
>
> I said, "I have nothing to do with these men!"
>
> This was the first conference on the Constitution. Everything was shaping up—I could sit here for four nights and tell you more.

Albert recalled a parallel prophecy dating back to two years before the Yellowface incident, when he was eight years old. "In a ceremony, a departed soul appeared. It said, 'Have the world's population kneel and pray for peace—even while the other half labors to make weapons. There will be no peace until all my prophecies come to pass.'" These two anecdotes were told to a class of education students at Red Deer College in 1983, recorded by Dr. Brigham Young Card, professor emeritus at the University of Alberta, who gave his notes to the author.

5. The 30" x 48" oil-on-canvas painting now resides in the Amon Carter Museum in Fort Worth, TX.

6. This hitherto unpublished narrative of Joseph Y. Card (1885–1956) was provided to the author by his son, Dr. Brigham Young Card, who gave permission to reproduce the account in Smallboy's biography. It appears here verbatim.

7. Joseph Y. Card concluded his narrative by saying: "The Book of Mormon was placed in their hands and there were those among them who could read it. Chief Yellow Face and Brother Parker became great friends. The Cree Indians camped for the winter months on the Church Ranch property as long as Brother Parker was manager there, and he was able to give them assistance in many ways when times were hard for them."

8. "Many of the things Yellowface foretold that winter have come to be," said Chief Smallboy. Nonetheless, Smallboy pointedly rejected the Mormonism espoused in modified form by Yellowface. Smallboy, "Prophecies," 106–7.

CHAPTER 7: A TUG OF WAR

1. Chief Bob Smallboy, "Living the Indian Way," trans. Gordon Lee, in "The Indian Way: The Memoirs of Chief Bob Smallboy," ed. Gary Botting (unpublished manuscript, 1984), 72.
2. Smallboy, "White Man's Education," 76 (see chap. 5, n. 3).
3. Smallboy, "Early Memories," 52 (see chap. 3, n. 19).
4. Chief Bob Smallboy, "Meeting with the Islamic Spiritual Leader in London, England," trans. Eugene Steinhauer, in "The Indian Way: The Memoirs of Chief Bob Smallboy," ed. Gary Botting (unpublished manuscript, 1984), 39.
5. Smallboy, "White Man's Education," 77–78.
6. Wessel, "Rocky Boy's Indian Reservation," 57 (see chap. 4, n. 14).
7. Chief Bob Smallboy, "To Become a Chief," trans. Gordon Lee, in "The Indian Way: The Memoirs of Chief Bob Smallboy," ed. Gary Botting (unpublished manuscript, 1984), 82–84.
8. Ibid., 84.
9. Wessel, "Rocky Boy's Indian Reservation," 57–58; Chief Rocky Boy to Indian Agent, 14 February 1916, and Little Bear to Jewell D. Martin, 26 February 1916, Series 8, FRC, Denver, CO.
10. Letters, Martin to Commissioner, 21 September 1915 and 26 November 1915, Series 2, FRC, Denver, CO.

11. Smallboy, "White Man's Education," 75.

12. Ibid., 76.

13. Chief Bob Smallboy, "Respect for Elders," trans. Gordon Lee, in "The Indian Way: The Memoirs of Chief Bob Smallboy," ed. Gary Botting (unpublished manuscript, 1984), 98–100.

14. York, *The Dispossessed*, 93 (see chap. 2, n. 28).

15. Ibid., 92–93.

16. *United States Statutes*, 38, no. 807.

17. Ewers, *Ethnological Report*, 133 (see chap. 2, n. 22); Dusenberry, *The Montana Cree*, 83 (see chap. 3, n. 1). Dusenberry seemed to have believed that Rocky Boy died "one year after the creation of the reservation named for him" (47). Earlier, he wrote in an article that Rocky Boy died in 1917, immediately before the Rocky Boy Reservation was established. The perpetuating error seems to have been introduced by Dusenberry's misquoting of the date of a newspaper article upon which he relied. However, it is clear that Rocky Boy died on 18 April 1916 (*Helena Daily Record*, 24 April 1916, p. 4, col. 2).

18. Rocky Boy, letter to Frank B. Linderman, Linderman Papers, Museum of the Plains Indian, Browning, MT.

19. Roger St. Pierre to Jewell D. Martin, 25 January 1916, Series 8; Martin to Commissioner of Indian Affairs, 1 April 1916 and 19 April 1916, Series 2, FRC, Denver, CO.

20. *Great Falls Tribune*, 23 April 1916.

21. Ibid. The letter was addressed to Thomas Gibson, who in turn submitted it to the *Great Falls Tribune* for publication. The text of the letter is contained in Dusenberry, "Rocky Boy Indians," 14 (see chap. 2, n. 64).

22. "Public Law 261" (7 September 1916), *Statutes at Large of the United States of America*, Vol. 39, 739.

23. Wessel, "Rocky Boy's Indian Reservation," 55. See also Roger St. Pierre to Commissioner of Indian Affairs Cato Sells, 8 February 1915, NARG; "Record of Employment, 1887–1925," (Fort Bellknap Agency), Series 12, FRC, Denver, CO.

24. Charles W. Rastall to Commissioner, 19 May 1916, Series 2, FRC, Denver, CO. See also Wessel, "Rocky Boy's Indian Reservation," 73–74.

25. Ibid.

26. Roger St. Pierre to Charles W. Rastall, 2 June 1916, 9 October 1916, and 24 March 1917, Series 8; Rastall to Commissioner, 19 May 1916, Series 1, FRC, Denver; Rastall to St. Pierre, 22 December 1916 and 28 March 1917, Series 4, FRC, Denver; Rastall to Little Bear, 9 August 1918, Series 8, FRC, Denver, CO.

27. Wessel, "Rocky Boy's Indian Reservation," 114.

28. Ibid., 119.

29. Ibid., 119–20.

30. Dusenberry, "Rocky Boy Indians," 14.

31. Malcolm McDowell, Board of Indian Commissioners, to all superintendents, 10 October 1917, Series 1, FRC, Denver, CO.

32. York, *The Dispossessed*, 93.

33. Smallboy, "White Man's Education," 78–79.

34. Dusenberry, "Rocky Boy Indians," 14.

35. Charles W. Rastall to Roger St. Pierre, 9 August 1916, Series 8, FRC, Denver, CO.

36. Charles W. Rastall to Cato Sells, 17 April 1917, Series 8, FRC, Denver, CO. See also Wessel, "Rocky Boy's Indian Reservation," 74–75.

37. Charles W. Rastall to Roger St. Pierre, 8 May 1917, Series 4, FRC, Denver, CO.

38. Wessel, "Rocky Boy's Indian Reservation," 76–77.

39. Ibid., 77.

40. The men were less likely to be given bizarre, diminutive names, although *Apitchitchiw* became "Short Young Boy" or "Shorty" in the Rocky Boy roll (rather than Small Boy) and Coyote became "Poor Old Coyote."

41. Dusenberry, *The Montana Cree*, 91 (see chap. 3, n. 1).

42. Chief Bob Smallboy, "Following the White Man's Tracks" (interview with Gordon Lee, recorded in London, England, 2 December 1981), trans. Gordon Lee, in "The Indian Way: The Memoirs of Chief Bob Smallboy," ed. Gary Botting (unpublished manuscript, 1984), 54.

43. Ibid., 53.

44. Conversation with author, 23 February 2005.

45. Marie Smallboy and Arlene Small have suggested that the proper translation of *Apitchitchiw* is "Small," which their father, James Smallboy, adopted as an alternate name (correspondence with Arlene Small, 14 August 2005). Ironically, Smallboy's older biological sister, Little Girl, married Joe Small of the Rocky Boy Band, who could trace his ancestry back to David Thompson's brother-in-law, Patrick Small, Jr.

46. Wessel, "Rocky Boy's Indian Reservation," 77.
47. Ewers, *Ethnological Report*, 77.
48. *Tentative Roll of Rocky Boy Indians*, 30 May 1917, on file at the Rocky Boy Agency.
49. "Changes in Employees, Fort Belknap Agency," May 1917, Series 15, FRC, Denver, CO.
50. The contrast in attitude between the two countries became evident in the recruitment process for the First World War. In Montana, the Army refused to enlist Indians unless "organization commanders" accepted them—and there was an unwritten agreement among commanders in the field not to do so. In Canada, Indians could enlist, as had Albert Lightning and dozens of other Indians. The war effort in Canada was already well advanced and required industry in other areas, including the production of food, an industry that, as Smallboy soon discovered, would be well rewarded.

CHAPTER 8: FAMILY AND THE FARM

1. Some authorities, including Marie Smallboy, have identified *Apitchitchiw* as Joe Smallboy or Joe Small, Sr., of the Rocky Boy Reservation, but this is unlikely: he was born in 1882, whereas *Apitchitchiw* was born in 1871.
2. Chief Bob Smallboy, "In-Laws," trans. Gordon Lee, in "The Indian Way: The Memoirs of Chief Bob Smallboy," ed. Gary Botting (unpublished manuscript, 1984), 97.
3. Ibid.
4. Charles W. Rastall to Roger St. Pierre, 19 February 1917, Series 4, FRC, Denver; St. Pierre to Rastall, 24 March 1917, Series 8, FRC, Denver, CO.
5. Smallboy, "White Man's Education," 79 (see chap. 5, n. 3).
6. Wessel, "Rocky Boy's Indian Reservation," 94 (see chap. 4, n. 14).
7. Ibid.
8. Smallboy, "Respect for Elders," 98 (see chap. 7, n. 13).
9. Commissioner of Indian Affairs Charles H. Burke to Secretary of the Interior, 10 February 1922, NARG 48, File 51.
10. Dusenberry, *The Montana Cree*, 228 (see chap. 3, n. 1).
11. York, *The Dispossessed*, 93 (see chap. 2, n. 28).
12. Document supplied by Chief Smallboy.
13. "Any Indian person found off the reserve without a pass was treated as a vagrant and summoned to court.... A treaty Indian was ordered back to his reserve; a non-treaty Indian was asked to decide which band he wanted to settle with. The alternative was jail." Snow, *These Mountains*, 53 (see chap. 1, n. 10).
14. Ibid., 106.
15. Ibid., 107–8.
16. Commissioner of Indian Affairs Charles H. Burke to Senator Thomas J. Walsh (Montana), 27 January 1925, NARG 75, File 92517.
17. Wessel, "Rocky Boy's Indian Reservation," 112–13 (see chap. 4, n. 14).
18. Ibid., 114.
19. *Great Falls Tribune*, 15 November 1925; John D. Keeley to Commissioner of Indian Affairs, 22 January 1925; Keeley to Commissioner, 11 December 1925, NARG 75, File 8601-100.
20. Hugh Scott, Board of Indian Commissioners, "Report on Rocky Boy's Reservation," August 1925, National Museum of Natural History, Archives, Smithsonian Institute, Washington, DC.
21. Smallboy, "The Oral Tradition," 61–64 (see chap. 1, n. 6).
22. Ibid.
23. Chief Bob Smallboy, "The Buffalo," trans. Gordon Lee, in "The Indian Way: The Memoirs of Chief Bob Smallboy," ed. Gary Botting (unpublished manuscript, 1984), 85–87.
24. Smallboy, "Buffalo Hunting," 88–89 (see chap. 5, n. 35).
25. Ibid., 89–92.
26. Ibid., 90.
27. Ibid.
28. York, *The Dispossessed*, 103.

CHAPTER 9: POLITICS

1. Meili, *Those Who Know*, 111–12 (see chap. 3, n. 25).
2. York, *The Dispossessed*, 93 (see chap. 2, n. 28).

3. Ibid.
4. Personal conversations with Nancy LeClaire, 1975–76; 1983. See LeClaire and Cardinal, *Alberta Elders' Cree Dictionary* (see chap. 1, n. 3).
5. Meili, *Those Who Know*, 79.
6. Personal conversations with Albert Lightning, 1982–83. Compare Meili, *Those Who Know*, 79–87.
7. Snow, *These Mountains*, x (see chap. 1, n. 10).
8. Smallboy, "Decision to Leave Hobbema," 113 (see chap. 1, n. 7).
9. Ibid., 118.
10. Ibid. See also Smallboy, "Respect for Elders," 98 (see chap. 7, n. 13).
11. Ibid.
12. Smallboy, "White Man's Education," 77–78 (see chap. 5, n. 3).
13. Ibid., 79.
14. Ibid., 118.
15. Smallboy, "Following the White Man's Tracks," 56 (see chap. 7, n. 42).
16. Ibid.
17. Smallboy, "Decision to Leave Hobbema," 113.
18. Ibid., 118.
19. Snow, *These Mountains*, xiii, 60.
20. Morris, *Treaties of Canada* (1880), 206 (see chap. 2, n. 1).
21. Marie Smallboy, interview with author, Hobbema, 13 January 2005.
22. Smallboy, "To Become a Chief," 84 (see chap. 7, n. 7).
23. Chief Bob Smallboy, "Leadership and the Exodus," trans. Alberta Native Communications Society, ed. Eugene Steinhauer, in "The Indian Way: The Memoirs of Chief Bob Smallboy," ed. Gary Botting (unpublished manuscript, 1984), 1.
24. Ibid., 2.
25. Ibid., 3.
26. Smallboy, "Decision to Leave Hobbema," 114–15.
27. Jessie Smallboy, interview with author, 17 April 2005.
28. Smallboy, "To Become a Chief," 84.
29. Smallboy, "Leadership and the Exodus," 1–2.
30. Smallboy, "Decision to Leave Hobbema," 115, 117.
31. Smallboy, "Leadership and the Exodus," 2.
32. Chief Bob Smallboy, "A Submission to the Queen" (25 February 1971), in "The Indian Way: The Memoirs of Chief Bob Smallboy," ed. Gary Botting (unpublished manuscript, 1984), 15.
33. Compare the contemporary observations of Cardinal, *The Unjust Society*, 7–8 (see chap. 1, n. 1).
34. Smallboy, "Leadership and the Exodus," 4.
35. Ibid., 5. See the parallel observations of Harold Cardinal about Robert Battle, then assistant deputy minister, in *The Unjust Society*, 105–7 and 117.
36. Ibid., 6.
37. Ibid.
38. Smallboy, "Submission to the Queen," 15.
39. Ibid., 15–16.
40. Ibid., 3–4.
41. Ibid., 4.
42. News Release regarding Smallboy's death, issued by the Four Bands, 10 July 1984, and circulated to the press at his funeral.
43. Smallboy, "Decision to Leave Hobbema," 112–19. See the parallel observations of Harold Cardinal in *The Unjust Society*: "In fact, the real power, the decision-making process and the policy-implementing group, has always resided in Ottawa, in the Department of Indian Affairs and Northern Development.... The bureaucrats have maintained the upper hand by subjecting durable native leaders to endless exercises in futility" (7–8). He gives a graphic hypothetical example, parallel to Smallboy's experience, of an old man being kept waiting all day by an Indian agent and his clerk. "The old man leaves the office at five-fifteen. He knows that he could have completed his business and left at nine-fifteen that morning. He knows that the agent kept him waiting just to show him who was boss.... The agent holds dictatorial powers over him and they both know it" (81–82).

CHAPTER 10: THE EXODUS

1. *The Western Canadian Journal of Anthropology,* 1, no. 1, 111–12. Although Marie Smallboy was a child at the time, she recalls camping on the Kootenay Plains with her father and grandfather (Johnny Smallboy) every year between 1964 and 1967, specifically to test the suitability of various sites, the better to make recommendations to the Chief. Marie Smallboy, interview with author, Hobbema, 13 January 2005.
2. *The Western Canadian Journal of Anthropology,* 1, no. 1, 111–12.
3. Ibid., 5–6.
4. Ibid.
5. Stan Reid, *Edmonton Journal,* 11 August 1968.
6. 20 October 1968.
7. Ibid.
8. Paul Grescoe, *Weekend Magazine,* 21 September 1968.
9. Meili, *Those Who Know,* 111 (see chap. 3, n. 25).
10. Gresco, *Weekend Magazine,* 21 September 1968.
11. Meili, *Those Who Know,* 112.
12. Cardinal, *The Unjust Society,* 35 (see chap. 1, n. 1).
13. Smallboy, "Decision to Leave Hobbema," 113–15 (see chap. 1, n. 1).
14. Meili, *Those Who Know,* 111.
15. Snow, *These Mountains,* 128 (see chap. 1, n. 10).
16. Ibid., 129, citing the letter to Premier Harry Strom.
17. Ibid., 130.
18. Ibid., 130-31.
19. Small, "Submission to the Queen," 17 (see chap. 9, n. 32).

CHAPTER 11: THE KOOTENAY PLAINS

1. Ironically, Smallboy may have been related by marriage to David Thompson through Thompson's Métis wife, Charlotte Small. The Smallboys of today claim a connection to the Smalls of yesterday; indeed, according to Marie Smallboy (who prefers the name "Small"), *Apitchitchiw* is more accurately translated "Small" than "Smallboy." Joseph Small, also known as Joe Smallboy, is thought to be a direct descendant of Thompson's brother-in-law Patrick Small, Jr. Joseph Small's wife, Little Girl (*Apisisisew,* phonetically almost identical to *Apitchitchiw*), was likely the elder biological sister of Chief Smallboy.
2. Smallboy, "Meeting with Islamic Spiritual Leader," 39–41 (see chap. 7, n. 4).
3. Ibid., 39.
4. See, in particular, his exhaustive diary entries for 1807 and 1810 in J. B. Tyrell, ed., *David Thompson's Narrative of his Explorations in Western America, 1784-1812* (Toronto: Champlain Society [1916] 1968); Richard Glover, ed., *David Thompson's Narrative, 1784-1812* (Toronto: Champlain Society, 1962); David Thompson, *Travels in Western North America, 1784-1812,* ed. Victor G. Hopwood (Toronto: Macmillan, 1971).
5. Marion Smith, *Koo-Koo-Sint: David Thompson in Western Canada* (Red Deer: Red Deer College Press, 1976), 50–58.
6. Ibid., 54.
7. Ibid., 56.
8. Morris, *Treaties of Canada* (1880), 198 (see chap. 2, n. 1).
9. Marie Smallboy, interview with author, Hobbema, 13 January 2005. See also Cardinal, *The Unjust Society,* 27, 31 (see chap. 1, n. 1).
10. Morris, *Treaties of Canada* (1880), 190.
11. Marie Smallboy, interview, 13 January 2005.
12. Ibid.
13. Ibid.
14. Morris, *Treaties of Canada,* (1880), 192–93, 241–42. Morris said that Big Bear explained that "he had been out on the plains hunting the buffalo, and had not heard the time of the meeting; that on hearing of it he had been sent in by the Crees and by the Stonies or Assiniboines to speak for them" (193).
15. Ibid., 193, 242.
16. Ibid., 29.
17. Cardinal, *The Unjust Society,* 27.

18. Snow, *These Mountains* (see chap. 1, n. 10), citing Peter Wesley, citing Wesley's mother, citing the lieutenant-governor of the North-West Territories, Lieut.-Col. James F. McLeod.

19. Ibid., citing Peter Wesley.

20. Ibid.

21. G. Stewart, *Canada under the Administration of the Earl of Dufferin* (Toronto: Rose-Belford, 1879), 491–93, cited in *Native Rights in Canada*, 187 (see chap. 1, n. 1).

22. Public Archives of Canada, Memorandum, J. D. McLean to Duncan C. Scott, Superintendent General of Indian Affairs [n.d. November 1910] (map attached); J. D. McLean to P. G. Keyes, 21 November 1910.

23. Cited in Snow, *These Mountains*, 88.

24. Ibid., 94–95.

25. Snow, *These Mountains*, 63.

26. John Laurie, "Home of the Kootenay Plains," *Canadian Cattlemen* (August 1950): 22–23. Chief Snow noted, "Peter Wesley's action was not without its counterpart in other tribes. Within the last decade, Chief Robert Smallboy, leader of the Ermineskin Band of Hobbema, took a similar trek into the wilderness because of the many problems on his reserve caused by the Department of Indian Affairs, and because he and his people were denied the opportunity to continue their traditional way of life."

27. See Cardinal, *The Unjust Society*, 119–37. Cardinal called the new Indian policy "a thinly disguised programme of extermination through assimilation" (1), "born and delivered of forked tongue" (27).

28. Trudeau, "Remarks on Aboriginal and Treaty Rights," 331–32 (see chap. 1, n. 1).

29. Chief Bob Smallboy, "On Breaking Up the Reserves," trans. Eugene Steinhauer, in "The Indian Way: The Memoirs of Chief Bob Smallboy," ed. Gary Botting (unpublished manuscript, 1984), 31–32.

30. Ibid., 32–33.

31. Dusenberry, *The Montana Cree* (see chap. 3, n. 1).

CHAPTER 12: A PROPOSAL TO THE QUEEN

1. Smallboy, "Submission to the Queen," 13–14 (see chap. 9, n. 32). The written submission, prepared in advance, was formally presented on 18 February 1971, along with a petition to the provincial government.

2. Ibid., 18.

3. Ibid., 18–20.

4. Chief Bob Smallboy, "An Indian Approach to Solving Some of the Problems Facing the Indians of Canada" (written submission dated 18 February 1971), trans. Eugene Steinhauer, in "The Indian Way: The Memoirs of Chief Bob Smallboy," ed. Gary Botting (unpublished manuscript, 1984), 25–26.

5. Ibid., 26.

6. Ibid., 28–29.

7. Chief Bob Smallboy, "A Request for Land," trans. Eugene Steinhauer, in "The Indian Way: The Memoirs of Chief Bob Smallboy," ed. Gary Botting (unpublished manuscript, 1984), 22–23.

8. Ibid., 23.

9. Ibid., 23–24.

10. Ibid., 24.

11. Ibid.

12. Smallboy, "Indian Approach to Solving Problems," 28–29.

13. Mike Steinhauer, "Personal Statement in Support of Chief Robert Smallboy's Request for Land," in "The Indian Way: The Memoirs of Chief Bob Smallboy," ed. Gary Botting (unpublished manuscript, 1984), Appendix c, 124–26.

14. Botting (1984), 30, 126–27.

15. Cited in Snow, *These Mountains*, 128 (see chap. 1, n. 10).

16. Botting (1984) 30.

17. Discussion following presentation of brief, recorded in minutes of "Third Annual Premier's Prayer Breakfast," 26 February 1971.

18. Ibid.

19. Ibid.

20. Ibid.

21. Snow, *These Mountains*, 16.
22. *Red Deer Advocate*, 5 November 1972, p. 4.
23. Smallboy, "Leadership and the Exodus," 184 (see chap. 9, n. 23).
24. Smallboy, "Submission to the Queen," 14.
25. See "Breakaway Indians Win Out: Ottawa Officials Pay Visit," *Edmonton Journal*, 20 October 1968.
26. Cardinal, *The Unjust Society*, 14, 33 (see chap. 1, n. 1).
27. Harold Cardinal listed Chief Smallboy first among many in his "Acknowledgements" in the 1999 edition of *The Unjust Society*. "I wish to express my gratitude to Chief Robert Smallboy who, through his wisdom, gave me the opportunity to gain a deeper understanding of Indianness in the twentieth century" (v).

CHAPTER 13: NATIVE RIGHTS AND THE CONSTITUTION

1. Earlier in the wilderness sojourn, another of the original leaders, Joe Mackinaw, had moved from the Smallboy Camp to Buck Lake, nearer civilization and within the boundaries of Treaty Six, taking six of the original twenty-five families with him.
2. Dorothy Smallboy, interviewed by Dianne Meili, *Those Who Know*, 112 (see chap. 3, n. 25).
3. "The Manitou Foundation," http://www.manitou.org/MF/articles.html, 2.
4. Tang G. Lee and P. J. Adams, "Preliminary Site Investigation of the Southesk Area for Habitation," Faculty of Environmental Design, University of Calgary (April 1980).
5. He carried the Union Jack in parades and occasionally at powwows.
6. In *Re Indian Association of Alberta* (9 December 1981), reported as "Indians' Application Fails," *The Times Law Report*, 10 December 1981 (Queen's Bench Division), per Woolf J.
7. *Parliamentary Debates (Hansard)*, House of Lords Official Report, Vol. 425, No. 3 (10 November 1981), 177.
8. Ibid.
9. Ibid., 178.
10. Ibid., 179.
11. Ibid., 180.
12. Ibid.
13. Chief Bob Smallboy, "Treaty and the Law" (speech given in London, England, on 2 December 1981), in "The Indian Way: The Memoirs of Chief Bob Smallboy," ed. Gary Botting (unpublished manuscript, 1984), 37.
14. Ibid., 36.
15. Smallboy, "Meeting with Islamic Spiritual Leader," 39–41 (see chap. 7, n. 4).
16. Smallboy, "Advice for Europe," 42–43 (see chap. 1, n. 2).

CHAPTER 14: BEING KIND TO THE SOUL

1. Smallboy, "Following the White Man's Tracks" (see chap. 7, n. 42).
2. Ibid., 56, 60.
3. Ibid., 59.
4. Ibid., 59–60.
5. Ibid., 56–57, 60.
6. Being kind to the body and kind to the soul was a repeated theme.
7. This anecdote, reconstructed from details supplied by Janet Omeasoo and embellished by Joe Smallboy, was confirmed, laughingly, by the Chief.
8. Chief Bob Smallboy, "Puberty Rites," trans. Gordon Lee, in "The Indian Way: The Memoirs of Chief Bob Smallboy," ed. Gary Botting (unpublished manuscript, 1984), 105.
9. Smallboy, "Following the White Man's Tracks," 58.
10. Chief Bob Smallboy, "Medicine," trans. Gordon Lee, in "The Indian Way: The Memoirs of Chief Bob Smallboy," ed. Gary Botting (unpublished manuscript, 1984), 117–18.
11. Smallboy, "Puberty Rites," 103–5.
12. Smallboy, "Role of the Elders," 69 (see chap. 5, n. 27).
13. Smallboy, "Being Kind to the Soul," 95–96 (see chap. 5, n. 25).
14. Smallboy, "Following the White Man's Tracks," 59–60.
15. Smallboy, "White Man's Education," 78 (see chap. 5, n. 3).

16. Ibid., 78–79. Smallboy's remarks echoed those of Harold Cardinal in *The Unjust Society* (see chap. 1, n. 1):

> Who can understand the white man? What makes him tick? How does he think and why does he think the way he does? Why does he talk so much? Why does he say one thing and do the opposite? Most important of all, how do you deal with him? As Indians, we have to learn to deal with the white man. Obviously, he is here to stay. Sometimes it seems a hopeless task. The white man spends half of his time and billions of dollars in pursuit of self-understanding. How can a mere Indian expect to come up with the answer?... He believes in equality, but apparently believes the white man is more equal than the Indian. He just doesn't make sense. Study of the white man will make a great field for future Indian psychologists and psychiatrists (63–64).

17. Cited in York, *The Dispossessed*, 90 (see chap. 2, n. 28).
18. Ibid., 89 (in Chapter Four: Hobbema: Oil and Suicide).
19. Ibid.
20. Ibid.
21. Ibid., 88–89.
22. Ibid., 90.
23. Ibid., 91.
24. Ibid.
25. Dion Resource Consulting Services Ltd., "Indian Lands: Social Impact of Petroleum Activity" (Edmonton, 1984), report commissioned by Department of Indian Affairs.
26. Ibid.
27. York, *The Dispossessed*, 95.
28. Smallboy, "White Man's Education," 80.
29. Ibid., 79.
30. Ibid., 80–81.
31. Ibid., 81.
32. Smallboy, "Following the White Man's Tracks," 60.
33. Ibid., 59.
34. Smallboy, "The Oral Tradition," 67 (see chap. 1, n. 6).
35. Smallboy, "Following the White Man's Tracks," 59. Ironically, a trust fund was set up in Chief Smallboy's name to sponsor a major medical scholarship for First Nations students, tenurable at any university with a medical school—where modern "white" medicine is taught almost exclusively and Native medicines, regarded as mere "remedies," are not given the time of day.
36. Ibid., 59–60.
37. News Release, Smallboy Camp, 10 July 1984.

EPILOGUE

1. Meili, *Those Who Know* (see chap. 3, n. 25).
2. Jeff Holubitsky, "A spiritual foothold in the wilderness," *Edmonton Journal*, 18 July 2004.
3. *Wayne Roan et al. v. Canada*, T-1576-97 (F.C.T.D.).
4. The decision to withdraw funding from the school may have also been influenced by the Native Claims Commission, which did not recognize the Smallboy Camp as a legitimate band, and by the Environmental Appeal Board, which held that the single issue to be determined was whether a decision by the board should await the decision of the Federal Court.
5. Holubitsky, "A spiritual foothold."
6. Snow, *These Mountains*, 63–64 (see chap. 1, n. 10).
7. As Chief Snow made clear in *These Mountains*, 63–64, 74–75, and 93–95, no attempt was made to consult the Stoneys who lived on the Kootenay Plains, although in 1909 there was talk of 23,680 acres of land on the Kootenay Plains being set aside for a Stoney reserve.
8. Department of Marine and Fisheries, *Handbook of Indians of Canada*, 2 George V, A. 1912, Sessional Paper No. 21a (Ottawa: The King's Printer, 1913), 477.
9. Ibid., 477–78, citing Treaty Eight (emphasis added).
10. Snow, *These Mountains*, 16.

Index